SMARTER PROPERTY INVESTMENT

Smarter Property Investment

Ways to make more out of residential property investment

3rd Edition

PETER CEREXHE

First published in 2001
Second edition published in 2004 by Allen & Unwin
Third edition published in 2008 by Allen & Unwin

Allen & Unwin
83 Alexander Street
Crows Nest NSW 2065
Australia
Phone: (61 2) 8425 0100
Fax: (61 2) 9906 2218
Email: info@allenandunwin.com
Web: www.allenandunwin.com

National Library of Australia
Cataloguing-in-Publication entry:

Cerexhe, Peter.
Smarter property investment: ways to make more out of residential property investment.

3rd ed.
Includes index.
ISBN 978 1741 754421 (pbk.).

1. Real estate investment - Australia. 2. Residential real estate - Australia. I. Title.

332.6320994

Typeset in 10.5/13.5 pt Sabon by Midland Typesetters, Australia.
Printed in Australia by McPherson's Printing Group

10 9 8 7 6 5 4 3 2 1

CONTENTS

TABLES AND FIGURES

Tables

Figures

ACKNOWLEDGEMENTS AND DISCLAIMER

In preparing this book I have drawn deeply from the well of my personal experiences as an investor and lawyer, and, believe me, over the years I have seen investment tactics that would turn your hair white. When it comes to matters of precise detail, including tables and graphs, I would like to acknowledge specifically the generous assistance and resources offered by the Australian Taxation Office, the Australian Bureau of Statistics, State and territory revenue offices, Colonial First State and the Real Estate Institute of Australia, without which this book would not have been possible. My heartfelt thanks go to Hans Kunnen, Geoff Stean, the subjects and sources of the various case studies and other anecdotes, the late Sid Conway and Katie.

I consider it unfair to talk about people and their money if doing so will identify them or their projects. Accordingly, I have changed the names of all those who shared their stories with me and any particulars which might reveal their actual development projects. The lessons are the most important aspects of the case studies.

The subject matter of this book traverses a huge range of facts, figures and opinion. Government regulation and industry practice are changing constantly and in important ways. While every care has been taken to ensure accuracy, readers must seek up-to-date information and expert personal advice before acting or refraining from acting on any information contained herein. In particular, readers should discuss their plans with a licensed financial planner; the author is not a licensed financial planner and intends by this book to provide information of a general nature only, not financial advice.

I hope you enjoy the read.

Peter Cerexhe

GLOSSARY

AAPR Abbreviaton for **Average Annual Percentage Rate**

allotment A block of land subdivided out of a larger section.

amenity The pleasantness of a place. The amenity of a street, for example, will be an amalgam of the type and number of trees and bushes, the air quality, whether it is a wide boulevard or a quaint, narrow lane, noise levels and traffic.

auction The public sale of property to the highest bidder on the fall of the hammer.

Average Annual Percentage Rate (AAPR) This is one of several methods of comparing one loan deal with another by incorporating the interest rate, any lower introductory rate, fees and charges. The aim is to quantify the true cost of the loan over a period of time. Other terms in use include 'effective rate' and 'comparison rate'. Each method will have its own way of making the comparison, so one set of figures might not actually be a fair comparison with another if they are worked out under different methods. See **Compulsory Comparison Rate.**

bank cheque A cheque issued by the bank on its account.

body corporate The council or committee consisting of unit owners which manages a strata/unit development including the buildings and common property.

bridging finance A short-term loan to help someone complete the purchase of a property before their existing property is sold.

capital Accumulated wealth—a lump sum of money or other assets after deducting debt.

capital gains tax (CGT) This is a Commonwealth tax payable on the increase, if any, in the value of an asset—such as shares or property—between the time it was purchased or acquired and the time it is sold or disposed of. The family home is generally exempt from CGT. CGT only applies to assets purchased or acquired after 19 September 1985.

capped loan A loan where the interest rate has an upper limit.

caveat A warning notice placed on the legal title to a property, claiming an interest in the property by someone other than the registered owner. The property cannot be sold while the caveat is present and it may be difficult to borrow money using the property as security for the loan.

CCR Abbreviation for **Compulsory Comparison Rate.**

CGT Abbreviation for **capital gains tax.**

community title This is the name given, in some States/territories, to a more recent form of property ownership designed for a range of uses—residential, commercial and even industrial—within the one development. It may be used to create a resort, for example, bringing together villas, apartments, shops, a golf course, marina and tennis court with roads and other infrastructure.

company title This is an older form of title, generally predating strata title, which uses a company structure to subdivide a property into separate units. Each property owner actually owns a share or number of shares in the company. Company title is now usually found only in old apartment blocks, some of which are run-down and others highly prized and exclusive. Company title properties often are more difficult to sell than strata/unit title properties, and this is reflected in generally lower prices. This is because there may be restrictive conditions in the company documents setting out the agreement between the shareholders. For example, it may be necessary to obtain the consent of the other owners to a prospective purchaser.

Compulsory Comparison Rate (CCR) This is a rate prescribed by legislation under the Consumer Credit Code which took effect nationally from 1 July 2003. This law requires financial institutions to specify the 'comparison rate' in their fixed-term consumer credit advertising and promotions (that is, it excludes 'indefinite' credit products such as credit cards and line-of-credit loans). The comparison rate is based on the loan's interest rate (including any cheaper rate during the initial period) plus fees and charges, calculating an all-up cost of the loan over a set period. The previous comparative scheme was called Average Annual Percentage Rate.

Consumer Price Index (CPI) A measure of the cost of living. It is used to measure inflation.

conveyancing The process whereby ownership of a property lawfully passes from one person to another. It generally involves checking that the vendor has full and proper legal title to the property free of any encumbrance or hindrance and registering the transfer of ownership. People usually engage a solicitor or licensed conveyancer to undertake this task, although there is nothing to stop an individual doing their own conveyancing.

covenant A restriction on the legal title to property that either benefits or burdens the land (for example, specifying what building materials can and cannot be used).

CPI Abbreviation for **Consumer Price Index.**

default To break the terms of your mortgage contract with your lender—for example, to miss the due date for a repayment, or to fail to keep the mortgaged property insured.

deposit It is almost universally required, under contracts for the sale and purchase of property, that the purchaser pays part of the sale price to the vendor at the time of entering into the contract, with the balance of funds to follow after a period of investigation of the property's legal title. The deposit is this first sum of money. Generally the contract for land will call for a deposit of 10 per cent of the agreed sale price. The purchaser can lose this deposit to the vendor if the purchaser fails to complete the contract within its terms.

deposit bond When buying a property which is not yet completed—such as an 'off the plan' apartment—a purchaser can avoid having to pay the usual 10 per cent deposit on exchange of contracts. Certain financial institutions will pay or guarantee the deposit for purchasers, charging a fee ranging from around 0.5 per cent to almost 2 per cent of the full purchase price of the property. The actual amount varies according to the time period until completion of the building and the amount the purchaser wants to borrow (the shorter the completion term and the smaller the amount, the lower the fee). This fee is not credited against the deposit, which must be paid either at settlement or when the bond term expires.

depreciation This is the writing off of the capital cost of an item of plant over the term of its effective life. There are two different methods to calculate the depreciation of an item: prime cost and diminishing value.

diminishing value This is a method of calculating depreciation of an item of plant where the benefit of the deduction is greatest in the first year. This is because each year the set rate (for example, 15 per cent) is applied against the written-down (depreciated) value of the asset from the previous year. Each year the value of the asset goes down. The rate applied is one-and-a-half times (150 per cent) the equivalent prime cost rate on eligible assets acquired up to 9 May 2006, and two times (200 per cent) thereafter. See also **prime cost.**

discretionary trust A legal structure for owning property (and other assets) controlled by a trustee, who determines which beneficiaries receive income and in what amounts. It is a structure used for tax planning and estate planning purposes.

drawdown To call loan monies from your lender/mortgagee and apply them to your purpose—for example, to pay for the purchase of your property or to pay out an earlier loan. In some situations, such as when building or renovating a property, there may be more than one drawdown of funds over a period of time.

easement A right—such as to walk or to drive—over the land of another. Generally, the owner of the encumbered land cannot build over the site of the easement or block the passage.

encumbrance A burden on a property giving legally enforceable rights to someone who is not the owner of the property—for example, a right of access, a driveway, a water course, a covenant (such as, restricting the use of certain building materials) or a mortgage. The existence of the encumbrance will be revealed by a search of the title documents or certificate of title for the property. A conveyancer must search for encumbrances on a property and report to their client (whether purchaser or mortgagee) on their meaning and impact.

equities Another name for stocks or shares in a company not bearing fixed-interest returns.

equity The net capital value of an asset free of all loans and debts. For example, if you own a property valued at $100 000 and it is subject to a mortgage of $38 000, your equity in the property is $62 000. This is not to be confused with 'equities'.

equity loan A loan secured against the equity in a property.

establishment fee Application fee for a loan.

exchange In many States/territories, counterparts of the contract of sale for property are signed separately by the vendor and the purchaser. The contract is made, or comes into existence, when those signed counterparts are swapped, so that the vendor ends up with a copy of the contract signed by the purchaser, and vice versa. This is the 'exchange' of contracts and is the moment when the contract comes into existence and from which any time limits specified in the contract start to run.

fee simple A legal interest in property or estate capable of being inherited without limitation. It is the highest form of ownership.

financial institution An organisation or company which deals in financial services, such as taking deposits and making loans. Examples include banks, building societies, credit unions and finance companies.

fixed rate A 'fixed rate' mortgage is one in which the interest rate will not vary during the term of the loan. It will remain unchanged even though the official cash rate rises or falls.

forfeit This means to take something from another. In the context of conveyancing, it generally means the purchaser has breached an important part of the contract and the vendor lawfully takes ('forfeits') the purchaser's deposit money.

freehold Ownership of property in fee simple.

gearing An investment is geared if the purchaser borrows money to finance its acquisition. When prices rise, gearing can enlarge the percentage capital gain, but should prices fall, gearing can enlarge percentage capital loss.

goods and services tax (**GST**) A consumption tax on most goods and services at the rate of 10 per cent. The tax was introduced on 1 July 2000. Note that residential rent is exempt from GST, but expenses are not.

gross In money terms, it is a total without taking out any deductions. For example, a person's gross wage is what their employer pays them without deducting income tax or any other amounts such as top-up superannuation (not the superannuation guarantee charge), Christmas club payments, union fees, etc. See also **net**.

GST Abbreviation for **goods and services tax.**

guarantee A contractual promise to do something (for example, to pay back a loan).

guarantor A person or company that gives a guarantee, generally for the benefit of another. For example, a parent might guarantee the fulfilment of the obligations under a loan contract entered into by his or her child.

IAS Abbreviation for **instalment activity statement.**

inclusions Objects included in the sale/purchase of property, such as carpets, blinds, curtains, light fittings, TV antenna, clothesline and so on.

instalment activity statement (IAS) A form for reporting PAYG instalments or PAYG withholding by certain investors or businesses which are not registered for GST.

interest Money paid by a borrower in return for the use of money lent by another, or money paid for not requiring a debt or loan to be repaid.

inventory A schedule of items included in a sale/purchase which are not attached to the property or fitted. For example, beds, cupboards, chairs, tables, rugs, mirrors.

item of plant An asset which depreciates in value over time.

joint tenants A legal mode of ownership of property by more than one person. Joint tenants own the whole of the property in equal shares. When one joint tenant dies, their share is divided equally between the remaining joint tenants. See also **tenancy in common.**

land tax A State/territory government tax on property ownership. See Chapter 8.

lease A legal agreement—not always in writing—by which the owner gives exclusive possession of a property to another, generally in consideration of the payment of rent.

lender's mortgage insurance (LMI) This is insurance to cover the situation where the borrower (mortgagor) defaults in payments to the lender (mortgagee) required by the mortgage and there is a shortfall when the property is sold. The premium is paid by the borrower, usually as a one-off payment at the commencement of the loan. It is not to be confused with income protection insurance, which replaces lost income if a person suffers illness or injury and is unable to work as before, or mortgage protection insurance (which covers loan repayments).

lessee The tenant.

lessor The landlord.

line of credit A loan account with a financial institution which the customer can use for deposits and withdrawals up to a pre-arranged credit limit. Interest is charged on any credit taken by the customer and, of course, there are various fees.

LMI Abbreviation for **lender's mortgage insurance.**

Loan-to-valuation ratio (LVR) The amount of debt (e.g. mortgage) relative to the value of a property, expressed as a percentage. For example, if a property is valued at

$100 000 and the mortgage is (or will be) $80 000, the LVR is 80 per cent.

low-doc Low-doc or low-documentation loans—see **non-conforming mortgage.**

LVR Abbreviation for **loan-to-valuation ratio.**

managed fund A unit trust that pools the investment moneys of a number of individual investors. It is managed on behalf of the investors by a professional manager.

managing agent A person appointed by the owner of a rental property to manage that property. Tasks would generally include finding tenants, collecting rent, arranging quotes for maintenance and repairs, lodging bonds with relevant State authorities, preparing and issuing all notices to tenants required by law or lease and handling disputes with tenants, including appearing before tenancy tribunals.

margin loan A loan generally for the purpose of buying shares or units in managed funds.

mortgage A loan against real estate—for example, the bank loan used to enable a person either to buy a property or to raise money for other purposes, which may have nothing to do with the property itself (such as, a business loan, or a personal loan to pay for a holiday or support a line of credit). The mortgage contract and associated legislation permit the mortgagee to sell the security if the mortgagor defaults on the loan.

mortgage broker A mortgage finder whose knowledge of the market for mortgages enables him or her to locate the mortgage best suited to a client's needs. The broker acts for the borrower, not the lender, although he or she is paid by the lender.

mortgagee The name given to the lender where the loan is over property. The mortgagee may be a bank, finance company or even a family member.

mortgagor The name given to the borrower (and owner of the property) where a loan is over property.

negative gearing A property used for investment is negatively geared when the net rental income, after deduction of operating expenses, is less than the interest paid on the mortgage used to purchase the property. Negative gearing lowers the overall taxable income of the investor for taxation purposes.

net In money terms, it is a total after taking out any deductions. For example, a person's net wage is what their employer actually gives them after deducting income tax and any other required or negotiated amounts such as salary sacrifice contributions and union fees. See also **gross.**

non-conforming mortgage A product designed for people who have difficulty conforming to the set pre-conditions for eligibility applied by most financial institutions for their mortgages. Interest rates tend to be around 1 per cent higher than those of a standard mortgage, the LVR for LMI can be lower than 80 per cent and there may be high exit fees and many other special conditions. See Chapter 10.

notice to complete The contract for sale of property includes a provision for a party to the contract to issue a notice calling on a party in default to fulfil its obligations—for example, calling on the purchaser to pay the balance of the sale price and complete the contract. It will specify what will happen if the other party does not meet its contractual obligations by the notice deadline (for example, the contract will be terminated and any deposit moneys will be forfeited).

off the plan The actual act of selling or offering for sale or purchasing a unit in a development before construction is complete, after inspecting the architectural drawings and building plans.

offset account An account with a bank or other financial institution which maximises savings by playing the tax rules. The account is linked to a mortgage so that any interest earned on savings is used to reduce the interest on the mortgage. The account holder doesn't actually earn assessable interest.

old system title The original form of legal title (ownership) in Australia—it has largely been replaced by Torrens title. Ownership of old system title property relies on being able to prove an unbroken chain of title leading up to the current vendor. The chain of title consists of the documents by which the property has been conveyed (sold), mortgaged and otherwise encumbered over the years, going back to what is called a 'good root of title'. State/territory legislation covers many aspects of the operation of old system title.

option In the context of property, this is a legally enforceable right to buy a property before the expiry of a deadline and at a pre-determined price. This privilege generally will incur a fee, which might be credited against the eventual purchase price for the property if the option is 'exercised', but this is not always the case.

outgoings Day-to-day expenses associated with owning and running an investment property. They include rates, gardening, managing agent's fees, insurances, strata/unit levies and maintenance.

Pay As You Go (PAYG) A system of income taxation whereby the self-employed, some businesses and many investors are required to lodge an annual or quarterly return with the Tax Office and pay tax on their income. From 1 July 2000, PAYG replaced the system of provisional tax, as well as a number of other taxes. See Chapter 13.

prime cost A method of calculating depreciation of an item of plant, using the cost of the item as the basis for the calculation. The relevant rate of depreciation remains the same over the life of the item. See also **diminishing value.**

principal The capital of a loan, as opposed to the interest charged on it.

private sale Sale of property by the owner without involving a real estate agent.

private treaty Private sale of property (as opposed to the public sale of property at auction).

property syndicate A group of investors who put their money together to buy one or more properties jointly; a syndicate usually has a fixed term of five to ten years, after which the assets are sold and the net proceeds distributed; there are restrictions on investors getting their money out earlier. See Chapter 16.

purchaser The buyer.

records Financial records to do with your investment—receipts, invoices, rent statements, bank statements and so on—must be kept for five years from the date you lodge your tax return. For capital gains tax purposes, you must keep the records of your ownership and capital improvements for five years from the date you sell or otherwise dispose of the property.

redraw facility A benefit offered by some types of loan contract—including many but not all mortgages—which allows the borrower to take money back out of their loan account provided they have paid more than the minimum requirement of the loan contract. For example, let's say your mortgage requires you to make monthly loan repayments (principal and interest) of $1200 but you accelerate your repayments by making monthly payments of $1500 (or you make a lump sum deposit into the account to reduce the loan principal); if your loan contract allows 'redraws' you might be able to withdraw some of the excess. These might be free of charge or, particularly with 'no frills' mortgages, could cost tens of dollars each time. It is a very positive feature to look for in a home loan.

refurbish To decorate or fix up a property into good order. This might include painting, and replacing floor coverings, fixtures and fittings.

rent The money a property owner receives from the tenant in exchange for letting the tenant live in the property. It is commonly paid weekly or monthly. It is regarded as income for taxation purposes.

reserve The purchase price set by a vendor at auction below which the vendor will not sell the property.

Reserve Bank The Reserve Bank of Australia is the central bank of the Commonwealth of Australia. However, it operates independently of the government. Its task is to keep the economy healthy through maintaining desirable levels of inflation, growth and employment. One of its chief tools by which it achieves these aims is by establishing the cash rate—the basic building block for the interest rates used by financial institutions—and the availability of money to service the national economy.

responsible entity The name given to the manager of a unit trust (managed fund or property syndicate, for example).

shared equity This commonly refers to a scheme whereby to facilitate the affordable purchase of a property a lender defers or waives interest on a proportion of the loan in return for a share of the equity on sale.

stamp duty A State/territory government tax. Among many other situations it is payable on the transfer of property or an interest in property. Generally, in conveyancing, it is payable by the purchaser, though this is not always the case.

strata (unit) title A form of Torrens title which allows a property allotment to be subdivided vertically or horizontally. An example is a block of home units, where each unit has a separate title and can be sold and owned independently of the other units.

syndicate See **property syndicate.**

tenancy in common A legal system of ownership of property by more than one person. Tenants-in-common own the whole of a property in such proportions as the title indicates—the proportions do not have to be equal. When a tenant-in-common dies, their share is passed according to the provisions of their will. It need not necessarily go to the surviving tenants-in-common. See also **joint tenants.**

tenant The person or company that rents property from a landlord.

Torrens title A form of legal ownership of real estate guaranteed by the State/territory government and based on a system of registration of interests and certificates of title.

transfer A document recording the change of ownership of real estate; it is designed to be placed on the public register at the Land Titles Office (or equivalent) and to change the details accordingly on the certificate of title.

trust See **discretionary trust.**

unit trust a managed fund which pools the money of investors to invest in jointly owned assets. It is not a separate entity for tax purposes.

valuation The worth of a property. A bank or financial institution will often require a valuation to establish if the property is in sound condition and to assess how much money it can safely lend using the property as security. The valuation can be a certificate from a licensed valuer, or simply a letter from an estate agent. In many cases lenders will use the purchase price of a property as its valuation, particularly where that property was purchased through public auction and the amount of the loan being sought is a moderate proportion of that price.

variable rate A mortgage is said to have a 'variable rate' when the interest rate is free to change, up or down, in line with the terms of the mortgage. Usually any change will follow a move in the official cash rate.

vendor The seller.

yield The yield of an investment is the ratio of its income to its value.

INTRODUCTION

You know what annoys me? Money books with smart answers. It's pretty arrogant to reduce the breadth of human financial experience to a number of pithy statements and inspirational anecdotes. What world do these people inhabit? We are bombarded by the success stories of those who stalked wealth with nothing more than a few thousand dollars in hand and a fearless attitude to risk-taking. What about all those who took the Big Risk only to crash and burn?

For years I worked as a lawyer in Sydney, when inflation, interest rates and housing prices were going through the roof; millionaires were being made and no quarter was given in negotiations. I saw smart investors go broke while fortune (for no good reason) smiled on charismatic knuckleheads. Intelligence didn't seem to be a prerequisite for successful investing.

Property investors are not stand-up comedians—'good timing' is not the key to success. Hard work, sound preparation, good negotiating skills and an affinity for money—these are the tools of this particular trade. Did school/university/college teach you how to negotiate? Or how to feel comfortable talking money? The aim of this book is to help you prepare for the negotiations to come.

What is it about owning your home—or hoping to own your home—that is so attractive? Is it the security it brings?

Is it the freedom to bang a nail in the wall and hang a picture where you want? Is it a kitchen that sparkles and shines, filled with clever little features? Do you hate the idea of moving and love the feeling of putting down roots? Well, whatever the reason, forget it! You're looking for an investment now, not a home.

Many of you will have bought and sold more than one home. That will stand you in good stead, but buying a home is *not* the same as buying an investment property to be occupied by a tenant. While there is an overlay, buying an investment property requires a different mindset, a less emotive perspective.

Australians buy their homes with their hearts. The decision is ruled, ultimately, by emotion. And in some cases the precise emotion is not love but greed. It's possible to become besotted with a property not because it will be nice to live in but because of its potential for capital gain. Nonetheless, it is still a decision of the emotions, not the mind.

The searcher for investment property must listen to the cool, calculating voice of reason, and this book contains the information you need to get your investment property based on a solid footing. It's a combination of:

- obtaining and understanding *finance*;
- *saving*, or *restructuring* your affairs, to provide your deposit;
- choosing your *target* property out of the hundreds or thousands on the market;
- making use of incentives in the *taxation* system to your advantage;
- understanding the bite of *capital gains tax*;
- minimising *land tax* liability;
- purchasing the correct *insurance* protection to secure your assets;
- understanding your attitude to *risk*;

- coming to terms with the rights and responsibilities of being a *landlord*;
- knowing in whose *name* to purchase the investment; and
- designing your *strategy*.

Australians are researching and buying property differently. The internet has dramatically increased opportunities to inspect properties and find finance. While it's not essential to be connected to the web, those who are will find their horizons expanded. Of course, a huge amount of real estate web content is unmitigated trash—junk information and tawdry PR, but I've recommended quite a number of websites, both in particular chapters and at the end of the book, which will let you sample the quality end of the market.

In various chapters, I have inserted case studies of ordinary people who have got into first-time property investment. What interests me is not their life histories but their experience of the process of buying and owning investment property. Out of respect for their privacy, therefore, I have changed their names. Their stories, however, are true.

This book is principally aimed at first-time investors. Accordingly, it is focused on residential property—providing someone's home. Options such as commercial or industrial property, or even vacant land, are outside the scope of this work as they bring additional layers of complexity and risk. Leave those for another day.

Think about the people you know who have got into property investment. Some I know are daring and flamboyant; others are quiet and conservative. Some are real go-getters who have the fire to start their own businesses from scratch; others remain dutiful employees the whole of their working lives. Big salaries, modest wages; university-educated, or didn't even finish school. What have successful property investors got in common? Precious little—except that at some point in their ordinary, busy lives they decided to stop talking and start doing, to get serious about investment and about providing for their financial future.

Section I
ARE YOU MOTIVATED?

Chapter 1

Why property?

Around 70 per cent of Australian households live in a home they own. If you're one of them, you are already a property investor in a substantial way. Add to that your superannuation—which your fund managers will invest partly in property—and it is likely that the greatest proportion of your 'wealth' is in property.

Property ownership is a defining characteristic of our culture. In many other countries, it is common to be a renter for life. Not so here. Strong growth in property values in many capital cities over the last few years has made the dream of property ownership harder to realise, but somehow Australians are still managing it. Despite the rising prices, the First Home Owner Grant and the general property frenzy have actually seen a reversal of the slow downward trend in home ownership. But it has been property investment which has flourished most. In 2003 the annual rate of growth of housing credit for investors passed 30 per cent, while housing credit growth for owner-occupiers remained well below 20 per cent. By early 2007 the rates of growth for investors had fallen substantially (to 12 per cent) but not significantly for owner-occupiers (16 per cent). However, the trend was up for investors seeking refuge from inflated share prices and taking advantage of falls in housing prices.

In June 2007 alone we borrowed almost AU$8.1 billion for investment housing.

Decades of government policy have encouraged us to own property, and in particular our homes. Just consider:

- First Home Owner Grants;
- stamp duty concession schemes;
- favourable taxation treatment for the home—capital gains tax exemption;
- favourable treatment for Centrelink pensions and benefits;
- in the past, artificially low (government-regulated) home loan interest rates;
- council and water rate concessions for low-income earners; and
- land tax exemptions.

You would have to be looking the other way to miss the signposts.

If you own your home, are you ready to invest more deeply in property? If you haven't yet purchased a property, are you thinking about buying an investment property and getting the Tax Office to help pay for it? Just what is your motivation for reading this book at this point of your life? Why are you looking at property rather than shares?

You must believe you are ready to invest. And you must feel a certain drive to find your own level of financial self-sufficiency. Property can help you reach your financial goals. Indeed, property is an essential element of financial planning, along with shares and fixed-interest investments. You don't have to own property directly (that is, in your own name)—there are other ways of putting your money into property (see 'property trusts' in Chapter 17), but without property there is no balance. It's almost inescapable.

WHERE PROPERTY FITS INTO BROADER INVESTMENT STRATEGIES

While investment fads come and go, property remains a constant. Yet if you feel motivated to invest seriously in property, it is important to get a perspective on where you are heading. You can rack up notional millions of dollars in property (and mortgages) and still be no further ahead. Put too much of your money into property and, despite the solid-looking bricks and mortar, your accumulated wealth is vulnerable.

HOW HAS PROPERTY PERFORMED?

In late 2003, as the boom came off the boil, the first reports began trickling through of 10–30 per cent price falls, with apartment developments being pulled off the market for redesign and even relaunch, to kick-start stalled sales campaigns. High vacancy rates, empty properties and rising interest rates through 2003 to 2006 reminded us of the risks.

Property is no longer the safe cure-all for guaranteed wealth creation. The 'good old days' are over. Piling up property after property will bring you only terrific costs and a significant array of taxes. The fabled 'magic' of negative gearing is a shadow of its former self, thanks largely to the year 2000 tax reform programme. Today, property investment strategies have to be precisely targeted. You need in-depth research and preparation. You must realise that, even in a boom city at the height of a buying frenzy, there can still be properties which lag in value. So you've got to ask yourself, 'Am I ready to invest?'

WHO INVESTS?

Thanks to surveys conducted by the Australian Bureau of Statistics we know a bit about residential property investors and renting.

- Twenty per cent of Australian households rent their homes from the private sector and 6 per cent are in public housing.
- Big corporations, employers and a host of organisations own a share of this private residential rental stock, but most property providers are ordinary people.
- Around three-quarters of private owner-investors are couples; more have children than live without them.
- In almost 70 per cent of investor couples, both partners are employed.
- This type of investment picks up after the age of 35 and hits its peak in the 45–54 age group.
- Ownership rolls off once people reach 65.
- Tax-saving is a key motivation for younger investors, turning to 'income from rent' as owners enter the retirement years. The most common motivation is that property is seen as a secure long-term investment.
- For around 21 per cent of young, single property investors, another motivating factor is the possibility of moving into the property themselves at some point.

According to the Reserve Bank, more than 10 per cent of Australian taxpayers now own a negatively geared investment property—this is an increase of around 50 per cent on the proportion in the early 1990s.

Government policy has a lot to do with the ongoing attractiveness of property, and investors should be aware of how policies adapt to changes in society. For example, Australians are buying their homes later in life and living at home longer, and considerable numbers are deciding they will never own their own home. From another angle, during the 1990s, the federal Coalition government promoted a policy of increasing assistance for low-income households—provided the extra money went towards renting in the private sector as opposed to public housing. There are lessons here for all property investors.

'I'm holding my breath'

Jean-Paul's first foray into property investment was the purchase of a $500 000 dollar–plus apartment in Sydney's CBD during 2000. He borrowed 100 per cent of the purchase price. He is holding his breath at the moment due to interest rates, debt and competition for tenants in the CBD.

Jean-Paul is a go-ahead businessman who reads widely about personal finance issues and has some formal financial qualifications. He and his wife owned their own home for some time before finally making the jump into broader property investment.

Jean-Paul did his research carefully. 'I started by choosing a number of areas where I thought capital appreciation would be good, based on historic records,' he says.

I looked for areas with low vacancy rates and where life was convenient—five minutes to get to work and five minutes to get home again. I wanted a property which had an underlying lifestyle element—for those who want to go nightclubbing or be part of the café society; it had to be close to entertainment. These factors let you charge a premium for rent.

When it comes to sourcing an appropriate apartment, it doesn't take much to find out that certain buildings are really on the nose. And this is for the most practical reasons. I heard of a beautiful building with wonderful views—but the owners and tenants were moving out because the walls were paper-thin and you heard every noise, every flush of the toilet.

The promotional brochures for the new prestige developments are getting silly now. I've seen 40-page glossies full of semi-naked men and women and nothing about the building!

I was only interested in buying a new property. Again, this lets you charge a rent premium as well as get the benefit of good depreciation allowances on the building and plant. Following this prescription, I was able to find a property with an above-average gross return—7 per cent per annum—and move towards being revenue-neutral on the deal.

When it came to sourcing finance, I went initially to my bank. They were not helpful. Next I approached the business manager at my job. There is a lot of paperwork and assessment involved when you want a loan for a deal like mine. I figured my employer's bank would know a lot about my employer and my job security and that this would count in my favour. In the end, I got the money I needed—and it came at a lower interest rate too.

My tip is that if you want to borrow more money, and you think you have the capacity to pay your way, tell the financial institution that, to you, property investment is not just a hobby but a business. They will see your professional attitude and will assess you differently.

SHARES VERSUS PROPERTY: WHICH IS BETTER?

Shares did very well for investors through the 1990s and into 2000, when the bull run started to falter, before picking up speed again in 2004. Property gains have been patchy or even flat in many parts of Australia, despite huge leaps in most capitals, major regional centres and selected suburbs in other locations around the nation.

How has property performed in Australia? Tables 1.1 and 1.2 use a *moving annual median* to show how values have risen. The moving annual median is the average of the median (mid-point) for four consecutive quarters. It is a more useful measure of trends than taking simple median prices, and is preferable for making comparisons over a period of time or from place to place.

Property prices show continual growth. But is it good enough? In newspaper and magazine articles, experts are keen to point out that shares have been 'a better investment than property'. Is this true? Over time, the All Ordinaries Index has outperformed housing in terms of broad growth. Individual circumstances such as tax and the nature of income generated by an investment will affect these indices but shares are still the winner. However, the ride has been much bumpier with shares than property.

Figure 1.1 shows us that your money performed better if it was in shares than in residential property. (It shows the weighted average of house prices in the eight capital cities, compared with the All Ordinaries share index—both sets of figures have been converted to index numbers so they start at the same point, with a value of 1000 at 30 June 1989.) The bald facts show that yes, it is true: shares have outperformed property as an investment. Indeed, shares have shot ahead dramatically since 2004.

But the short answer ignores the more complex realities of life. There is a time to buy shares and a time to buy property. In many ways, the timing has less to do with events in the marketplace and more to do with family life, available resources and overall investment strategy. From this perspective, the question 'Do shares outperform property or does property outperform shares?' is of little value to the long-term investor. A balanced investment portfolio will involve both, as well as some fixed-interest cash-based investments.

Figure 1.1 Shares vs property

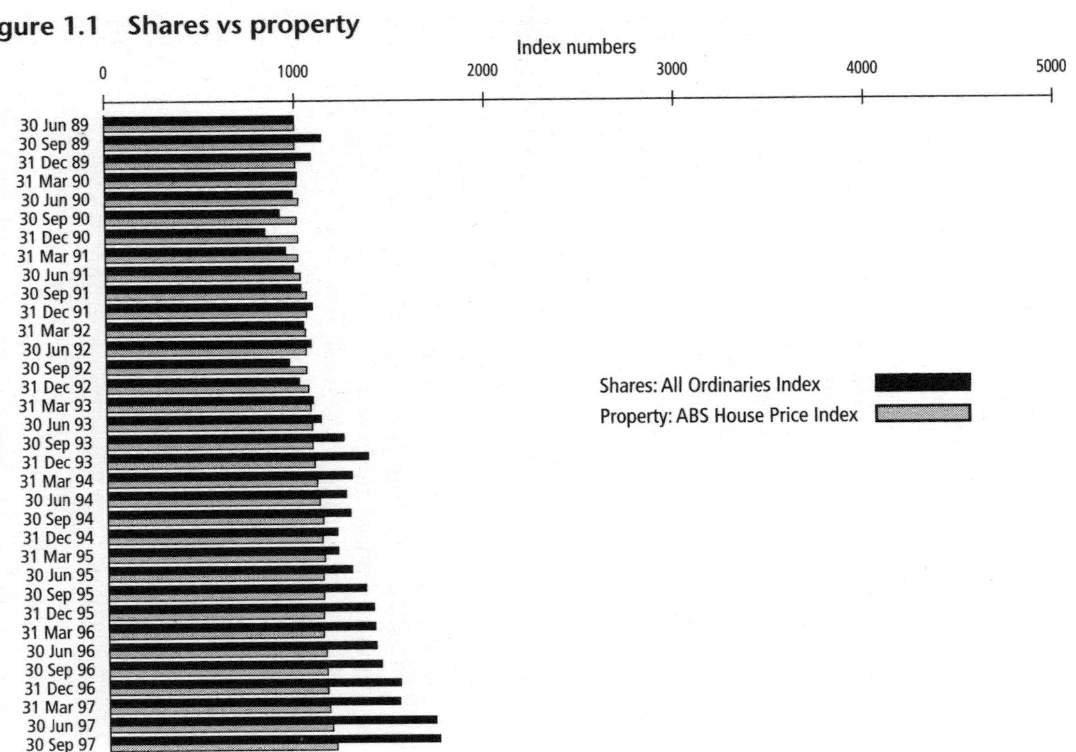

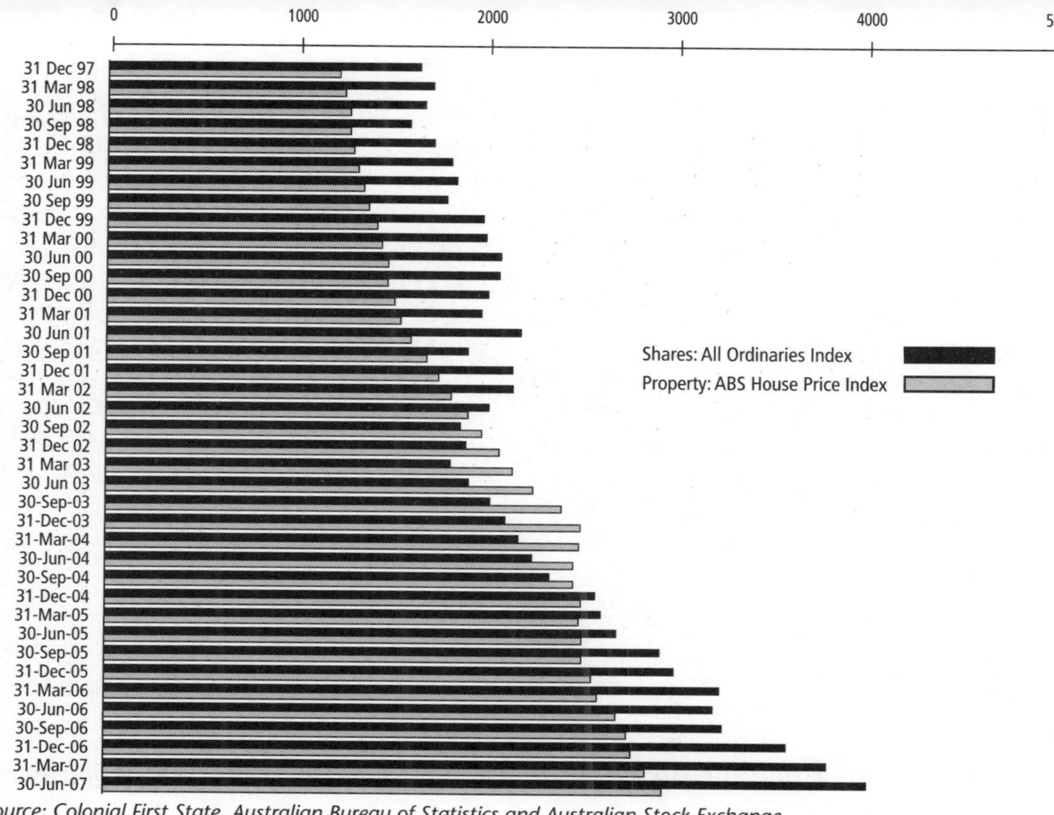

Source: Colonial First State, Australian Bureau of Statistics and Australian Stock Exchange

Table 1.1 Twenty-four years of established house prices—moving annual median, June quarter each year

Year	Sydney ($)	Melbourne ($)	Brisbane ($)	Adelaide ($)	Perth ($)	Canberra ($)	Hobart ($)	Darwin ($)
1984	84 500	61 300	56 900	59 800	47 000	77 400	na	na
1985	89 300	74 400	60 200	73 900	50 500	86 900	na	na
1986	97 900	82 700	61 200	77 400	54 300	92 300	na	na
1987	109 600	86 400	60 000	76 400	59 500	90 200	na	na
1988	141 300	98 600	65 800	78 300	65 200	93 500	na	84 500
1989	206 000	126 400	86 100	88 800	98 500	110 000	na	87 300
1990	184 300	140 000	103 000	100 500	97 500	117 500	na	97 400
1991	172 800	138 800	108 500	107 300	94 300	126 000	na	103 200
1992	179 800	136 500	118 500	107 800	97 500	147 500	91 400	120 300
1993	179 300	140 300	122 300	110 600	104 300	159 100	99 900	142 100
1994	182 800	144 300	127 300	112 400	118 900	160 500	108 000	150 100
1995	199 300	146 600	132 500	112 800	125 400	158 300	110 000	166 100
1996	203 700	146 300	133 800	110 200	127 100	155 500	108 500	162 400
1997	230 000	170 000	140 000	149 000	135 000	155 000	105 000	178 000
1998	260 000	198 000	144 000	120 300	144 000	160 000	107 000	180 000
1999	280 000	226 000	145 000	125 000	148 500	158 000	115 000	176 000

	Sydney ($)	Melbourne ($)	Brisbane ($)	Adelaide ($)	Perth ($)	Canberra ($)	Hobart ($)	Darwin ($)
2000	315 000	253 000	149 200	135 000	157 800	184 000	130 000	190 400
2001	316 000	291 000	180 000	148 200	165 700	203 000	120 300	187 000
2002	388 000	327 500	230 000	170 000	185 700	227 600	130 000	200 000
2003	465 000	359 000	289 000	220 000	210 200	305 000	180 000	206 000
2004	559 000	376 000	295 300	245 500	246 800	366 300	227 500	237 400
2005	537 800	356 800	306 600	270 800	277 000	354 400	263 000	268 600
2006	520 500	363 600	320 000	279 800	351 500	366 200	275 600	328 300
2007	522 300	393 800	345 200	299 500	451 900	412 800	296 000	385 000

Source: *Real Estate Institute of Australia*
Note: na = not available

Table 1.2 Twenty-four years of established unit and other dwelling prices—moving annual median, June quarter each year

Year	Sydney ($)	Melbourne ($)	Brisbane ($)	Adelaide ($)	Perth ($)	Canberra ($)	Hobart ($)	Darwin ($)
1984	65 100	46 500	57 700	46 800	38 400	54 800	na	na
1985	67 100	58 100	57 100	59 200	36 900	68 600	43 800	na
1986	69 200	62 900	57 200	64 300	41 800	74 100	57 100	na
1987	74 900	68 500	61 800	62 700	46 900	83 200	59 800	na
1988	99 700	76 000	62 800	65 900	49 800	80 700	59 500	na
1989	137 100	91 700	78 800	69 900	69 800	88 500	66 400	na
1990	138 300	111 200	88 500	77 500	76 800	95 600	73 200	na
1991	134 200	113 400	91 300	82 800	75 800	95 700	72 600	na
1992	138 400	105 600	98 000	85 100	75 200	119 400	74 800	na
1993	139 400	107 800	100 400	91 400	77 700	129 700	79 300	na
1994	148 600	111 400	101 400	92 000	82 000	129 300	83 800	na
1995	154 800	114 100	107 000	92 600	87 900	129 500	86 500	na
1996	161 600	113 600	116 900	92 400	86 700	123 700	86 400	na
1997	185 000	126 000	132 500	103 200	91 800	127 800	75 300	na
1998	220 000	148 000	159 000	92 500	97 500	136 000	72 500	137 000
1999	236 000	173 000	140 000	93 800	105 900	126 000	86 000	150 000

	Sydney ($)	Melbourne ($)	Brisbane ($)	Adelaide ($)	Perth ($)	Canberra ($)	Hobart ($)	Darwin ($)
2000	250 200	190 000	135 200	87 500	113 200	135 000	97 500	160 000
2001	283 000	230 100	164 300	110 000	122 300	145 000	85 800	148 000
2002	330 000	266 400	171 800	130 000	140 300	185 000	87 000	155 000
2003	365 000	279 000	207 000	165 000	159 000	255 000	121 000	164 500
2004	377 300	292 800	227 100	185 100	192 800	287 000	176 800	163 800
2005	370 300	294 900	238 300	204 900	220 600	298 000	212 300	188 100
2006	362 200	306 500	267 900	213 800	280 300	308 300	221 900	248 600
2007	358 400	328 100	289 800	226 900	352 800	317 900	229 800	282 200

Source: Real Estate Institute of Australia and State institutes
Note: na = not available

Table 1.3 Shares vs property

Shares	Property
A small outlay will get you started—$1000 will do	A large outlay required—at least $15 000–$50 000, including expenses
Lower purchase expenses	Higher purchase expenses
Fast transaction time—buying or selling can be done in a day	Much slower transaction time—allow at least two to three months to buy and three to twelve months to sell
No ongoing costs	Ongoing costs include insurance, repairs, maintenance, breakages, rates, levies, possible land tax, managing agent's fees, and more
Potential for high growth, or high losses; share prices can be very volatile; occasionally some shares become valueless	Potential for high growth in select areas; losses do occur but stagnation or modest losses are more likely than high losses
Share prices can be artificially inflated by fashion or the frenzy of a rising market	Property prices, particularly in 'hot' suburbs, can be inflated by fashion or the frenzy of a rising market
Rising interest rates and rising inflation can hurt share prices as companies face higher costs of operation	Rising interest rates can hurt property investors (they are a disincentive for property purchasers), but rising inflation can lead to increased prices
Dividends supply some income	Rent supplies income—except when the property is vacant

Shares	Property
You can borrow money to buy shares, but if the share values fall substantially you might be required by the lender to put more of your money into the loan; this can be tense and difficult	Property mortgages are very competitive and even when property values fall, you do not usually have to put more money into the loan (for example, you can extend the loan term)
You can't improve your shares	You can usually do something to improve the value or saleability of your property—property has potential for improvement by your hand, but at your cost

If you want to get serious about investment you should start not by putting a few thousand dollars into the latest public float of a well-known company, nor by buying an investment property, but by creating an investment plan for yourself and, where relevant, your family. You can do a lot of the planning yourself—but at some point you should discuss your strategy with one or more people with experience and an objective perspective.

If you haven't already done so, contact a licensed financial planner. I know it can sometimes be difficult to find someone who you feel has an interest in you, and I have come across a number whose interest level drops to zero as soon as you indicate you want to invest in property rather than high-commission managed funds. But from time to time every investor needs an outside expert to look coolly at their pile of varying investments—term deposits, sundry shares and a home—and correct the mix.

To be licensed, financial planners must have undertaken courses of study and demonstrated a degree of professional skill. They will hear what you have to say about your aims and resources and draw up a profile of your attitude to risk and reward. Only after assessing you, the investor, and having understood where you want to head and how fast and aggressively you are prepared to travel, should your adviser begin planning how to get you there.

Some people might prefer to do it all themselves, or might have an aversion to surrendering control to a financial adviser. Even then they should write down an investment plan and seek opportunities to discuss their plan with other, more experienced investors, their accountant, lawyer, bank manager, and so on. Being responsible for their own portfolio, the DIY investor must read widely and keep up-to-date on developments with their investments and in the marketplace.

A time for each

People will always argue about whether shares should take precedence over property in a person's investment planning. But there is one important factor which is regularly left out of such discussions, particularly in the media: you need substantial savings to purchase a property.

Have you got a spare $1000? You can buy some shares. But $1000 will get you nowhere when it comes to buying an investment property. At some point in your life you will find you have a chunk of money to your name. It might be because interest rates have fallen and you are getting ahead with repayments on your home mortgage. It might be because your children are old enough for school and your household returns to being a two-income family after having got by on one income for some years. An inheritance or lottery win can suddenly dump a lump sum in your lap.

At this point you can either spend your newfound cash (or home equity), or decide to invest it. If you decide to invest it, you should consider the pros and cons of shares and property. No matter how attractive the sharemarket might appear, you should ask yourself: 'Will I ever have this amount of spare cash again in my life?' You might have the full deposit for an investment property, or just the makings of a deposit. Don't spend it, even on good investments, until you consider the place of direct property investment in your portfolio. As you will see in Chapter 17, you can always get into property by buying units in a property trust—a spare $1000 will get you started there—so you need not feel locked out of the property sector. But by buying shares you may be shutting the door on ever owning an investment unit or house in your own name.

If your windfall or savings are not sufficient to let you buy a property, by all means consider putting the money into growth investments such as shares until you can afford to buy property. My point being that in our lives we don't often have a real chance of buying an investment property, yet we will have many opportunities to get into the sharemarket. Recognise these moments when they occur.

At the very least, property investment is a good savings plan. Like the Tar Baby, it doesn't let go easily. You have to keep up the payments and you don't get your money out until you sell the whole thing.

LOOKING FOR BALANCE

Is there balance in your investment portfolio? Take a look at this example and write down your current exposure to these broad areas of investment: property, shares and fixed interest/cash. Underneath each heading, write down what assets you have in that category, along with their monetary value and any debt.

Example:

Property	Value ($)
Home	600 000
Mortgage	(350 000)
Superannuation	60 000*
Total:	*310 000*

Shares	**Value ($)**
Telstra	9 600
Westpac	9 250
Foster's	2 150
Superannuation	80 000*
Total:	*101 000*
Fixed interest/cash	**Value ($)**
Term deposit	10 000
Cash management account	2 000
Superannuation	30 000*
Total:	*42 000*
Proportions	
Property	68%
Shares	22%
Fixed interest/cash	10%

* Check the latest report from your superannuation fund to find out in what proportions your super is split across the various areas of the economy. Shares, for example, might divide into local and overseas proportions.

THE LIFE STAGES LADDER

What are the proportions of your assets? Your home (if you have purchased one) gives you an enormous 'credit' under the property heading. You might have a few shares resulting from high-profile company floats. It is easy to be very light in the fixed interest/cash corner. As people get older, financial security becomes more important (see Figure 1.2), and the balance shifts to more capital-secure investments. In retirement, the cavalry of wage income won't come and rescue you after a financial disaster.

Figure 1.2 Life stages ladder

60+ Retire so as to withdraw your superannuation tax-free

55+ Evaluate your existing investments: consider moving part of your money into capital-secure investments and gradually out of higher-risk shares and property if their uncertainty troubles you; investigate rollover funds and retirement planning options generally—be prepared for retirement

45–65 Look at your superannuation: obtain advice on 'topping up' your superannuation with extra payments

40–55 Consider further direct property investments; consider greater involvement in the sharemarket, here and overseas

35–45 Consider direct property investment; learn about tax advantages and investment; structure your loans so that you have access to emergency cash (perhaps through a redraw facility)

30–40 Try to bring your home mortgage down by making extra repayments (lump sums or fortnightly instalments instead of monthly, for example); if not done yet, get expert advice for preparation of a financial plan for your life

25–35 Buy your first home; purchase shares in a few companies—directly or via managed funds; consider carefully any prominent company floats; learn about how the sharemarket works

START 17–30 Save for a home deposit; ensure you are receiving superannuation from your employer; consider moving your cash out of the low-interest bank account and into a cash management account, for example

Direct property investment—that is, where you buy a property yourself, not through units in a managed fund—is not for everyone. It might not suit your temperament or be out of your financial reach. Over the years, some very smart retirees have told me that as the retirement years roll on they are moving out of direct property investment. They are doing this to avoid the kind of high-impact cost which can come out of nowhere with this type of investment—such as the need for a new roof, new carpets or kitchen cupboards. Owners of a unit in a high-rise building might be hit with special levies to replace an unreliable elevator or to fix concrete cancer in the balconies. It might be far harder in retirement than at other times of life to find a few thousand dollars to deal with a property maintenance issue. Like everything else, there is a natural flow, a pattern, a life-cycle for the investor.

Figure 1.2 is an indicator of the life stages of the investor. It won't be the same for everyone, but you can use it as a pattern against which you can compare yourself and how you are travelling. Any hiccup in life—serious illness, divorce, retrenchment—will put the brakes on your progress. You might have to climb back onto this ladder several times through your life.

GETTING YOUR DEPOSIT TOGETHER

If you don't have enough money for a deposit, how do you get there? There are many books and magazine articles that will help you decide the right strategy for your situation, but if you are finding it difficult to put enough money together you should consider seeking expert advice from a range of professionals.

Generally speaking, there are only a handful of ways in which to acquire that all-important first deposit. Fads come and go, but these have not really changed since the days of the pharaohs:

- You inherit it.
- Your family provides you with the deposit.
- You marry it (or similar).

- You cheat someone out of their money.
- You win at the races.
- You study hard and qualify yourself for a better paid job.
- You start your own successful business.
- You save like squirrels and invest strategically not randomly.

Joking apart, any method you choose will work at least twice as fast if you have a stable long-term relationship and an enthusiastic partner who shares the same goal.

Saving starts with a plan and a budget. Prepare your household budget (any number of finance books will show you how) and, when you realise you spend more than you earn, look at trimming the expenses. Do you need two cars? Do you need even one car? Look at what convenience is costing you. What about the mobile phones or that $10 each week on videos? You have to sort it out yourself—no one's going to hold your hand the whole way through the process.

For many of us, it is pretty pointless to plan to save whatever money is left over at the end of the month. All too often, it just seems to evaporate, so you might have to put your savings away first.

Where should you put your money? An adviser will look at your circumstances and make recommendations. Growth-oriented investments will be an important part of your discussions, as even a term deposit will only put you ahead of inflation by around 1 or 2 per cent after you've paid income tax on the interest. If you have a five-year-plus time-frame, you might want to consider managed funds (in a rising market) which will accept regular direct debits from your account. And placing piddly amounts of cash into three or four stocks (shares) is often a recipe for losing your money rather than making it. Many investors have discovered the high interest rates and convenience of using online savings accounts (in late 2007 this was paying around 6.3 to 7.0 per cent).

If you already own a home, you might look at using the equity to help finance a second acquisition: see Chapter 11.

SUMMARY

- Shares have frequently outperformed property investment in Australia—but so what? It is not the right issue for the investor. The issue really is: how and when do I add property to my investment portfolio.
- The investor's portfolio requires balance across the main sectors: property, shares and fixed interest/cash.
- See a financial planner—you need expert advice to establish your financial plan before you start investing seriously.
- There is a life-cycle of investment. What stage are you at now?

Chapter 2

Guru peril: Separating motivation from information

Having spent many years reviewing personal finance books, I feel compelled to pass on a warning to Australian investors: don't rely on what you read in a personal finance book written outside Australia. A similar concern applies to local seminar programmes with overseas-based speakers. Their information can, in key respects, be incorrect or unsuitable for our marketplace conditions.

This becomes more of an issue where a book has been a best-seller overseas. On its release in Australia, it will receive a big marketing push and plenty of media exposure. Thousands of copies will be sold. But what if the book has not been adapted for Australian investment conditions? We can't expect an investment formula which might work in the United States or the United Kingdom to be successful in Australia. The most obvious sticking point is taxation.

The US tax system is fundamentally different from the Australian tax system. And it is taxation which so often makes or breaks an investment.

Here's an example. Home ownership advice from the United States can be summarised as: 'your home is a liability'. Speaking in sweeping generalisations for the moment, this might well be true for the United States but it most certainly is not true for Australia. In the United States, a home-owner's mortgage instalments are tax deductible and, consequently, a type of capital gains tax is charged when the home is sold. There is not the same absolute divide between the tax treatment of a residence and an investment property that exists in Australia.

The family home is the most fundamental wealth-creation investment in Australia; abroad, investors' money might better serve their needs by targeting other growth strategies rather than staying tied up in the home.

It is a complicated matter to assess an investment book or magazine article for its relevance to Australia. Apart from taxation (income, deductions and capital gains), there are issues to be considered such as social security implications, death duties, interest rates, inflation, corporate regulation, investment regulation, landlord and tenancy law (rights and obligations), local supply and demand, to name but a few. It is unfortunate that some Australian book publishers and distributors do not get successful overseas books assessed for local conditions before releasing them here. Some could do with a sticker on the cover saying: 'Wealth Warning!' So file them under 'fiction'.

A second reason not to place too much reliance on these books is that reading the neat and tidy maxims of the overseas investment gurus is damnably seductive. These pithy sayings claim to be the key to secret knowledge hidden from the masses and imparted only to the initiated few. Human nature is attracted to the quick answer, the shortcut, the easy way to wealth—just like the 'no exercise' diet. Take a look at your local bookshop's investment or finance section and see how often the writers and editors dangle words such as 'secret', 'myth' or 'what they don't teach you in school' in front of you. They are telling you that you too—yes, even you—can become a member of this fun-loving gang of success stories.

The thing I find most disturbing about certain successful overseas titles is the streak of naked greed that runs through them. Working hard to be a smart investor is not necessarily a good thing for everyone and it can only ever be one strand of a person's life. Sometimes the model of a successful investor we are being encouraged to imitate is a person who has led a far from admirable life, dragging their poor family through crisis after crisis, living in high-risk territory in the hope of fulfilling the dream of great wealth.

Well, thanks but 'no thanks'!

In the end, you have the choice to agree or disagree with an author's ethics or worldview—a choice that only you can make. All that I would ask is that you look first at the publication details overleaf from the title page and check whether the book you are holding is an Australian edition or simply a repackaged overseas edition. Check the date of publication as well. Since 2000, the Australian situation has changed remarkably for the investor, with major amendments to income tax, capital gains tax, interest rates and much more. Following the 2007 tax changes, superannuation has become much more attractive. A book quickly becomes out of date, even if it has been written specifically for Australia.

Online information suffers from the same problem, particularly as it is expensive and time-consuming for any business to continually monitor its website and ensure the information it presents is accurate—'high-tech' presentation doesn't guarantee the latest and best information. Think of the internet first and foremost as a business marketing tool,

WHAT WAS I THINKING?

Here are my Top 10 property investment mistakes:

- Buying for the tax break.
- 'Debt isn't as risky as it used to be.'
- Believing what you hear at dinner parties.
- Having an unbalanced portfolio.
- 'I will manage the property myself.'
- 'I don't need expert advice.'
- Buying a property in a run-down condition when you haven't first set aside money to get it into sound—and fast—lettable shape.
- Daring the tenant to 'Just try it, bud!'
- Creative accounting: 'Everyone is doing it—I won't get into trouble.'
- Believing 'The vendor says he only has the property's figures for the last financial year'.

a place where reliability comes a distant second. Trust is thin on the web.

For this reason, as an investor you should always confirm your proposed course of action with a licensed financial adviser, accountant or banker before proceeding with any plan derived from your reading and research. The same principle applies to this book too—there can be *no* exceptions.

Always get your information updated before investing a cent. And understand what is motivating you to take this investment path: property investing isn't like a flutter on Lotto.

SHARKS ARE CIRCLING

The last few years of the property boom made many people wealthy—not necessarily through investment, but through catering for the hungry investor market. Along with rising property prices, we have endured a raft of scams and questionable sales tactics:

- over-priced, over-hyped and over-positive seminars which engender unreal expectations;
- two-tier pricing, such as the scandal of Queensland properties being sold cheaper to locals than to interstate investors;
- financial or investment advice being provided by estate agents, solicitors, financial consultants and financial institutions in situations of arguable conflict of interests;
- unconscionable conduct such as high-pressure sales tactics and the use of interstate flights to take potential investors away from the things they know; saying an offer was 'special' and 'for a limited time only' to encourage a hasty commitment;
- property investment schemes where there were links between some or all of the promoter, the financier, the estate agent and the vendor;
- finance offers for unsecured loans being provided by a friendly company to customers who lack a solid asset base;
- 'churning', which is what happens when mortgage brokers encourage their customers to refinance their loans—with a view to maximising the broker's commission; and
- property investment programmes which place your home equity at risk through the constant accumulation of additional properties and debt.

We've seen the collapse of a number of high-profile property investment syndicates and schemes, from Westpoint to Fincorp and Australian Capital Reserve, as well as seminar presenters in trouble with the regulator.

Investors should be under no illusion that property is a liquid investment that will always increase in value. The risks are real, both from genuine market operations and from business failures. But whatever happens, be prepared to fend off the sharks and hold on tight to your money and assets.

SUMMARY

- It's OK to take your investment inspiration from the United States, but get the facts from Australia. Don't confuse the two.
- Always update your information and be prepared to pay for expert, up-to-the-minute advice that is personalised for your situation, your needs and your attitude to risk.

Section II
RESEARCH

Chapter 3

The broad canvas

You don't need an economics degree to become a property investor—in fact, it might count against you. The more you try to analyse world economic trends, the more paralysed you might become. There is always trouble brewing on the horizon. Yet, as the real estate agents say: 'Today is a good day to sell . . . today is a good day to buy.' Another favourite saying is that a little knowledge is a dangerous thing. And that would be true if you were asked to run the Reserve Bank of Australia for a day or two.

When it comes to residential property, economic trends are often signalled a long way in advance. If you keep your ears and eyes open, you generally will get plenty of warning that interest rates are moving up or down, for example. Of course, our own greed can blind us to the bleeding obvious, and all of us find it hard to sell at a loss.

Part of your research should include broad economic trends. When it comes to residential real estate, I believe domestic social trends are also important. After all, that's where the tenants are coming from. Here are some of the ways these factors can affect property investment strategies.

LOOKING FOR TRENDS—CLUES FOR ACTION

The early part of this new century shows several patterns emerging or settling down about the finances of the average

Australian household. An understanding of how the household is travelling is important if the investor is to get a feel for future directions of the national economy, including inflation and interest rates, property prices and consumer confidence. There is much we don't know about how the average Australian household gets by (and much we wouldn't want to know), but research has uncovered some useful information.

Debt is going up

Australian households carry substantial amounts of debt—and the burden is getting heavier. The debt carried by the average household is now roughly one-and-a-half times its disposable income. Just a decade ago, Australia was a country with a low debt-to-income ratio, but we are now on a similar level to households in Canada, the United Kingdom and the United States.

Where does the debt come from? We buy a lot of things on credit, using cards or personal loans. Loyalty schemes and frequent flyer points are relatively new phenomena which have kicked along and encouraged the use of debt for items ranging from overseas holidays to the weekly shop. Increasingly we are using our home loans as the borrowing vehicle to buy consumer goods (cars, new kitchens, and so on).

A large component of Australian household debt is the home mortgage. Low nominal interest rates in a low-inflation environment, plus huge promotional campaigns and hot competition between the financial institutions, have seen Australians borrow larger and larger amounts for their homes. Household credit grew by 11 per cent over 2005–06, while credit for housing investors grew by 12 per cent.

Assets are going up

Debt gets most of the media attention and hype—we seem to love to hear the worst about ourselves. However, the other side of the coin—our wealth—is arguably an even greater story than our ongoing debt blowout. The ratio of household debt to assets in late 2007 was sitting at around 17.5 per cent (it was 12 per cent in 1998). As frightening as our debt has become, those of us with well-located property assets have enjoyed a period of incredible asset growth which has created quite a buffer between what we own and what we owe. But it is part illusion. Much of this increase in wealth has been unearned, in the sense that we didn't do much except passively own a home. I'm not sure that this teaches us much about investing, risk and reward!

Still, there has been a splurge in converting equity to debt, borrowing against our assets to finance lifestyle expenses such as holidays, cars, school fees, plasma/LCD televisions and DVD collections, but also to acquire other assets such as shares, investment property and renovations. According to the Reserve Bank, the money we spend on alterations and additions now represents around 40 per cent of overall dwelling investment. We are raiding our home equity piggy banks: loans with a redraw facility now account for 14 per cent of all credit secured against housing. Thirty per cent of mortgages are refinanced in any year—often with a view to releasing equity for spending, as well as obtaining more favourable loan conditions and facilities.

Debt has risen but so have household assets. What can the investor draw from this? Our high levels of debt, even if looked at just in nominal terms, mean Australians are vulnerable to increases in interest rates. We have been piling on the debt when rates have been low, and if interest rates climb too high or too fast we might not be able to afford our assets. We last had high interest rates in 1990/91—a time before many of us even became investors. Are we really taking adequate precautions to limit our risk exposure? Interest rates rose four times in 2005–06 before another lengthy pause and rises in August and November 2007. More could follow.

While household liabilities (debt) relative to assets show modest increase, household debt levels relative to disposable income have risen consistently. This increased debt remained affordable when the servicing costs (interest rates) were falling in the late 1990s and early 2000s. It seems we are prepared to borrow more and more money, as long as it doesn't actually cost us any more (as a proportion of our income). Surely this leaves us vulnerable to any move in the economy which will impact on our disposable income? We love our homes and mortgages, but we don't want our lifestyles to suffer too much.

Financial institutions are having great success in influencing Australians to borrow money. Incentive factors such as special introductory rates (the one-year honeymoon mortgage rate) and more flexible borrowing conditions (redraw facilities and shared-equity loans) have been effective in bringing us in.

Wealth is not shared equally across the nation. A few selective spots (parts of Sydney, Perth and Melbourne, for example) are where the assets have been growing fast. National 'averages' which make our society's financial statistics look good conceal disturbing levels of homelessness, unemployment, stagnant home prices and poverty.

Once prices start rising our debt vulnerability will lead to pressure on wages. This process is already underway, with substantial increases in petrol, water, electricity and building costs. Senior executive salaries have soared—an inequity which fuels labour discontent. Inflation is back in the news again.

The Australian dollar bounces back

It was early 2001 when the Australian dollar hit historic lows against the US dollar. By late 2003 it had bounced back; in early 2004 it passed the US 80-cent barrier; by mid-2004 it was see-sawing around the 70-cent mark; and in 2007 it briefly hit new records above US 86 cents. This affects our trade position and the cashflow of the business community here. Investment decisions, to a degree, ride on the back of what is happening internationally and our local take on these moves. When our dollar buys precious little overseas, we spend and invest more at home. A rising dollar opens up fresh opportunities offshore.

We are buying homes later

As prices rose sharply through 2002–03, the proportion of first home buyers fell from around 25 per 100 households (in 2001) to 13 per 100 (in 2004). It rose back to 17 per cent in mid-2007. Housing affordability, as measured by the Commonwealth Bank/Housing Industry Association affordability index, hit record lows through 2007.

Young people in particular are delaying the purchase of a home—1.88 million adult Australians aged 15–34 live with one or both parents (Census 2006)—but they are not the only ones. Many Australians only buy their first home after the age of 55. Are they preparing themselves for retirement? Our understanding of housing—where we live, how we live—is undergoing change. People are renting for longer or they are living longer with Mum and Dad.

Migration

Migration of all kinds—from overseas and within Australia—can have an impact on our deliberations on property investment. We shouldn't make too much out of it, but certain locations have seen quite large numbers of new inhabitants. There are definite flows across the continent. While the raw numbers should not be seen as a kind of direct link to property prices rising, we should look to see whether new construction in those areas matches or keeps

Table 3.1 Australia's population—past, present and future

Year	Population (millions)
1997	18.5
1999	19
2021	22–24.8
2051	24.8–33.3

Source: Australian Bureau of Statistics

pace with the inflow and whether there is pressure on landlords to raise or lower rents.

Where do the migrants come from? As at 2005, the largest group had been born in the United Kingdom (24 per cent of all overseas-born persons), followed by those from New Zealand (9 per cent), Italy (5 per cent), and China and Vietnam (4 per cent each). There is another record to look at as well: in the year 2004–05, Australia experienced the greatest *outflow* of permanent residents in a single year, with 62 600 people leaving these shores for good—an increase of almost 12 per cent over the previous year. Clearly they were looking for something else.

Migration puts pressure on housing markets. Table 3.2 shows the population movement (net population gains after deducting population losses through leaving Australia) over a five-year period.

There are also movement patterns within Australia. Queensland—especially the Gold Coast, Tweed region and Brisbane—remains the preferred place to live. By 2041 Queensland is expected to overtake Victoria as Australia's second most populous State (after New South Wales). There's plenty of action in the west of the country too, with Mandurah (south of Perth) becoming the fastest growing region in Australia.

Table 3.2 Immigration on the rise again

Year	Net overseas migration
1989–90	157 400
1991–92	68 600
1992–93	30 300
1999–2000	107 300
2003–04	100 000
2004–05	110 100

Source: Australian Bureau of Statistics

Table 3.3 Where the migrants settled

State/territory	Proportion of (net) overseas migrants moving there (2004–05) (%)
New South Wales	33
Victoria	29
Queensland	16
Western Australia	15
South Australia	6
Australian Capital Territory	< 0 (a net loss)
Northern Territory	< 1
Tasmania	< 1

Source: Australian Bureau of Statistics

Victoria's population is on the increase. Interestingly, the focus for high-income earners has shifted from their traditional home in the eastern suburbs of Melbourne to more fashionable inner-city suburbs. Indeed, contrary to national trends, the average age of the population in these trendy suburbs has fallen.

Australians are on the move, in the search for better jobs or a better lifestyle. Table 3.4 shows the movement patterns (net population gains after deducting population losses) for 2004–05.

Table 3.4 Moving between States/territories

State/territory	Net interstate migration
Queensland	+ 31 500
Western Australia	+ 1 500
Tasmania	+ 187
Northern Territory	+ 5
South Australia	– 1 620
Victoria	– 2 400
Australian Capital Territory	– 3 500
New South Wales	– 25 700

Source: Australian Bureau of Statistics

Overseas migrants want to live in New South Wales, Western Australia, Queensland and Victoria; but within Australia, many are departing the southern States—perhaps because of rising property prices. The Northern Territory, Australian Capital Territory, South Australia and Tasmania are also leaking population as a long-term trend. High property prices and opportunities continue to push the population from one corner to another.

And keep an eye on what young people are doing—they are highly mobile. One in three interstate moves is made by a person aged 20 to 34. A subset of this is the constant drift from the country to urban centres.

The national Census provides a wealth of information about Australians—who they are, how they live. This gives real insight into the dominant social characteristics of the many different parts of the country. Here are some examples of findings drawn from the research. As you read them, ask yourself what signals they give to the property investor:

- Lake Macquarie in regional New South Wales is the area with the most 'double income—no children' families. Good income and particular housing needs?
- The suburb with the most university students is Randwick in New South Wales (near the University of New South Wales).
- The suburb with the highest average age is Nudgee Beach in Queensland.
- You'll find the most babies (aged from birth to four) in Penrith, New South Wales.

The national Census of 2006 gives a detailed snapshot of action within the social fabric of Australia. Some of the matters revealed by this huge survey have implications for housing design and provision. Smart investors can consider acting in ways which are in tune with these needs:

- From 1996 to 2006 the population grew by 11 per cent.
- Family households fell (from 71 per cent to 67 per cent) while single-person households rose (from 22 per cent to 23 per cent).
- Nine out of ten 'young families' comprising mum, dad and young kids were most likely to live in a four-bedroom house. These families are also likely to have two cars—hence the great desire for garaging and off-street parking. Two-thirds of these families are paying off a mortgage, except in the Northern Territory, where 43 per cent are renting.
- Median weekly gross personal income for those aged fifteen years and over was $400 to $599.
- Eighty-three percent of one-parent families were headed by a mother, and the average size of this family was three persons.

- The average Australian is aged 37—up from 34 just ten years earlier.
- The areas with the oldest populations in Australia were Bribie Island in Queeensland, Queenscliffe in Victoria and Victor Harbor in South Australia. Other retirement capitals include the Great Lakes area of New South Wales and Victoria's Mornington Peninsula. Generally Queensland has the highest proportion of babies and toddlers.
- Over the decade from 1996 to 2006 the proportion of dwelling homes that were owned without mortgage fell from 41 per cent to 33 per cent, while the proportion of homes with a mortgage rose from 26 per cent to 32 per cent. The proportion of homes being rented dropped from 29 per cent to 27 per cent.

Woeful savings

According to the Reserve Bank, household savings started going negative in 2002 and have continued in this manner ever since. The truth is that we don't actually save much money anymore. Most of our wealth seems to come from rises in property prices and share values. Compulsory superannuation is playing a role, but that is forced upon us. In one sense, our wealth is 'unearned'. It is not as though we are all dutifully and actively saving for the future by carefully putting aside 10 per cent of our wage each week.

In the late 1990s, Australia was ranked twentieth among OECD nations for saving, with a savings rate about one-quarter that of leading nations Greece, Belgium and Italy. Australia's savings ratio (household consumption to net disposable income) has fallen from around 17 per cent in the mid-1970s to 0.7 per cent in 2005–06 (ABS). We might be well down the list of saving nations, but Australia is in pretty good company, with the United States, Sweden, Denmark, New Zealand, Finland and Norway nearby. Still, we're only saving half of what the Canadians manage to squirrel away, and one-third of the average stash of the Germans, Dutch and Japanese.

Fortunately, the property and share booms have helped, with household net worth increasing by almost 10 per cent, on average, over the past decade.

More retirees

Retirement is going to have a huge and increasing impact on how we plan our property investments. In the last century, it was possible to ignore retirees. Now their future needs—nay, demands—will affect every aspect of the property market.

We all know that the Australian population is ageing. The number of retired people in Australia will double in the period up to the year 2021. As a percentage of the population, official estimates show an increase from approximately 11 per cent to about 16 per cent over this period. By 2030, there will be five million Australians aged 65 or over. Increasing longevity, particularly of females (with an expected average life span approaching 87 years), is a contributory factor. Of great concern to government is the growth in numbers of very old Australians (generally those aged 85 or more), whose proportion of the population will increase much faster than the above figures suggest because average life expectancy has increased by six years over the past 30 years.

The baby boomers are starting to hit retirement age. For decades this broad group has controlled TV programming, the movies and the biggest music acts (from the Rolling Stones and Hendrix to any singer/guitarist who reminds them of Joni Mitchell). Baby boomers are used to getting their own way, are frequently politically informed and active, know how to stand up for themselves, have enjoyed good education and, on the whole, have experienced helpful economic conditions.

When the baby boomers start saying what they want from the property market, we would all do well to see that it is served up. It is a huge customer base both for tenants and for potential purchasers of your investment when you want the cash out. For six years I was editor of a national magazine for retirement planning. The feedback I had from people at or near retirement raises several issues for potential landlords and developers:

- *Security*—there is a broad fear of personal violence and assault; retirees want to know they can lock the door and head off travelling without having to worry excessively about burglary.
- *Privacy*—many feel the cities, in particular, are becoming crowded. On the street, the boomers love the clamour and colour of a vibrant suburb or city, but at home they want to be left in peace without feeling that someone is always looking over their shoulder.
- *Food*—cooking and eating are very important for this group. They won't put up with broken-down kitchens; many want to live near good cafés and restaurants.
- *Backyard*—the traditional backyard is losing its hold. Apart from the real enthusiast, many actually prefer a small, private, low-maintenance courtyard or balcony. (The shed is optional.)
- *Space*—homes require more storage, an area for an office and computer, and a secure place to park the caravan or boat.

But it would be wrong to think that this huge group is homogeneous. At the one end are those with the money; they will achieve most of their material dreams, even if they have to move to a cheaper suburb, town or city to do so. At the other end are those without the cash—and they are not just the majority, they are the vast, vast majority.

DERAILINGS

The next question is, what are we doing about these trends in our society? It's a bit like going to the races—we're prepared to put our money on a couple of nice-looking horses (our home and a few shares) and hope they put in a good finish. Our passivity, I believe, renders us vulnerable to the harsh realities of the wider economy. Will we know what to do in the event that share prices fall and big-borrowing purchasers pull out of the heated property auction market? Then we might actually have to earn our wealth, not just bury our hopes in our Telstra and Virgin Blue shares and a three-bedroom home in suburbia.

If you are sufficiently motivated to have attended a range of investment seminars, you may have been left feeling a bit inadequate. Are you being left behind? Are you a scaredy-cat, afraid of making your fortune? Maybe you don't even deserve to be wealthy!

It may be an exciting message that the gurus give us, but so what? Passive investment has worked well in Australia. Buy a home, a few shares, let the money pile up in compulsory superannuation, and you will acquire substantial asset wealth during your lifetime. You don't have to do a lot in order to benefit from the way the system works. Save hard for that first deposit, choose your first home carefully and stay in employment. It's not the way to become a multi-millionaire but, thanks to compulsory (for many) superannuation and the age pension, you'll be OK.

Yet increasingly something is going wrong with this easy-going, very Australian formula. The fault does not lie with the mechanics of wealth creation. The rules are easy to learn and the economy drives them along happily. Too often, however, the dream run loses steam. As you contemplate becoming a property investor, think about these three major causes of derailment—otherwise known as financial disasters.

Financial disaster #1: Retiring with only one major asset—your home

A 2004 survey by the Association of Superannuation Funds of Australia (ASFA) found that we were anticipating retirement at an average age of 59, although increasing numbers of people were indicating they would continue to work after reaching 65. The superannuation changes brought in by the 2006 Federal Budget will accelerate the desire to hold on to work until at least the age of 60, and we know the Federal Coalition is keen for us to consider working to 70 (and to be self-supporting thereafter too). It also seems likely that more and more of us will opt to make use of the transition-to-retirement rules to phase ourselves slowly out of the workplace while drawing some income from existing super.

Three in ten of those surveyed by ASFA believed it was likely they would achieve the income they required in retirement. Around 18 per cent intended to sell their home as part of their retirement planning. It is too easy to reach retirement age in this country and have the bulk of your savings caught up in your home. The only way to maintain a desirable lifestyle is to sell up and move out. According to the Reserve Bank of Australia, in mid-2007 household debt accounted for 17.5 per cent of total household assets, up from 13.5 per cent just seven years earlier.

What happened to all those people who took the step to home ownership in their 20s or 30s but failed to make the next leap to long-term financial independence? Only financial planning will help us avoid hitting retirement as asset-rich but cash-poor.

Financial disaster #2: Losing your job or your health

Passive investment strategies rely on a lifetime of steady, if not spectacular, income. A high income is not as important as a lifelong income when it comes to passive investment. Job security can no longer be taken for granted, as it was in the past. Indeed, many of us might not even want the 'job for life' that was once so attractive in our society. We may find ourselves walking out the door in the search for stimulation, travel, new horizons and challenges. Or a tough job and modern stresses may bring us to the point of burnout. Unemployment and illness contribute to the failure of passive investment in creating self-funding retirement. As Australia moves closer and closer to the US model of 'underemployment'—where you're working a shift almost every day but for a total of only twenty hours per week—we have to move to more active strategies for creating financial independence.

Financial disaster #3: Relationship breakdown

Separation and divorce, often involving children who must be supported, is a sure-fire way to wreck your financial security and derail your plans. Drawing a thick blue line through the assets acquired by the partnership, we turn a potentially self-supporting economic unit into two or more under-resourced households. Take a moment to ask yourself this question: does your current investment strategy offer any ways of coming out of a relationship breakdown without financial meltdown?

SUMMARY

- Before you can invest in property, you must do your research. Social and economic trends are important.
- Our household level of debt is increasing.
- Our level of assets is also increasing.
- Our currency is vulnerable; international markets have a great impact on our domestic economy and on our investment strategies.

- We are buying homes later.
- Our population is highly mobile. Some States/territories are moving ahead while others are losing their people.
- We remain a nation of poor savers.
- Retirees are becoming a powerful force in our economy.
- Passive investment has left a legacy of retirees who are asset-rich but cash-poor.
- We must create more active investment strategies—leave our passive investment strategies in the past and take a stronger interest in our financial affairs.

Chapter 4

Location, location, location

It's not how much you spend that counts . . . it's where you spend it. 'Location, location, location' (otherwise known as the First Rule of Real Estate) remains the fundamental catchcry of the real estate agent. And in this, at least, the agent is correct.

Yet 'location' isn't quite as clear as perhaps it once was. We've seen plenty of evidence that a 'poor' location in a large city—for example a run-down, traditional working-class suburb—can become a fashionable hot-spot, with frantic buyers throwing down obscene amounts of money to secure a lifestyle location that was once the home of a poverty-stricken factory worker.

Violent fringe neighbourhoods have become trendy suburbs, defying much of the popular sentiment that they make poor investment choices. Here, of course, there is a catch: the 'good location' starts about 30 metres above the ground, in a luxury high-rise development with spectacular views of the harbour, river, ocean or parkland. On ground level you have to negotiate the used syringes, the homeless people camped in doorways, the prostitutes, drug dealers and petty criminals. Pray your car doesn't break down on the way into the underground security parking.

WHAT MAKES A DESIRABLE LOCATION?

Let's ignore the aberrations for the moment and concentrate on the main game: finding a good location. Location is so important because it's the one thing you can't fix later. That patch of land is what it's all about. You can buy an investment property with a tired kitchen, a mould-encrusted bathroom, only one bedroom, rising damp or worse. And, by throwing money at the problem, you can improve the situation and add value to your investment. But you can't shift the house ten blocks across town. If you make a bad location choice, sometimes the only remedy is to sell the property and buy again—thereby throwing away at least $40 000 (plus your wasted time and energy).

The land is the irreplaceable factor. A good location is made a great location because it is in short supply. You can always build a pile of small units where a beachside family home once sat, but you may have noticed that quality houses in great locations are gradually disappearing under the pressure to develop every good site. A huge part of the value lies in the dirt, along with the right to expand into the airspace above.

In my view there are six hallmarks of a good location:

Proximity

It should be close to desirable things such as:

- the beach, river or harbour;
- beautiful parks;
- schools;
- a university;
- a hospital;
- a major shopping centre; and
- workplaces (CBD, hospital, university, etc.).

Distance

It should be well away from:

- factories and industrial estates;
- anything that emits strong odours;
- highways;
- rail lines (unless the property is within easy walking distance of a station);
- airports;
- aeroplane flight paths;
- rubbish dumps;
- clubs and pubs;
- nuclear reactors;
- electricity substations; and
- major overhead powerlines or microwave towers.

Services

It should give the occupants (your tenants) good access to:

- public transport (buses, trains, ferries); a local train station or ferry wharf to the CBD is highly valued;
- car service stations (so you can drop off the car for servicing on the way to work and pick it up near home again);
- a local convenience store (for the last-minute necessities of life, from the litre of milk to fresh croissants on Sunday morning); and
- even, in some areas, a Centrelink office.

Amenity

This is a piece of jargon, but it's one you should get used to. 'Amenity' means literally the pleasantness of a place—how 'liveable' that little corner of the town or city is. Does it have:

- leafy streets filled with beautiful trees;
- wide, generous boulevards or intimate courtyards;

- grand old homes here and there, imposing their gracious charm on the street scene;
- houses in a ring around a tidy patch of park;
- streets that are not used as a shortcut or thoroughfare by through traffic;
- fresh and sweet-smelling air; and
- the sounds of happy children playing, cats purring and a sprinkler playing softly on a well-cared-for lawn?

Do you get the picture? Of course the ideal amenity for one person might not be perfect pleasantness for another. You might prefer a more vibrant amenity, characterised by:

- traffic;
- lots of cafés and restaurants;
- nearby nightclubs;
- people out on the street at all hours of the day and night;
- neon lights flashing through the dark night sky;
- music spilling from open doorways; and
- a sexy 'buzz' to the area.

Demand

No matter how wonderful the physical location is, it must be situated in an area experiencing a constant, strong demand from outsiders to move in, or from locals to move to better housing.

Location and demand are like a couple joined at the hip. You cannot separate them in your thinking and planning. Australia is full of towns and suburbs with streets which meet the above criteria with flying colours, yet they remain poor investment choices due to a lack of demand and/or an oversupply of quality accommodation.

Potential

There are three ways you can make money from your investment property: rent, capital gain and by developing the site. When you assess a property, look for the potential to:

- add a family room;
- add a bedroom;
- add an ensuite bathroom to the main bedroom;
- add offstreet parking or a lock-up garage;
- increase the storage;
- extend upwards or out into the backyard;
- turn one dwelling into two flats;
- add a dwelling in the backyard; or
- fix an architectural problem—aluminium windows, for example—and restore period authenticity.

Of course, no property has every one of these attractive attributes. Property selection is, at all turns, the art of compromise. The target property might be near a wonderful park, but also close to a highway; it might have water views, but be under a flight path.

Bear in mind that one major drawback can wipe out a whole host of good features. Try these:

- The telegraph pole is directly outside the bedroom balcony—you're looking straight into the wires.
- The house is up against the 10-metre-high brick wall of the former shop next door.
- The bus shelter is right at the front gate—with queues of yawning people every morning.
- There is a sewer 'stink pipe' jutting out from the shrubbery in the backyard.

When you are targeting a particular spot, prepare a list of the area's good and bad features and a second list of good and bad features about any particular property in which you are interested. Before you make your lists, pull out the street directory and open the relevant map. Get out any information you have on the property itself, whether a leaflet or brochure supplied by the estate agent or simply the picture from the local newspaper.

You are looking to secure an investment location for a tenant, not yourself. What you love—or hate—about a location is relevant only to the extent that your sentiment's are shared by a wide cross-section of the renting public. For example, if you currently drive to work, you might be inclined to rate poorly a nearby railway station with all its dirt and noise. Others who rely on public transport will love the proximity of the station. A leafy block will look cool and peaceful to one person but suggest damp and poor security to another.

There can be considerable overlap between what owners and tenants want from a property and location. When you prepare your property profiles, try to consider things from the perspective of the likely tenant population in that area. Test your own values and challenge what you love about the property and its location. For example, there are parts of Sydney where investment apartments with harbour views remain vacant for long periods of time. While it's easy to fall for the view, there will be critical reasons why potential tenants are not queuing up to move in.

Tip: Don't confuse what *you* want with what your tenants will want.

THE WORST HOUSE

You may have heard of the Second Rule of Real Estate: 'Buy the worst house in the best street'. That holds great truth for your home. But is it quite the same when considering an investment property?

Let's return to the prospective occupant: what will tenants be looking for? In some suburbs the majority of tenants might want a property where all the hard work has been done. The kitchen is up-to-date, the bathroom is immaculate—they have made a lifestyle decision to rent (and get the standard of home they could never afford to buy) rather than buy a home in a less expensive area. This sort of tenant is demanding and will not readily accept a 'renovator's delight'.

Know your tenants! If you invest in a fixer-upper you could soon find your managing agent on the phone, suggesting you put some money into the place so that it becomes easier to find tenants and to achieve the rental returns the property deserves.

When it comes to selling your investment, you are again looking at attracting owner-occupiers (as well as investors), and the potential of the site rises in importance once more.

BUYING OFF THE PLAN

Would you invest in a hole in the ground?

If you are interested in investing in brand-new property, you will find it is possible to buy a house or an apartment in a building which has not yet been constructed. What you see is most certainly not what you get. This strategy has some real potential advantages:

- You are securing a property at today's price yet not having to pay the full purchase price until construction is complete—usually many months later.
- You are buying a new property and may be able to take advantage of special depreciation rates for new constructions as well as depreciation off the new price of fittings and furnishings. This improves your cashflow.
- You don't have to come up with the full stamp duty on the full purchase price at the time you enter the contract.

By the time you settle the purchase, the property might even have increased in value, making it possible to extend your approved mortgage amount if you need to. Sometimes, however, there is a decrease in value before settlement.

- At the time you enter the contract, you don't have to start the full mortgage running. A bank guarantee or deposit bond will hold the place for you until settlement—you won't even have to provide the usual 10 per cent deposit up front. There is a fee for this, and bear in mind that this is an extreme example of leveraging your investment over the construction period, but it remains a useful tool. For more on deposit bonds, turn to Chapter 7.
- Tenants like moving into brand-new homes—you may be able to charge a rent premium.

BUT you are shopping blind. What can you do to protect yourself?

- Buy from a name with a good reputation. Local estate agents know which property developers have a good name and which leave a mess behind them. A mess turns into high ongoing maintenance charges and long vacancies.
- Find the addresses of other developments by this company. Go and inspect them. Do they have high vacancy rates? Are the cracks appearing?
- Check with your State/territory builder licensing authority and consumer affairs/fair trading agency to find out whether any warnings exist about the builder.

You should ensure your solicitor or conveyancer takes a good look at the contract. Be prepared to negotiate on the contract conditions if they are unfair. The contract should include:

- specifics about fixtures and fittings, clearly described and, where relevant, noting model brands and product numbers. Check them off your list: air-conditioning/heating, washing machine, hot water service, taps, bench-tops, stove—gas or electric?, carpets, tiles, bath (enamel acrylic/spa?), numbers of light fittings/power points, internet access, pay TV and cable access points, etc.;
- the strata plan, identifying the lot you are purchasing, any car space or garage, storeroom, private outdoor space, etc.;
- the schedule of finishes—number of coats of paint to be applied, cornicing and architraves, the quality of fittings, etc.;
- a copy of the building plans and specifications as approved by council;
- a floorplan of your unit *drawn to scale* so you can do your own figures and see if you really can fit into such a small space;
- a condition that sets a completion date for construction. The term should state that if this date passes you can get out of the contract if you so choose;
- a condition saying that the builder will only use new materials of the highest quality;
- a condition laying out a procedure for dealing with any dispute you might have with the builder/developer/vendor. In particular, check out the arrangements for handling variations of the contract which emerge or are necessitated as the works progress; and
- a condition specifying the time limit for any construction defects to be remedied.

Local rental agents will tell you the gossip about the developer and the development. Keep in touch.

'Get to that first meeting'

Roberta had an eye to the demands of retirement living when she purchased a brand-new two-bedroom apartment off the plan. She understood that good two-bedroom apartments in Sydney were appreciating faster than larger apartments, so she looked into a two-bedroom and planned to sell her present four-bedroom unit when she retired.

'I won't necessarily move into my investment property,' said Roberta, 'but what I've done is secure today the value I will have to pay for an equivalent apartment when I retire.'

Roberta purchased a unit in a new development so she could claim the depreciation allowance on her tax, enabling her to improve her cashflow position. However, she has an important warning to deliver:

'My tip is that it is essential, in a new building, to go to the first meeting of the body corporate. I was surprised how many people missed it. At that meeting some very important things take place which set the scene for years to come—for example, the budget is approved and the managers appointed.

'Some experienced owners acted unscrupulously at the first meeting, seeking personal advantage through the passing of special by-laws which would permit the fitting of ugly exterior air-conditioning boxes and the enclosing of balconies.

'The lengthy budget papers revealed that the managers had sweetheart deals going for the placement of insurance and service contracts. They had to state their expected commissions in the budget, but these figures were buried and you had to go looking for them. By insisting on obtaining further quotes we were able to save more than $20 000 in annual insurance premiums.

You have to be really active, especially in that first year.'

LOCATION WARNINGS

It's a heady thing finding you can finally raise the cash to buy an investment property. It can be tempting to see yourself as someone who has financial status and significance, particularly with real estate agents and bank managers eager to sell you their wares. Every stage of the process of buying an investment property, including selecting your location, has its traps. Here are my Top 5 pitfalls to avoid.

Warning #1: Avoid anything too fashionable

Fashions come and go. Some new or refurbished apartment blocks are now being put on the market with celebrity launches. This means you get an invitation to an opening party where you will (let's just say, 'might possibly') get to meet well-known or minor celebrities who have bought into the building. Oh, the glamour—and you can be part of it! But if the location is poor ultimately the glamour will disappear. And with it the celebrity neighbour. Fashion walks out the door when the general public walks in.

Warning #2: Avoid any location in which you would not be caught dead yourself

If the area is seedy it will not hold on to quality, peace-loving tenants for long. At certain ages and stages of our lives, we may be attracted to the gritty realism of life on the streets. It's an aphrodisiac for those leaving home for the first time or anyone seeking to escape safe, dull suburbia. That's a great time to move into a colourful part of town and experience this slice of life. But the attraction fades, for most, when a family member or dear neighbour is mugged, or their child picks up a syringe off the footpath. You are limiting your range of potential tenants and eventual purchasers if the subset of occupants for your investment is restricted to those who can handle the presence of danger and personal risk.

Warning #3: Don't be lured too far from home

In my view a good place to start your investigation of potential investment property is your own suburb or a suburb where you once lived. You might find it is too expensive to invest in an area where you can only just afford to buy your own home, but if you make notes about the pros and cons of the area and target particular properties, you can bring to bear your considerable experience and familiarity with living conditions.

When your eye moves far from familiar territory you become more vulnerable to the influence of others. 'This part of the coast will become the new Noosa!' says the local authority. It might be the inside tip of your life. Or it might take 30 years to come true. Or it might just be a fantasy (if not a downright lie). Some of us can afford to make wrong decisions. But if *you* can't afford it, then be wary about investing far from home.

Warning #4: Avoid 'holiday syndrome'

When holidaying, do you find you are drawn towards the shopfront windows of the local real estate agents? In a quaint, history-rich country town, a grand Federation home or snug timber cottage can seem incredibly inexpensive. With the sound of the ocean waves crashing in the background, and the itch of summer sand in your swimming costume, the exorbitant prices charged for beachside real estate might speak to you of the inevitable upward spiral of capital gain in such a carefree spot.

The holiday spirit can cloud the mind for hard investment decision-making. Look in the agency windows, sniff the air, wander the street . . . but don't make any sudden moves to commit. If you liked the place, plan a special investment trip for later. Do your research first, make some appointments, get someone to send you the property pages of the local newspaper for a few months, then go back well-armed. The person who walks up to you in the street and suggests a rendezvous to inspect a fabulous property investment is not offering you a hot insider tip.

Queensland's Gold Coast is a classic location for holiday investment syndrome. Some strike it lucky; many others find only fool's gold. It is a very tricky and demanding market. On a recent trip to the Gold Coast I was amazed to see the number of houses for sale and the empty shops standing out like a toothless grin. And still the cranes filled the sky, constructing hundreds more units with breathtaking views.

A good location is much more than a pretty place to live.

Warning #5: Beware of oversupply

All property investors, particularly in the eastern States, should now be aware that the construction and investment boom over 2003–07 has created areas of oversupply. Huge estates have been built and thousands of apartments launched onto the market, leading to difficulties finding tenants (but no corresponding problem finding buyers!). Lenders have become suspicious of the real value of many of these units. In some cases, lending criteria have tightened substantially—especially for small one-bedroom and studio apartments.

This doesn't mean investors should avoid these properties totally. There are still very good reasons to consider an investment in or near the CBD—if you pick your property carefully and ensure your bank or financier will back you up. Chapter 5 takes this further.

SUMMARY

- The First Rule of Real Estate is 'location'—get the location right.
- A good location has these six hallmarks: proximity, distance, services, amenity, demand and potential.
- Buying 'off the plan' can save you money—but you must take steps to research the deal fully.
- Don't confuse what you want from a property with what tenants will be looking for.
- Watch out for holiday syndrome—and beware of your vulnerability when you are searching far from home.
- Tread carefully in the CBD and inner-city apartment market, where there has been oversupply of product and reduced finance availability.

Chapter 5

The CBD sonic boom

Six years have passed since the first edition of this book was published. Back in 2001, this chapter began: 'Have you noticed the boom in inner-city high-rise living? Should you be joining the rush?' The bare statistics of the time were impressive. Over a ten-year period (1986–96) the resident population of Melbourne's CBD and inner city shot up by 215 per cent. Sydney followed on 55 per cent, with Brisbane on 28 per cent and Adelaide 25 per cent. Almost 19 000 people were living in the heart of Sydney. Cranes hung over the skyline of the major capital cities.

Interestingly, Brisbane's 28 per cent increase, huge as it was, merely reflected the growth rate for the city as a whole. Brisbane had become very popular (and remains so). On the other hand, the leap of 25.5 per cent in Adelaide was more than three times the city growth rate—people were flocking to Adelaide's CBD. Adelaide's inner-city boom was closer to the ground, with only 10 per cent of inner-city private dwellings rising four storeys or more in height.

The boom looked set in concrete. The marketing push was dynamic—much of it focused overseas. I have heard of apartment developments where 20 per cent of purchasers lived overseas. Now *that's* good marketing penetration!

However, it wasn't long before the signs of trouble emerged. In 2001 this chapter carried a number of warnings:

> When you look at this list [of benefits] it all sounds too good to be true. Yet in the late 1990s the losses started to appear. Studies in Sydney and Melbourne showed that around 50 per cent of sales in selected inner-city apartment buildings resulted in a capital loss to the investor (after allowing for inflation). While the losses were not great in dollar terms, they carried a real sting because investors had missed out on two or three years of growth.

Now we have seen examples of straightforward capital losses—along with some continuing success stories. It is not all doom and gloom by any means. So what has been going on?

- *Oversupply*. For a few years after 2000, oversupply of apartments was the big issue, with double-digit annual increases in construction of high-density housing. In many parts of Australia this problem has eased in more recent years.
- *Evidence of waning demand for CBD apartments*. Developers reported difficulties meeting required pre-sales figures; they reported rising construction costs.
- *The plug was pulled*. Several developments were deferred; some were cancelled—particularly publicly in Melbourne's CBD and the Gold Coast. This news set the market on edge.
- *Crisis of confidence*. News stories scared us about construction problems—noisy buildings, poor-quality materials and concerns over the use of private certifiers to approve construction work carried out by the contractors who were paying them.

- *The banks pulled back.* There were reports of investors having offers of finance (verbal and, in some cases, in writing) withdrawn or varied—not just from major banks but from a range of lending institutions. This occurred even where the relevant apartment projects had been fully sold. Rumours of a tightening of lending criteria spooked investors and lenders alike. In 2003–04 several banks announced they had dropped the threshold for requiring lender's mortgage insurance from a loan-to-valuation ratio (LVR) of 80 per cent down to 50 per cent in some instances.
- *Record borrowings.* As mentioned in Chapter 3, borrowing for property investment had reached record levels.

Even Sydney wasn't immune to problems here. Take, for example, the popular Darling Harbour/Pyrmont/Ultimo region—water views, granite benchtops, European kitchens, security parking, close to entertainment and shopping precincts. Sounds good? Over a two-year period in the late 1990s, around 5000 new apartments were constructed here. Average rent returns in the late 1990s hit 7 per cent compared with a more common 5–6 per cent for much of this region of Sydney (in 2007 the return was more like 2–4 per cent). Rents were high—if you could find and hold on to a tenant. Or were prices falling? It seems a lot of people did not want to live there, despite the views and features. At street level, much of the area remained grimy and stuck somewhere nearer the industrial nineteenth century.

When they are brand-spanking new, inner-city apartments tend to sell at a premium price. Once it comes to reselling a unit, this premium will have disappeared and the investor must hope there has been natural growth in value to replace it. Historically, units do not increase in value as rapidly as houses. These issues affect their investment potential.

WHY ARE PEOPLE MOVING TO THE CBD?

Despite all the negativity, there remains a genuine interest in inner-city living, because it offers:

- access to the best shopping;
- good public transport access: trains, buses and ferries;
- entertainment and culture: museums, art galleries, music venues and clubs;
- savings on commuting time, transport costs and parking if tenants work in the city;
- possibly no need to own a car; certainly you will use it less and save accordingly;
- proximity to beautiful parks, harbour or river shores;
- good views—even from ordinary high-rise apartment buildings;
- security buildings; and
- the fact that it is becoming easier to live there: supermarkets have returned, as have doctors, health professionals, gyms and more.

Danger signs for the inner city

Here is a list of cautions which exist at the present time for those planning on investment in CBD or inner-city apartment developments. The cities most affected are Sydney, Melbourne and Brisbane.

- Are you a first-time property investor? Some financial institutions have initiated tougher requirements for first-timers. Be prepared to go elsewhere. Of course, if a number of lenders are knocking you back, maybe you should reconsider your investment strategy.
- A high loan-to-valuation ratio (LVR). The LVR is one of the major ways the investor can get caught. If your lender says it is lowering the LVR for your property, you would be wise to do some comparison shopping. With

monthly budget targets and strong competition, you ought to be able to find a good finance deal. Or perhaps you should take a fresh look at what you are letting yourself in for.

- Lender's mortgage insurance (LMI). There are a number of mortgage insurers out there, so approach a few lenders with your proposition and see the range of premiums for LMI.
- Small is on the nose. The properties most affected by finance restrictions are inner-city or CBD one-bedroom apartments and studio apartments less than 50 square metres in size.
- Too ordinary. There is some hesitation over run-of-the-mill developments. The best developments—great location, big-name architects, etc.—seem to be better supported by financiers.
- Who is your tenant? There is concern, too, about particular types of tenants and accommodation: for example, student lodgings and old hotels/motels reshaped into apartments.
- Certain locations. Some 'good' suburbs and parts of town have attracted a reputation for being difficult investment propositions. Surprisingly, perhaps, some of these are beside the water—a traditional 'safe harbour' for investors.
- Variation of terms. Many who have got caught by finance withdrawal first purchased their apartments up to two years before the tightening took force—they were buying off the plan. Yet financial institutions reserve the right to alter the terms of the financing to suit conditions at the time of settlement. If circumstances have changed since entering the purchase contract you might find your finance arrangements have altered. Consider the merit of locking in the necessary finance—even if you have to pay a fee for this.

STRATEGIES FOR CHOOSING A GOOD CBD APARTMENT INVESTMENT

Go for a good location

The suburb, the street and the general amenity must be good on the ground, not just up in the air. A 'bad' neighbourhood does not always mean the property is a poor investment selection, but you limit the number and type of potential tenants and purchasers. You can get helpful statistics on property in a suburb which is traditionally residential in character, but there is less guidance available for researching new residences in traditional industrial zones.

Go for ready tenants

While we are in a 'settling down' phase of the apartment boom, it pays to look for an apartment which already has a tenant in place or where there is a high localised demand—for example, close to a university, college or hospital. If you have a tenant, you can approach your financier with greater confidence that it will back your deal more fully.

Go for quality

There is some evidence to support the proposition that high-quality apartments—in terms of construction, finishes and fittings—fare better than more basic apartments. There is some suspicion in the marketplace that construction is getting faster, cheaper and more prone to high ongoing maintenance costs, particularly with some of the huge developments comprising hundreds of units. With the building boom ahead of the introduction of the GST (1 July 2000) and the drain on national resources brought about by the enormous construction demands of the Sydney Olympics (September 2000), it became difficult to find professional tradesmen, materials were in short supply and construction costs escalated as demand outstripped supply. This building boom continued through the following years and has been particularly noticeable in Perth over 2006–07. Accordingly, concerns have been voiced that buildings are being 'thrown together' at great speed. Whether or not this is true, people have been talking about it—investors, journalists, estate agents and bankers among them. Hence the greater interest in apartment blocks which clearly display quality and attention to detail. Ask the selling agent when the building was constructed.

Go for something special

When a single apartment block or development might comprise literally hundreds, sometimes thousands, of units, you can always expect a few to be on the market at the same time—particularly when the building first opens for occupation. This competition can push prices down. That's handy when you're a buyer but a nuisance when you turn into a seller wanting to enjoy your capital gain. When assessing an apartment, look at how it will appear to a potential buyer when there are other, similar units for sale. Seek a *lasting* advantage in the one you choose. Perhaps this will be a slightly better view, a more accessible car space or garage, a better courtyard, greater privacy (fewer common walls, for example), the sunny side of the building or an architectural detail.

Go for views

Views are the classic 'something special' of an apartment. But they are more than just that. Panoramic views are one of the few areas where an apartment really has it all over most houses as an investment property. On the one hand is the issue of capital gain. Clearly a good view adds dollars to the value of an apartment. From a second perspective, like a bird's colourful feathers, it is a way of attracting a mate (well, a tenant). You might only have to attract a buyer once every five or ten years, but over this period it is likely you will have several changes of tenants. Your investment must be a 'tenant attracter'. A good, open view makes an apartment feel larger and less claustrophobic. It lets in more light and makes a real asset out of a balcony. Which views are best? Water—ocean, harbour, lake, river—is probably number one, followed by parkland, a golf course, or just the lights of the city by night, a rocky escarpment or peaceful bushland (in no particular order). A view straight into a neighbouring block of flats is almost invariably a negative.

Go for a developer with a good reputation

It takes a lot of muscle to put together a high-rise development in the heart of a capital city. There will be fights to be fought and won against community or neighbour opposition and the local council; perhaps there will be heritage destruction issues. And then there's the cost of putting the deal together and financing construction or renovation of a tired old building. It's not a game for wimps. On the other hand, the tough 'can-do' attitude of some developers can result in a poor-quality project, churned out with minimum acceptable standards of construction, rather than a superlative apartment block. Some developers gain an enviable reputation for quality work, while others suffer from poor word-of-mouth reports. So, for example, if estate agent A is selling the units in a new apartment block, speak to estate agents B and C in the suburbs about the development and the builder. They should be able to point you to other developments in the region completed by that builder in the last few years. Hunt them down and take a look around.

Tip: Local competing estate agents will be quick to tell you about problems with particular apartment blocks.

Go for low ongoing costs

Smart investors are always looking for ways to keep ongoing costs down. High ongoing costs will eat away at a good rent. You can expect higher ongoing costs where the building boasts a gymnasium, pool, sauna, spa, elevators or extensive landscaping. If there are commercial tenants on the lower floors, watch that they don't railroad the body corporate/council into spending a fortune on issues of prime concern to them, such as 'excessive' cleaning of the common areas.

Go for a second bathroom

Apartments are often rented to people who are not in a relationship—students, coworkers, people who answer an advertisement on a noticeboard for a share household. If each bedroom has its own bathroom your apartment has set itself up nicely to attract a wide range of tenants who don't necessarily want to know too many intimate details about the people they are sharing with.

Go for secure offstreet parking

The car is king—and is probably your tenant's most valuable possession.

Be wary of mixed-use developments

While it can work to your advantage to have a convenience store or friendly café on the ground floor of the block, it can be quite a different story if there is a discount computer shop or greasy takeaway lurking on street level. If some of the floors of the block are given over to commercial use—such as a small hotel or college—your tenants might have to fight their way through the lobby or for a position in the lift.

Tip: If an estate agent already manages other units in that block, they might agree to reduce their commission rate to manage your property as well.

Buying in the CBD is, at the end of the day, a decision to limit your choice of potential tenants and purchasers. Don't be misled by the recent boom: the statistics look impressive but the number of households here remains small relative to suburbia or even the broader inner-city region. Above all, the CBD is a fabulous place to live *if* you want colour, bustle and action. It is a positive lifestyle choice, but a more difficult investment choice.

There is sense in waiting to see how a particular apartment block develops over time. Some go on to become 'classic' residential buildings, while others fall into decay. The reasons, in either case, are hard to pick while the plasterboard is still wet. How much money would you bet on a horse which has no track record?

SUMMARY

- Since 2000 there has been a boom, a bust and a second boom in inner-city and CBD apartments, with much overpricing, oversupply and concern on the part of financial institutions. There are powerful lifestyle decisions involved—and inner-city apartments are not for everyone.
- Many developments are huge, which creates competition for tenants and purchasers among almost identical units.
- Many apartment blocks are being built in dirty and dangerous neighbourhoods. Will tenants stay long?
- Choose a quality development—maintenance levies can escalate sharply as the building ages.

Chapter 6

Down to the dirt: Assessing specific properties

Now you're ready to start looking for a good prospect, where is the best place to begin the search? There's no standard way of undertaking this task—some people love walking the streets endlessly while others want to stray no further than the internet. Whatever your strategy might be, consider these avenues of research:

- the internet—useful websites;
- real estate agents;
- your friends;
- newspapers—scan the advertisements;
- information from the Real Estate Institute—rents and vacancy rates;
- specific suburb reports;
- location profile—the suburb or area under investigation; and
- location profile—the specific property.

The first four are obvious avenues of inquiry. Prices, figures and anecdotes will all be rubbery, but you don't want to overlook the obvious just in case there's a bargain hiding there.

USING THE INTERNET

The internet has brought much chaos to the business sector. Some services are following the dodo into extinction, while others are enjoying the exquisite pleasure of being able to reach potential customers in vast numbers and at little cost per customer.

Among the great winners are those people who want information—such as the property investor. Here's an example. You're looking for an investment to buy. You go through the Saturday newspaper and find something interesting in the property pages. You telephone the real estate agent named in the advertisement. You get their voice mail—you can only leave a message to return your call.

The minutes tick by. The more you think about the property, the keener you are to move quickly. That blasted agent hasn't called back! You read and re-read the three-line ad, but you want to know more. It says 'ocean views' —are they extensive or just a glimpse between two blocks of flats? It says 'open-plan lounge'—does that mean the kitchen is exposed to the lounge?

You decide to phone the real estate office. A receptionist answers your call, but says all the agents are out of the office, attending to auctions and inspections. You leave a second message to return your call.

Soon it is five o'clock and no one has phoned. At some point during the day the agent picked up both your messages, but now is too tired to call, or is rushing to change clothes and head out on the town for some relaxation after a hectic day. He or she makes a note to phone you on Monday (although in my experience this note often seems to get lost!).

The day is over; you have missed your opportunity to

strike quickly. Soon you will be back at work and too busy to think about potential properties. It's a headache you didn't need.

However, these days you can chase up the ad on the agency's website. If it's not included in the advertisement, the agency office should be able to supply their website address. A good estate agency website will display further particulars along with helpful, revealing photographs of each property for sale. You might find more photos than there were in the newspaper advertisement and they are usually in colour. You can enlarge them on your computer to see details more closely.

The best real estate websites offer a 'virtual tour' of their properties: you stand in the middle of the main room and turn around through 360 degrees. Some properties will display more than one room in this fashion.

While on the agency website, you can compare the property which caught your eye with others for sale in that area. You can print pictures and text to pass around family members and friends, or to place in your bag and take to work (when you will phone the agent once more!). You can email the pics to your partner.

The great thing is that you can get moving on a target property without first having to contact the selling agent.

Apart from real estate agents, there are many services on the web which are helpful to investors. You can find:

- information on current interest rates from a range of lenders;
- information on current loan fees;
- a calculator to let you work out the amount of your potential mortgage instalments;
- a calculator to tell you how much interest you will pay over the term of the loan, and how much you will save in interest by paying off the loan earlier;

- a calculator which tells you how much principal you will have repaid at each stage of the loan's term; and
- information on State/territory stamp duty on a purchase of real estate.

Helpful websites to get you started include the following:

- *www.yahoo.com.au* and *www.ninemsn.com.au* Follow the link to personal finance. Here you will find current updates on a whole range of personal finance issues, from news to feature articles. There are home loan rates and interest rates for other products such as credit cards and term deposits. Information includes up-to-date stock prices for shares on Australian and overseas stockmarkets.
- *www.domain.com.au* As well as finance calculators (interest rates, etc.), you can search actual properties as potential investments. You will find demographic information as well as average property prices for a neighbourhood. Other useful information includes council rates for different suburbs, as well as direct links to some real estate agencies.
- *www.rba.gov.au* The Reserve Bank of Australia website is where you can learn more about the role of the Reserve Bank in controlling monetary policy (interest rates and money supply) and exchange rates for our currency. Speeches made by the Governor of the Reserve Bank, and other officials, will give you a feel for the language and targets pursued by this important statutory authority. Media releases summarise developments and are a good place to start your browsing.
- *www.fpa.asn.au* The Financial Planning Association is the professional association for qualified financial planners in Australia. From its site, you will be able to find a referral to a financial planner and the views of the

association on matters in the news (such as government regulation of financial planning and financial planners, and government reviews into financial sector reform). You can also work through a question-and-answer test which aims to provide you with a financial health check, exposing areas where you might benefit from professional advice. There is also a mortgage calculator, and a budget calculator to help you identify where savings could be made. Phone 1800 626 393.

- The banks and other lenders have their own sites of mixed value. It's worth checking for special deals and savings when you are selecting a lender. You can also find interest calculators and other spreadsheets to assist your overall financial planning. The lender's name generally leads you to the web address—for example, www.westpac.com.au; www.anz.com.au; www.stgeorge.com.au; www.commbank.com.au.
- Try the obvious, www.property.com.au, www.yourmortgage.com.au and www.moneymanager.com.au.

More websites are listed in 'Contacts, websites and further research' at the end of this book.

Is there comfort in the country?

'Buying a residential investment in my part of regional Australia has a better cash flow than buying in Melbourne. This means you can either put in less equity or buy more property,' argues Geoff Stean, licensed real estate agent and a director of Stean Nicholls Pty Ltd, real estate agents in Albury, New South Wales.

Geoff believes that purchasing an investment property in rural or regional Australia is less about matching the capital gain available in some capital cities and more about affordable cashflow and a host of other reasons.

A lot of those who invest in Albury plan to live here when they retire. A farmer, for example, will purchase a house in town when he's had a good year with his crop. Over the years he will rent it out, pay off the loan and then move in when he retires and enjoy the convenience and facilities.

Contrary to popular perception, it *is* possible to find good capital gain outside the big cities. When one Albury residence sold for $1.1 million there were five interested underbidders at the auction—there is healthy demand out there.

As a research project, Geoff investigated Albury central residential property prices and rent over a twenty-year period from 1970 to 1990.

The pattern was consistent in these high inflation years. Whatever your weekly rent, you would find the same average weekly capital gain in the value of the property. For example, if the rent was $100 per week you could expect the property to increase in value by an average of $100 per week over the twenty years.

Geoff says this relationship has flattened out in the low inflation era, but the right purchase decision can still lead to regular long-term growth. His tips are:

- Buy central property—it is the land value that increases, not the structure on it. Land is cheap on the fringes of town and this keeps values down out there.
- Don't buy property which is past its use-by date. The children of the baby boomers will

not put up with the types of housing their parents would accept. Old barracks-style unit developments are not good investments.

- Buy property which is either well situated or has very good modern design and architectural features.
- A new building has the bonus of a good depreciation rate—on the construction and on the fittings and chattels—which will help your cash flow.
- Look for a town with a large or increasing population and which is prosperous.
- An emerging market is in housing for senior citizens and retirees who don't necessarily want to mix with younger people in rented accommodation.

'It's all part of having confidence. Investors in regional Australia want to know: "If I buy it will I be able to sell it?" Well, our office clearance rate is 79.5 per cent of the properties we list,' says Geoff. 'That's as good as you'll get in Melbourne.'

REAL ESTATE INSTITUTE RESEARCH

The Real Estate Institute gains much valuable information from its huge network of estate agents. You can tap into this research through a local estate agent or by contacting the relevant State or territory branch of the Institute. Copies of research are available for sale and summaries can often be found online at the Institute's websites. You'll find out about property trends in different localities as well as median sales price and rent information.

RENTS

How have rents been faring? Tables 6.1 and 6.2, based on Real Estate Institute figures, show the broad trends in the capital cities for houses and units. Even at this gross, city-wide level we can see areas of growth and areas of concern for the investor. Institute tables take this issue into much greater depth than is possible or desirable here. People oftne say that apartments are not as good investment as houses. Well, in ten years the median rents for apartments doubled in Perth and Canberra, for example. Capital gain might not be as great with apartments, but such rent increases really help with the investor's cashflow. In other words, your choice of property will have a lot to do with the potential for rent increases.

VACANCY RATES

Perhaps the greatest fear facing the property investor is having no income deriving from his or her property. We can forgive slow capital gain, and maintenance is a necessary evil. But a vacant property sucks the lifeblood out of your investment and out of your other savings (assuming the place is mortgaged).

A vacant period can drag on for weeks or, in bad cases, months. In the world of commercial and industrial property, it is not uncommon to see properties vacant for years. Some will never again house a tenant—changing trends and needs will pass an unsuitable property by. It might be a case of the wrong place at the wrong time, or a property which just needs too much done to it, at too great a cost, to make it an attractive proposition. Fortunately, almost any piece of residential real estate can find a tenant once again. It takes an awful lot to render a house or unit completely undesirable at any price.

Table 6.1 A decade of median weekly rents for three-bedroom houses, as let, December quarter each year

Quarter	Adelaide ($)	Brisbane ($)	Canberra ($)	Darwin ($)	Hobart ($)	Melbourne ($)	Perth ($)	Sydney ($)
1997	150	165	180	260	150	183.5	145	200
1998	160	170	170	250	150	196	155	220
1999	165	185	190	240	150	185	161	225
2000	160	175	210	220	155	190	154	235
2001	180	200	235	235	165	200	166	240
2002	185	200	260	230	180	210	178	245
2003	195	220	290	260	195	210	179	250
2004	210	230	300	270	230	220	190	250
2005	230	250	310	300	250	230	225	260
2006	245	270	330	315	260	240	270	275

Source: Real Estate Institute of Australia

Table 6.2 A decade of median weekly rents for two-bedroom units and other dwellings, as let, December quarter each year

Quarter	Adelaide ($)	Brisbane ($)	Canberra ($)	Darwin ($)	Hobart ($)	Melbourne ($)	Perth ($)	Sydney ($)
1997	120	165	140	190	120	162	123.7	210
1998	120	145	150	185	125	169.4	127	230
1999	130	150	170	185	120	165	135	240
2000	125	160	190	180	125	175	138	260
2001	140	185	230	190	135	185	138	270
2002	150	180	238	180	150	195	141	270
2003	155	200	260	180	150	200	146	280
2004	165	215	270	210	160	210	155	290
2005	175	230	290	220	190	220	200	300
2006	190	260	300	240	200	240	250	310

Source: Real Estate Institute of Australia

We measure the demand for rental property by looking at vacancy rates, and Table 6.3 shows us average vacancy rates for all rented dwellings in the June 2007 quarter.

So how are vacancy rates defined as good or bad?

- *A good vacancy rate*: anything lower than 3 per cent is regarded as a good environment for the landlord, with high demand for rental properties.
- *A disastrous vacancy rate*: you're in trouble at 4 per cent, and heading over the cliff at 7 per cent.

Table 6.3 Average quarterly vacancy rates

	All rented dwellings June 2007 (%)	Annual change (% points)
Sydney	1.4	– 0.7
Melbourne	1.4	– 0.3
Brisbane	1.5	– 0.7
Adelaide	1.3	– 0.3
Perth	2.1	– 0.6
Canberra	2.4	+ 0.4
Hobart	2.3	+ 0.1
Darwin	1.2	– 1.2

Source: Real Estate Institute surveys of real estate agent property managers

Tip: A low vacancy rate generally goes hand-in-hand with rising rents. A high vacancy rate generally goes hand-in-hand with falling rents.

It is possible, however, to have both a high vacancy rate and high rents. Take Darwin, for example, where there has been substantial development of upmarket apartments, many of which front onto the sea. If you want to live in one of these beautiful developments, you have to be prepared to pay a serious rent. But landlords are content to keep their properties vacant rather than lower the rent to find just any old tenant.

Back in 2003 and 2004, vacancy rates of 4–5 per cent were not uncommon. Some agents reported a doubling of vacancy rates—but their angst was a truer sign of the depth of the problem, something which figures cannot really show. There were stories of 9 per cent vacancy rates in particular locations. In 2007 vacancy rates for the capitals were falling sharply.

Crucially, don't just look at what the rates are now. Ascertain the extent of planned construction work in that area: look to the future vacancy rate easing or increasing.

Averaged figures are only a guide, however. Table 6.3 gave us a taste of very broad trends across these cities. Upon further investigation you will find a range of vacancy rates in each suburb, each nook and cranny, each street and each development. That's the sort of material you might wish to track down when you are narrowing your search for a desirable investment property. Ask an estate agent to provide you with the necessary local research. Compare local information with city-wide trends and, most importantly, with vacancy figures for specific properties of interest.

Remember, an advertised rental return of $20 000 per annum is actually only $15 000 per annum if the property has been vacant for three months each year. Ask the agent for figures for the last three years, if they are available. (They will exist, despite what hurdles might be put in your way!) And if the agent or owner won't show you the vacancy figures, walk away from the deal.

A 'bargain' is not truly a bargain if it has a history of substantial vacancy—unless you intend bulldozing it and redeveloping the site. And that is beyond the scope of this book.

Purchase specific suburb reports

Major newspaper groups and research houses are selling suburb-specific reports with details of actual sales. You no longer have to make guesses about what is really going on.

Here are some examples of places to purchase property reports:

- Domain uses Australian Property Monitors' Home Price Guide www.homepriceguide.com.au
- Property Value www.propertyvalue.com.au
- Real Estate Guide www.realestateguide.com.au/propertyvalue
- Residex www.residex.com.au
- RP Data www.reports.rpdata.com.au

LOCATION PROFILES

In Chapter 4 we considered the attributes of a good location or a poor location. I suggest you prepare some blank tables in the format below so you can summarise the *location* issues; one for the suburb and one each for the property itself and its immediate vicinity, concentrating on issues of location.

Finally, when you actually inspect a property, prepare a *property* report (page 87). This time you want to note features and attributes of the house/apartment, inside and out. Include little details (such as strong colours) so you can visualise a specific property when you are reviewing a number of property profiles. Make particular note of areas that will require work before the property can be let.

These examples are quite brief—some people suggest forms as long as your arm. Run some blank forms off on your printer (or use the post office photocopier). Include all the things you think are important, including the name and phone number of the agent and the price or price range. Ask the agent what sort of rent the property could demand. Without a system, you will soon start to jumble and confuse the attributes of the different properties you have inspected.

Location profile: Suburb of Seaford

Good features	**Bad features**
Nice park	Southern part of suburb is under flight path

Good features	**Bad features**
No smells from industry	Used car yards along Darling Street
Plenty of historic buildings	Several prominent historic buildings have been subject to crass renovation
Train station and bus route to city	
Substantial homes near park and in east	Crappy 1970s home unit developments clustered in south
State primary and good high school	
Grass nature strips on many footpaths	
Major shopping mall in next suburb	Old local shopping centre is starting to fail; several vacant shops

Location profile: for 16 Sandcastles Lane, Seaford

Good features	Bad features
One block from park	No views from here
Wide street	Potholes in road
Good-quality houses in street	Next-door house is in poor repair
Tree planting in street	
Corner convenience shop 50 metres away	
Plenty of street parking—most houses have garages	
400 metres to train station	Noise from trains, particularly in early evening; dirt?

Property report: 16 Sandcastles Lane, Seaford

Good features	Bad features
3 bedrooms; mirrored wall in master bedroom	1970s kitchen needs substantial renovation—stained orange benchtops ($$); daggy knobs (replace)
No major cracking	Hall and kitchen need urgent repaint
Large, open-plan lounge/dining	No additional family/rumpus room
Bathroom clean, unbroken surfaces, no bath	Signs of water damage (roof leak) in master bedroom
Good rental bathroom	
High ceilings	Carpet in laundry! Stained (replace)
Light and airy apart from the minor bedrooms	Timber in entertainment deck is rotting in places
Garage	Neighbour has noisy dog

SUMMARY

- Walk the streets and talk with the real estate agents; stare in the windows.
- Ask your friends—what's the gossip?
- Scan the advertisements in the weekend newspapers.
- Get onto the web: research loan products or use a calculator programme.
- Obtain information from the Real Estate Institute about the locality prices, rents and vacancy rates—try your estate agent for this.
- Purchase specific suburb reports from newspapers and research companies.
- Prepare location profiles—the suburb, the street and the property under investigation. These will help you review your efforts.

Section III
COSTS

Chapter 7

Can I afford to buy it?

When you are concentrating on the main game, it is possible to miss the big hit coming from left field. I have seen people so fixated on putting together the purchase price that they fail to set aside sufficient funds to cover the other significant purchase costs. Even for a modest investment purchase, these up-front costs can set you back $30 000. Government stamp duty is the really significant charge (see below).

The six categories of fees and charges at this point are:

- finance;
- taxes;
- legal costs;
- inspection reports;
- mortgage insurance; and
- building and contents insurance.

FINANCE COSTS

Lending institutions primarily compete for your business on the basis of their interest rate—the lower the better. They know, however, that they can claw back a fair bit of lost revenue through fees and charges. The three main up-front finance costs are:

- application fee;
- valuation; and
- legal fees.

With a bit of haggling, you should be able to minimise or even avoid them.

The application fee—also called the establishment fee, entry fee or administration fee—is to compensate the lender for the time it spends assessing your loan application. Application fees currently range from nil to more than $1300. As a reference point, the main banks hover around the $600 mark for their traditional product. Some intermediaries—such as an agent who helps locate a mortgage for you—may charge a flat percentage of the amount borrowed (e.g., 0.5 to 1 per cent of the loan), although this is less common now than it used to be. An intermediary these days is likely to be reimbursed by the lender and charge you nothing directly.

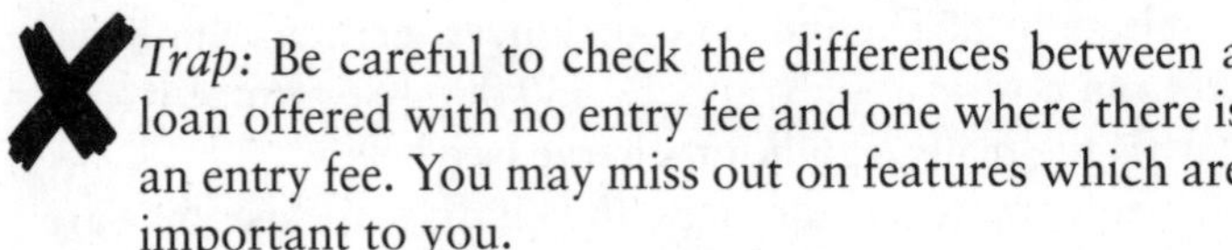

Trap: Be careful to check the differences between a loan offered with no entry fee and one where there is an entry fee. You may miss out on features which are important to you.

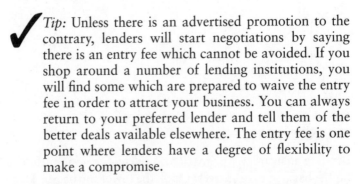

Tip: Unless there is an advertised promotion to the contrary, lenders will start negotiations by saying there is an entry fee which cannot be avoided. If you shop around a number of lending institutions, you will find some which are prepared to waive the entry fee in order to attract your business. You can always return to your preferred lender and tell them of the better deals available elsewhere. The entry fee is one point where lenders have a degree of flexibility to make a compromise.

A second fee is for property 'valuation'. Again, in the past it was more common for institutions to require some kind of formal valuation—hence the fee. Lenders often did a 'drive by' and checked the look of the property (if it was in their locality) from the car window. Today, lending institutions are more inclined to rely on the negotiated purchase price for the property and, if any doubts remain, to hedge their bets with a requirement for mortgage insurance.

Nevertheless, some lenders still charge for valuation. This is generally in the range of $150 to $300—not a big deal, but in many cases still an almost unnecessary leakage of your funds.

✔ *Tip:* If you are borrowing less than 75–80 per cent of the value of the property, tell the lending institution you see no reason to pay a valuation fee.

The third category is legal fees. The lending institution will have some legal expenses. This legal work (approving the legal title to the property, preparing the mortgage documents and registering them on settlement) will be performed either by the lender's employed staff or by an outside firm of solicitors working for the lender. This is usually where a legal fee could arise. Expect to pay between $100 and $500.

✔ *Tip:* Where a lender charges legal fees, you should expect a lower application fee. As a rule of thumb, the entry fee, application fee and legal fee, when added together, should be no more than a couple of hundred dollars more than the application fee charged by a lender which does not also charge the other fees.

If a lender insists on imposing the full impact of these fees, it would have to be a very attractive interest rate or a very indulgent lender (prepared to overlook a flaw in your credit history) for you to proceed with their offer.

TAXES (STAMP DUTY AND DUTIES)

State and territory governments raise taxes at two main points on the purchase of real estate:

- stamp duty on the transfer of property; and
- stamp duty on the mortgage.

Both lots of stamp duty must be paid by the purchaser on or before settlement of the purchase. In some cases, the lender will settle first and pay the stamp duty later, but this is not a typical scenario. You'll need to build these substantial taxes into your calculation from the earliest stages. Table 7.1 shows stamp duty on the transfer of investment property in the various States and territories. Concessions may be available for those buying their first home or for people on low incomes. These vary from State to State and over time, so contact the appropriate revenue office—see 'Contacts, websites and further research' at the end of the book.

Mortgages attract their own tax regime, which varies from State to State—see Table 7.2. There is no mortgage duty in the Australian Capital Territory, Northern Territory, Tasmania and Victoria, and there are plans to reduce or abolish mortgage duty in the other States. In Queensland, mortgage duty will be cut by 50 per cent from 1 January 2008 and abolished from 1 January 2009. In Western Australia, which has already halved its rate, it will be abolished from 1 July 2008. New South Wales will abolish mortgage stamp duty for investment housing from 1 July 2008. South Australia took one-third off its rate from 1 July 2007 (see Table 7.2), with another third to come off a year later and the final third by 1 July 2009.

LEGAL COSTS

The purchase of real estate involves getting one set of names removed from the title documents and putting another set on to them. It is not a process you want to mess up. After all, buying real estate is not the same as purchasing a cheese sandwich. What you see is not always what you get. All sorts of people could have a legitimate interest in your chosen property, which is not obvious until someone checks through the title documents. For example:

- The house next door could have a right to use the side driveway on 'your' property.
- A government department could have a right to put a road through the backyard or to put an electricity sub-station on the corner.
- There might be money owing to the local council for unpaid rates.
- There might be a 'covenant' on the property limiting the types of building materials that can be used.
- And the big one . . . the person named on the contract as 'vendor' might not even own the property.

I have seen all of these situations. And yes, they cause nightmares all round.

This is what you pay a solicitor or conveyancer for. First, you pay them to ensure that when you hand over the balance of the purchase price you will be in a position to have your name put on the certificate of title to that property. Second, you use a solicitor or conveyancer because if they make a mistake, you can claim against their professional indemnity insurance.

There are do-it-yourself conveyancing kits out there, and the process has become much simpler in recent years. But competition has brought down the price for professional conveyancing too. If you don't feel comfortable leaving your car in the hands of the local mechanic for a service, why would you risk up to hundreds of thousands of dollars by taking shortcuts on your conveyancing?

To find out the cost, call a local conveyancer (see the *Yellow Pages*) or your State's or territory's Law Society or Law Institute (Victoria). Where competition is strongest, fees are as low as $450 to $800. Otherwise, aim to spend

Table 7.1 State/territory stamp duty on purchase or transfer of investment real estate ($)*

Price	ACT	NSW	NT	Qld	SA	Tas	Vic	WA
75 000	1 500	1 203	1 941	1 663	1 955	1 675	1 600	1 500
100 000	2 000	1 990	2 750	2 350	2 830	2 425	2 200	2 200
125 000	2 875	2 865	3 641	3 163	3 830	3 175	3 160	3 200
150 000	3 750	3 740	4 613	3 975	4 830	3 925	4 660	4 200
175 000	4 625	4 615	5 666	4 788	5 830	4 800	6 160	5 200
200 000	5 500	5 490	6 800	5 600	6 830	5 675	7 660	6 200
225 000	6 500	6 365	8 016	6 413	7 893	6 550	9 160	7 200
250 000	7 500	7 240	9 313	7 225	8 955	7 550	10 660	8 200
275 000	8 500	8 115	10 691	8 100	10 143	8 550	12 160	9 450
300 000	9 500	8 990	12 150	8 975	11 330	9 550	13 660	10 700
325 000	10 875	10 115	13 691	9 850	12 580	10 550	15 160	11 950
350 000	12 250	11 240	15 313	10 725	13 830	11 550	16 660	13 200
375 000	13 625	12 365	17 016	11 600	15 080	12 550	18 160	14 450
400 000	15 000	13 490	18 800	12 475	16 330	13 550	19 660	15 700
425 000	16 375	14 615	20 666	13 350	17 580	14 550	21 160	16 950
450 000	17 750	15 740	22 613	14 225	18 830	15 550	22 660	18 200

Price	ACT	NSW	NT	Qld	SA	Tas	Vic	WA
475 000	19 125	16 865	24 641	15 100	20 080	16 550	24 160	19 450
500 000	20 500	17 990	26 750	15 975	21 330	17 550	25 660	20 700
525 000	21 938	19 115	28 350	16 975	22 705	18 550	27 160	22 050
550 000	23 375	20 240	29 700	17 975	24 080	19 550	28 660	23 400
575 000	24 813	21 365	31 050	18 975	25 455	20 550	30 160	24 750
600 000	26 250	22 490	32 400	19 995	26 830	21 550	31 660	26 100
625 000	27 688	23 615	33 750	20 995	28 205	22 550	33 160	27 450
650 000	29 125	24 740	35 100	21 995	29 580	23 550	34 660	28 800
675 000	30 563	25 865	36 450	22 995	30 955	24 550	36 160	30 150
700 000	32 000	26 990	37 800	23 995	32 330	25 550	37 660	31 500
800 000	37 750	31 490	43 200	28 425	37 830	29 550	43 660	36 900
900 000	43 500	35 990	48 600	32 975	43 330	33 550	49 500	42 300
1 000 000	49 250	40 490	54 000	32 475	48 830	37 550	55 000	47 700
1 500 000	83 000	67 990	81 000	59 975	76 330	57 550	82 500	74 700
2 000 000	116 750	95 490	108 000	82 475	103 830	77 550	110 000	101 700
3 000 000	184 250	150 490	162 000	127 475	158 830	117 550	165 000	155 700

* Rounded to nearest dollar, as at 1 January 2008

Table 7.2 State stamp duty on mortgages ($)*

Mortgage	NSW	Qld	SA	WA
50 000	141	100	142	100
100 000	341	200	292	200
150 000	541	300	442	300
200 000	741	400	592	400
250 000	941	500	742	500
300 000	1 141	600	892	600
350 000	1 341	700	1 042	700
400 000	1 541	800	1 192	800
450 000	1 741	900	1 342	900
500 000	1 941	1 000	1 492	1 000
550 000	2 141	1 100	1 642	1 100
600 000	2 341	1 200	1 792	1 200
650 000	2 541	1 300	1 942	1 300
700 000	2 741	1 400	2 092	1 400
750 000	2 941	1 500	2 242	1 500

Mortgage	NSW	Qld	SA	WA
800 000	3 141	1 600	2 392	1 600
850 000	3 341	1 700	2 542	1 700
900 000	3 541	1 800	2 692	1 800
950 000	3 741	1 900	2 842	1 900
1 000 000	3 941	2 000	2 992	2 000
1 500 000	5 941	3 000	4 492	3 000
2 000 000	7 941	4 000	5 992	4 000
3 000 000	11 941	6 000	8 992	6 000

* Rounded to nearest dollar, as at 1 January 2008

less than $1000 (a bit more in Tasmania and Western Australia) by finding someone who will negotiate. On top of this will be the cost of 'disbursements', such as inquiry certificates, photocopying and postage, courier fees, registration fees and some report fees. These could easily amount to $400 to $800, plus registration fees. There is significant variation here too, depending on the practice of the conveyancer you choose. Much of this money will go to government departments for search, inquiry and registration fees (on your transfer of title and mortgage).

Tip: When getting a quote from a conveyancer, always ask for their fees and, separately, their typical disbursements.

As land titles offices put more and more of their documents in electronic form, we are getting closer and closer to 'virtual' conveyancing. Many of the necessary inquiries which form part of the conveyancing process are already available in this way.

Online conveyancing should be cheaper and quicker. It is arguable, at this point, whether it will be safer. Will you understand what you are reading? Who will alert you to a potential problem? Easements and rights of way, for example, are often difficult to interpret without personalised, expert assistance.

INSPECTION REPORT COSTS

The conveyancing process gives you the opportunity to check you are getting what you paid for (that is, the legal title to the property) and that what you are buying is in good condition (or at least the condition which you think it is in). You don't want nasty, expensive surprises, such as finding out the floors need replacing due to termite damage.

You should consider getting the following inspections and reports:

- *Building/structural*—safety, quality of workmanship, areas where work is required. This can be performed by a builder or architect. Look in the *Yellow Pages*. Look for businesses which specialise in this work, such as the Archicentre.
- *Building compliance*—that all constructed work was approved and to the building code.
- *Pest*—check for termites, borers and other destructive creatures.
- *Strata/unit council report*—if buying a unit or apartment in a strata or company scheme, someone should check the records of the body corporate or company, looking for the health of its finances, evidence of disputes within the building, repairs which have been signalled, and much more. Again, there are specialist businesses which will do this for you.
- *Survey*—the point of getting a surveyor to inspect the property is to confirm that what you see is in fact what you are buying (and not the property next door, due to confusions over the legal title documents) and to ensure that the building work does not breach local council requirements. Often an old survey will be attached to a contract, but if there has been recent construction work you might be advised by your conveyancer to get a fresh survey. A unit, however, generally does not require a survey, but it's always a matter to raise with your conveyancer.

Every State and territory has its own list of inspection priorities, but it is prudent to check the most important things even before you enter the contract to buy the property and while you are free to walk away from the deal without pain. These certainly would include the building report but, particularly in high-risk areas, also the pest report. Check carefully the terms and limitations of any guarantee that comes with the report.

LENDER'S MORTGAGE INSURANCE

If you apply to borrow a large proportion of the valuation of a property, you will most likely be required to obtain mortgage insurance. It will cost a lot and, let's be clear, it is not what you might immediately think of when you hear the the word 'insurance'.

Basically, it is an insurance scheme which insures the loan, not you as the borrower. It means if you default on your loan repayments, the lender will recover its money from the insurer. The insurer might then seek to recover these sums from the defaulting borrower.

Do not confuse lender's mortgage insurance with an insurance policy which covers the borrower who, through circumstances such as ill-health or loss of employment, falls behind in their loan repayments. It is not like your parent putting a hand in his or her pocket and handing over a few dollars to get you out of trouble.

If you want to cover yourself against ill-health or injury that stops you working and earning, ask your insurance broker—or phone a life insurance company—for 'income protection insurance'. Premiums are expensive, but commonly tax deductible.

Mortgage insurance, however, is none of these things. It is usually required when a purchaser wants to borrow more than 80 per cent of the valuation of the property (although this will depend on the lender's rules and your personal situation). Your lender will organise the insurance and get you to sign the necessary papers. As a guide, the premium—which is on a sliding scale and attracts stamp duty—is between 0.2 per cent and 3 per cent of the loan principal.

The smaller your amount of equity in the property, the higher the rate of your mortgage insurance will be. It is a one-off payment for the term of the loan.

Trap: The need for mortgage insurance (and the amount you will pay for it) is based on the valuation of the property you are financing. This is not always the same amount as the price you are paying when buying the property. The insurer is not particularly interested in what you are prepared to pay for it. The insurer is much more concerned with the price the property might fetch if it had to be sold for non-payment of mortgage instalments. Often a more formal assessment or valuation of the property will be required. If a valuation puts the property at less than you paid for it, you might find yourself faced with a shortfall in the amount you can borrow against it. This can create a crisis when settlement is looming.

Trap: Concerns over the value and vacancy problems affecting many CBD and inner-city apartment complexes in Sydney, Melbourne and Brisbane (particularly studios, company title, motel conversions and small one-bedroom units) have led some lenders to require mortgage insurance at much lower LVRs, such as 60 or even 50 per cent (instead of 80 per cent). Check whether your investment unit might be affected by this before you purchase it and factor the costs into your calculations.

BUILDING AND CONTENTS INSURANCE

Don't leave insurance costs out of your budgeting. Once you own the property, it is at your risk. This means that if it burns down, for example, you lose the value of any damaged or destroyed improvements on the land. If you are buying a house, you should insure the building and contents. If it is a unit, the body corporate or unit council/company looks after the building, but you should insure contents such as carpets, blinds, curtains, light fittings, cupboards and so on. A full 'landlord's' insurance policy should give you appropriate cover—discuss this with an insurance broker.

Take out a covernote from commencement of the contract (the Australian Capital Territory, Queensland, South Australia, Tasmania, Victoria and sometimes the Norhtern Territory) or from settlement or earlier if given possession of the property (New South Wales, Western Australia and sometimes in the Northern Territory depending on the form of contract used).

Trap: Don't assume that because the property will be rented, you as owner have no contents worth insuring.

How much am I up for?

Property

House in Melbourne purchased for $600 000 and financed with a mortgage of $450 000.

Here are the types of fees and charges you will have to pay on or before settlement of the purchase of the property. I've chosen to use a Victorian example as Victoria's stamp duty and fees push it towards the expensive end of the scale. There are quite a number of variables where figures could change considerably—for example, inspections and conveyancing fees.

Finance

Loan application fee	$600
Property valuation	$300

Legal

Conveyancing fees	$700
Inquiry certificates and sundries	$500
Registration fees	$1 435

Tax

Stamp duty on purchase	$31 660
Stamp duty on mortgage	nil

Inspections

Pre-purchase building inspection	$450
Pest inspection	$450

Mortgage insurance $3 929

Insurance

Building and contents	$1 200

Total $41 224

SUMMARY

- You will need to save or borrow a substantial amount of money to cover the costs and fees due at or before settlement of the purchase.
- The six categories of fees and charges at this point are: finance; taxes; legal; inspection reports; mortgage insurance; and building and contents insurance.
- Many of these fees are negotiable, including legal and finance charges.
- You can save on lender's mortgage insurance by keeping your loan-to-valuation ratio below the lender's threshold.
- Stamp duty is a State/territory tax and is the largest single cost.

Chapter 8

Can I afford to keep it?

Ongoing costs can be a killer for any investment plan. Do yourself a favour and pay close attention to these costs when comparing one property against another. Once you have purchased your property, you should look at how best to keep costs low.

If you are a first-time property investor, you will discover you are supporting a whole industry of workers, from the gardener and odd-job person to the local council officers. Everyone smiles when you walk past.

When assessing a potential purchase, make a list of the ongoing expenses:

- rates—council and water;
- levies—where the property is a unit in a larger development;
- insurance;
- pest inspection;
- gardening;
- repairs and maintenance;
- managing agent's fees and charges; and
- land tax.

RATES

The local council and the water authority—which, in many parts of Australia, are one and the same—charge each property for the services they provide. These services may include roads, drinking water, sewerage, garbage collection and town planning functions. The charges ('rates') can be substantial.

Trap: Don't assume someone—tenant or managing agent—will be active in alerting you to property costs. Get on to leaky taps promptly and install water-saving shower roses—or you will end up with an excess water rates bill.

Tip: Rates are usually the largest regular outgoing associated with your property investment. Pay them quarterly if you can, rather than as a single, annual amount. Make sure you have budgeted for the rates, as they come in big chunks and you might not have enough rent income in hand to cover them.

PROPERTY LEVIES

If the property shares facilities or the building itself among a number of owners, there will be a levy to cover common expenses. It could be a strata title, unit title, company title, community title or the like.

The levy will be raised by the body corporate, owners corporation; unit committee or whoever is the managing group. It covers such things as insurance, gardening, maintenance of common areas and the building structure, repairs, common electricity and water usage, cleaning the swimming pool, maintaining the elevator, and so on.

Laws cover this situation and late payment of your levies can result in interest being charged.

INSURANCE

An essential part of any good investment strategy is the recognition that you need to protect the gains you have made. This is the role of insurance. You've clawed the savings together to make your deposit; you've purchased your investment property; now you don't want to lose your money if the property burns down. Fire is the most obvious threat to your investment, but there are other risks which you can insure against. Here is a basic list of insurances for the property investor.

Building

The bricks, mortar, timber, tiles, metal roofing, plasterboard and flooring are all covered under a standard building policy. Buy insurance which covers loss or damage due to fire, storm, impact (car, tree, etc.) and, where possible, flood. Not all policies will protect you against loss from flood, yet in many areas this is a major potential risk.

Trap: Think twice before purchasing a property in a low-lying area with a history of flood. Check with the local council and ensure your insurance policy covers you for flood.

Contents

'Contents' include carpets, cupboards, blinds, curtains, fridge, washing machine, beds, tables . . . soft and hard furnishings of all kinds. Provided they are owned by you, you can insure them against damage or loss. Even where your property is a home unit—and the building is insured through the owners corporation or committee—there will be furnishings inside your unit which are worth insuring.

Public liability

This protects you against injury claims from the public.

Workers' compensation

Over the years, many tradespeople will work on your property, doing things from mowing the lawns to replacing elements in the stove or cleaning the carpet and replacing tiles which have fallen off the walls. Many of these workers will carry their own insurance, but some will not. If they are injured while working on your property, they might make a claim against you. By taking out workers' compensation insurance you cover yourself against claims by tradespeople and others injured while working there. Claims can run into millions of dollars (in a worst-case scenario), so this type of insurance buys a lot of peace of mind.

Loss of rent

If the property is damaged and rendered 'unliveable', either the tenant will move out or will have a right to ask for the rent to be reduced until such time as the property becomes fit for living in. It might be stormwater damage, or a fire, or a tree might have fallen through the loungeroom roof. You can insure against the rent you lose in this way. Note, however, that this type of policy does not cover you for a vacancy period where you have not been able to find a new tenant.

Many of these separate items can be covered in a single landlord's policy. Discuss this with an insurance broker.

'They can't take that away from me'

Bill retired some years ago. He owns his home, has a fair amount of money in term deposits and shares, and also owns a small apartment which is rented out.

Bill is not eligible for the pension under the assets and income tests, although he could probably restructure his affairs to achieve this. 'It would feel wrong to me to get the pension when I have some money of my own,' he says. His investment property has a fair bit to do with him failing the assets test.

However, Bill is not selling.

'There have been times when the share market has been in retreat and low interest rates have kept the term deposits from being very productive. At those times it has only been my investment unit which has kept me in funds. It is important to have your money spread across a number of sectors or you are at the mercy of the markets.

'From time to time, there is maintenance to carry out and to pay for. This can coincide with a period of vacancy in the unit, meaning no rent income. It's a double whammy.

'It's a problem when you have to refurbish the unit, get new carpet and so on. But over the twenty years or so that I've owned the place it really hasn't happened all that often. My tip is to arrange the tradesmen yourself. If you leave it to the managing agent it could drag on for weeks—and all the time you're getting no rent. You've got to keep an eye on your investment and step in when necessary.'

PEST INSPECTION

Properties are subject to attack from a whole host of living pests. Some, such as spiders and cockroaches, simply make it an unpleasant place to live in. Termites and borers, however, can threaten the structure itself. It is not uncommon for termite damage to create a repair bill running into tens of thousands of dollars.

Termites move quickly through wood. They also move unseen and largely unheard. This means you should make periodic inspections for termites—a job which generally is best handled by a pest inspection company. Inspectors should crawl under the floors (where possible), climb inside the roof and wander around the garden checking trees, fencing and any landscaping timber (such as railway sleepers).

Tip: If you see a pest inspection company treating a property near your investment, get your own property checked out. It means termites are active in your area, and they might well be looking for a new home!

GARDENING

If your investment property has a garden, the rental agreement (as opposed to an owners corporation lease) might make it your responsibility to maintain it—mow the lawns, trim the edges, prune the bushes, remove the waste. When negotiating with a gardener to perform these tasks, remember that gardening is a more pressing need in the spring and there can be less to do in winter. Don't simply assume there must be activity every week or two. If you engage a managing agent, you will be advised how much to pay and how often the gardener should visit. You can, of course, choose to perform the gardening yourself—although this will bring you into close contact with your tenant.

REPAIRS AND MAINTENANCE

You can assume there will be expenses for ongoing repairs and maintenance of your investment. This might involve painting a room, repairing leaking gutters or replacing tiles that have fallen off walls.

Major improvements are not tax deductible in the year in which they occur. Instead, they are treated as part of the value of the property itself—a matter of capital. Before you spend money on your property, it is important to be clear about the difference. The cost of a repair or maintenance item is deducted from your income for tax purposes that year. This eases the financial burden. See Chapter 12 for more details.

Major improvements and building works might, in some cases, attract depreciation allowances over time or get deferred until the owner sells or otherwise disposes of the property, whereupon they are added to the *cost base* of the property for calculation of capital gains tax. This means you could be waiting a long time for the tax system to reward your expense with an allowable deduction. The demarcation line between a repair and a capital expense can be tricky. For example, it is a repair if you buy a few new palings to replace a rotting section of a fence, but it is a capital expense if you replace the whole fence or even a large section of it. Pulling up the carpet and sanding the floors is, strictly, a capital improvement which you will have to carry.

MANAGING AGENT'S FEES

The managing agent's job is not an easy one. It is emotionally draining and can easily lead to burnout. People deserve to be compensated for this difficult task. But how much is too much? An agent's fees usually comprise:

- a commission on all rent received;
- the first week's rent—this should cover the costs of finding a tenant, including any advertising costs;
- preparation of a lease—this should be only a small sum;
- sundries, such as photocopying, stamp duty, postage and bank fees; and
- some arrangements include advertising costs as part of the commission; others add this separately.

In a large city, managing agents charge a commission of around 5–8 per cent. In country areas it might be more like 6–10 per cent plus GST. Check with a number of agents before committing yourself, and get competitive quotes. Ensure you can review the contract and terminate it by giving a month's notice.

Example of management costs

Bob and Renae own a two-bedroom home unit at Bounty Beach and have appointed Manage Pty Ltd to manage the property for them. It is currently vacant.

Manage Pty Ltd has a large space in the local newspaper and in the main city newspaper each week. It includes a line or two about Bob and Renae's unit: 'Bounty Beach: 2b/r, int laund, garage, $180 pw'.

Bob and Renae do not contribute directly to the cost of the advertisement. When Manage Pty Ltd find a tenant, they take a bond and rent in advance.

Over the course of the next twelve months, if the tenant stays that long, Manage Pty Ltd will charge Bob and Renae:

First week's rent	$180.00
Lease fee	$15.00
Sundries	$12.00
Management fee (52 × $180 × 6.6%)	$617.76
Total	**$824.76**

Manage Pty Ltd's account might also include any expenses which Bob and Renae have authorised them to deduct from rent received. These could include levies, insurance, gardening, maintenance, rates and the like.

CHOOSING A TENANT

You'll keep your ongoing costs down if you put some effort into getting the right tenant. A poor choice here will mean:

- extra costs for cleaning and repairs (although the bond might cover this if the expenses are small);
- delays in payment of rent—and you're left paying the same mortgage month after month;
- potential legal expenses to evict the tenant;
- extra charges from your managing agent for preparing a new lease and replacing one tenant with another;
- hassles with the body corporate or neighbours;
- stress; and
- friction between you and your managing agent.

Your managing agent should handle most of the advertising and selection process for you, just getting in touch to secure your approval. This process must involve the checking of references, particularly the applicant's previous landlords. The agent should inform you of any problem which comes to light.

Remember that you have a legal obligation not to discriminate between one applicant and another on matters such as race, sex, age and so on. Your agent will guide you on these matters or you can contact your State/territory anti-discrimination authority for detailed information on your rights and responsibilities in this regard.

DIFFICULTIES FINDING A TENANT? SOME STRATEGIES

In times of high vacancy rates, it is very likely that prospective tenants will want to inspect your property. But the main problem will be getting them to commit. After all, the property choice before them will be wide, and many owners will be prepared to sacrifice much in order to land a tenant. So, faced with a negotiating tenant, what strategies can the owner adopt? Here are some suggestions.

- *Drop the rent.* As unpalatable as this is, it is cheaper than doing major renovations to attract a 'prospective' tenant. For example, a new kitchen might cost you $12 000 to install. A split air-conditioning unit at $3000 (installed) will take something of the order of three to six years to recoup if you value it as an improvement which, at other times, would justify a weekly rent increase of around $10 to $20.
- *Consider offering two or more weeks 'rent free'.* The tenant might look at this and average it into the total cost of renting over the likely term, but you can still present your 'typical weekly rent' to lenders at the higher level. That can be handy if you are part-way through a programme requiring further borrowings and need your income figures to look their best.

  On the other hand, if you are looking to sell in the near future—and you expect the purchaser to be an investor with an eye to yield—it's the total dollars through the door which count.
- *Discuss property management with other agents.* Should you shift the management contract? Things might have changed among local agencies since the last time you chose one. Look for:
  - an active presence in the local newspaper and main city paper;
  - a great internet site that gives due space to rental vacancies and which is not totally devoted to sales;
  - evidence of street signs for rental vacancies (not just sales); and
  - an office which is open on weekends.

- *Renovate.* In some situations your best strategy will be to bring the property in line with the expectations of tenants in your building or area. Take a critical look at what your competition is offering. Are there new apartment developments with pool, gym, granite benchtops and concierge? What is the market offering? You could consider improvements such as new carpets, fresh paint, adding appliances (a dishwasher or washing machine), installing a new bathroom or kitchen, polishing timber floors, improving security (doors, bars, surveillance), adding or improving heating and cooling, installing built-in wardrobes, providing internal laundry connections, turning a car space into a carport or a carport into a lockable garage.
- *Be flexible on the term of the lease*—it doesn't have to be a straight six or twelve months. What works for you?

Illustration: filling a vacancy

A studio apartment in Mortville has become vacant in May. While the previous tenant was paying $210 per week, the owner is having difficulty finding a replacement. Along comes a potential tenant who is a student. She makes an offer of $180 per week—a drop of $30 per week. She says she only wants the place for six months, as she hopes to use the First Home Owner Grant to buy her own place. Then she'll be off. 'Take it or leave it,' she says to your managing agent, who sheepishly passes this delightful quote on to you.

The benefits

- It's a tenant—at least the place is not vacant.
- Rent is coming in.
- Your mortgagee is happy.
- There will be no more advertising costs to cover.
- Your insurance policy conditions will be met—you can't leave a property unoccupied for lengthy periods (see the policy—it might be 60 days, for example) or you risk losing insurance cover.

The drawbacks

- Your income from the property is reduced substantially—though not fatally.
- The tenant will know you are vulnerable and may require improvements week by week.

However, this new tenant intends vacating at an inconvenient time: mid-November. Your agent tells you that the best estimate for finding the next tenant will be mid-December or mid-January, so you could well have another vacancy for four to eight weeks at that point!

Strategy

Agree to the lower rent but make the term of the lease either seven months (mid-December) or eight months (mid-January) instead of the usual six months. If the tenant has not considered any option other than a typical six-month lease, or found a property to purchase, it might in fact be desirable to her to stay put over Christmas.

There may be other factors which can form the basis of beneficial negotiations. For example, in return for a good deal on the rent, your tenant might be prepared to offer a benefit in return—such as painting the flat without charging for labour. Your gain as landlord is twofold: first, you could save $1000 to $2000 in labour (or you could split this with the tenant); and second, this maintenance task would take place without the usual vacancy. A six-month tenant who paints your flat for you is saving you something in the order of $40 to $80 per week over that period. That makes a loss of $30 per week on the rent look like a bargain.

You can make a deal about almost anything:

- gardening;
- decorating;
- walking your dog;

- shampooing the carpet;
- putting up with renovations; or
- accepting the property with an oven which does not work.

Obviously a lot depends on the prospective tenant. Some will see a certain fairness in a tit-for-tat arrangement while others will simply try to get every dollar they can twist out of the landlord. Why stand still and accept a slaughter? Ask a few questions about the person and what they do for a living and as hobbies or interests—and why not surprise them? Are they asking to pay $30 per week less than the current rent? Offer them a saving of $40 per week . . . if they just do something for you. Seize back the initiative—and don't come across as desperate. In a tight market the desperate landlord is standing on the precipice of free-fall.

✓ *Tip:* See a period of vacancy as an opportunity to fix up the place while there is no tenant in residence. You have a clear run to get the property set up for the next six or eight years of investment. Use the time wisely.

✓ *Tip:* Managing agents often leave it until very late to let you know a tenant is leaving. OK, they don't want to be the bearer of bad news, but this really messes the owner around. If you are forewarned you can put plans into place—for renovation, repair or simply to advertise earlier for a tenant. Instruct your agent to inform you *at the earliest opportunity* of any impending vacancy and of any lease expiry (even where the tenant has not indicated he or she might be departing).

What are other landlords and developers offering as inducements to attract tenants? Almost anything goes: free gym membership, appliances which the tenant can keep (e.g., a microwave oven or TV), internet and cable/satellite TV connections, prize draws, holidays. Note that these are usually corporate deals for units rather than private rental deals, but it's good to know what you're up against.

Tip: Remember, your loss is also a tax deduction: losing \$30 per week—\$1560 a year—might ultimately hit your pocket as a genuine \$1000 loss in cash terms.

LAND TAX

One way or another, we seem to be paying tax every time we blink. And that's all well and good if we enjoy the benefits of nice parks, clean beaches and streets, well-maintained roads, top-notch hospitals, well-resourced schools, and so on. I'm not against taxation.

Some taxes pop up when we buy things or use services—the goods and services tax (GST); some come straight from our income—income tax; others arise when we sell or dispose of an asset—capital gains tax. One in particular attaches to the ongoing ownership of property—land tax. It is a wealth tax.

Under our federal system, income tax and GST are the domain of the Commonwealth government. State governments benefit from the GST, but continue to raise their own taxes. Property is hit by a number of State taxes, including stamp duty on the transfer of property (such as on purchase) and land tax.

The fact that land tax is a State tax determines its procedures and, at the same time, suggests how to plan for the tax. (The Northern Territory is the only place where there is no land tax.) Land tax is a complicated little area affecting the property investor. Before going into the specifics—a whole list of inclusions and exclusions—here are the five main principles which must be grasped:

1 Your home is, in most cases, excluded from land tax.
2 Tax is assessed on the *unimproved* land value of your investment property—excluding the value of any buildings and fixtures—above any tax-free threshold.
3 Many, but not all, States and territories have a tax-free threshold. If your land value is below the cut-off point, you are not liable for land tax (see below).
4 Property values may be added together across a number of properties in sole or joint names, thereby passing the threshold.
5 Tax mounts up quickly—it is worthwhile planning your investments so that you minimise its impact.

The big exclusion: Your home

Your principal place of residence (that is, your main home) is, in most cases, exempt from land tax. That comes as a great relief to most homeowners. However, there are two main exceptions to this rule operating in some parts of Australia:

1 where your home is on a very large block of land; or
2 where the land is used for primary production.

There are other exemptions which are sometimes available:

- land (improved or not) purchased with the intention of being solely used and occupied as your principal place of residence within two years—provided you don't already own your principal place of residence;
- land for a retirement village; or
- proportional exemption for a principal place of residence where part of the land is occupied by someone else (for example, a flat which is rented out).

In short:

- The home must be your principal place of residence.
- Only one home gets the exemption. Your holiday home, for example—even though not rented out—is not exempt.
- The Land Tax Agency looks at your family situation. You can't get away with saying, 'This is my home—and that is my wife/husband/partner's home.'

Land value only

The valuation does not include the value of any building or improvement (such as a swimming pool, garage or shed) on the land.

Tax-free threshold

You can own investment property without necessarily having a land tax liability—it depends on the value set for the tax-free threshold (see details below). If the land value of your property falls below this point, you are not liable for land tax in that year. Of course, at some future date your land value might pass beyond the cut-off point and you will have to pay the tax.

As one example, in Western Australia in 2007 the threshold value was $150 000 (for land owned at midnight, 30 June 2007). Remember, this is land value only.

Do you own more than one property? A major confusion about land tax comes about at this point. The land values of all properties you own or part-own (other than your home or other exempt property) will be added together. For example, if you own one property in your sole name and a second property (not being your home) jointly (equal shares) with your wife/husband/partner, the value of your two interests will be added. You might find that the total value crosses the tax-free threshold—and you will be liable for land tax. This will be the case even where the properties' land values, taken singly, are each below the threshold.

Assessment of land tax

Each State and territory has a different way of assessing land tax, as briefly summarised below. Land tax adds up quickly to become quite a burden, so it is useful to see the differences—particularly if you are contemplating potential investments in more than one State or territory. There is no GST on land tax.

Australian Capital Territory

Land tax is assessed on the total unimproved value of your assessable land holdings, including investment properties, on a quarterly basis as at 1 July, 1 October, 1 January and 1 April.

Your principal place of residence is exempt from land tax.

Tax is calculated by multiplying the average unimproved value by the rate of the number of days in the relevant quarter divided by the number of days in the year. A sliding scale is used, depending on what is called the Average Unimproved Value (AUV).

You have 30 days to notify the Commissioner for ACT Revenue that you have begun renting out a residential property. It's a tax default to fail to meet this deadline.

Average Unimproved Value (AUV) ($)	Marginal rate for residential property (%)
Up to 75 000	0.60
75 001 to 150 000	0.89
150 001 to 275 000	1.15
Above 275 000	1.40

Source: ACT Treasury

These figures and information were correct as at April 2007. Different rates are used for non-residential property. Please check for changes, exemptions and updated information at:

ACT Treasury
www.revenue.act.gov.au
Phone (02) 6207 0047

New South Wales

Land tax is assessed on the total unimproved value of your assessable land holdings, including investment properties, as at midnight on 31 December in the previous year.

Your principal place of residence is exempt from land tax. The way the land tax threshold is calculated has changed in New South Wales. For the 2007 and future land tax years the land tax threshold will be averaged. The threshold will be the average of the 'indexed amount' for the new tax year and the previous two land tax years, as calculated annually by the Valuer-General.

Land tax is charged at the rate of 1.7 per cent of the assessable value of your land holdings above the threshold of $352 000 (for 2007). The rate will fall to 1.6 per cent from the 2008 tax year plus $100.

These figures and information were correct as at April 2007. Check for changes, exemptions and updated information at:

Office of State Revenue
www.osr.nsw.gov.au
Phone 1300 139 816, or (02) 9689 6200 outside New South Wales

Northern Territory

There is no land tax in the Northern Territory at present.

This information was correct as at April 2007. Check for changes and updated information at:

NT Treasury

www.nt.gov.au/ntt/revenue
Phone (08) 8999 7949

Queensland

Land tax is assessed on the total unimproved value of your assessable land holdings, including investment properties, as at midnight on 30 June each year.

Your principal place of residence is exempt from land tax.

Taxable value of land ($)	Rate of tax
500 000 to 749 999	500 plus 0.70%
750 000 to 1 249 999	2 250 plus 1.45%
1 250 000 to 1 999 999	9 500 plus 1.50%
2 000 000 to 2 999 999	$20 750 plus 1.675%
3 000 000 and above	1.25% on full value

Source: Queensland Office of State Revenue

A number of general and special rebates apply.

These figures and information were correct as at April 2007. Check for changes, exemptions and updated information at:

Office of State Revenue
www.osr.qld.gov.au
Phone (07) 3874 4088 or 1300 300 734

South Australia

Land tax is assessed on the total unimproved value of your assessable land holdings, including investment properties, at midnight on 30 June each year.

Your principal place of residence is exempt from land tax. No land tax is payable on total land value up to $110 000.

Total taxable site value ($)	Rate of tax
Up to 110 000	Nil
110 001 to 350 000	30 cents per $100 or part thereof above $110 000
350 001 to 550 000	$720 plus 70 cents for each $100 or part thereof above $350 000
550 001 to 750 000	$2120 plus $1.65 for each $100 or part thereof above $550 000
750 001 to 1 million	$5420 plus $2.40 per $100 or part thereof above $750 000
Over 1 million	$11 420 plus $3.70 per $100 or part thereof above $1 million

Source: RevenueSA

These figures and information were correct as at April 2007. Check for changes, exemptions and updated information at:

RevenueSA
www.revenuesa.sa.gov.au/taxes
Phone (08) 8204 9870

Tasmania

Land tax is assessed on the total unimproved value of your assessable land holdings, including investment properties, as at 1 July each year. The value is multiplied by an adjustment factor imposed by the government.

Your principal place of residence is exempt from land tax. No land tax is payable on total land value up to $25 000.

Taxable land value ($)	Rate of tax
Less than 25 000	Nil
25 000 to 349 999	$50 plus 0.55% above $25 000
350 000 to 749 999	$1837.50 plus 2% above $350 000
750 000 and above	$9837.50 plus 2.5% above $750 000

Source: Tasmania's Department of Treasury and Finance

These figures and information were correct as at April 2007. Check for changes, exemptions and updated information at:

Department of Treasury and Finance
www.treasury.tas.gov.au
Phone (03) 6233 3068 or 1800 001 388

Victoria

Land tax is assessed on the total unimproved value of your assessable land holdings, including investment properties, as at midnight on 31 December of the previous year.

Your principal place of residence is exempt from land tax. No land tax is payable on total land value below $200 000 for an individual. The tax is assessed using a valuation multiplied by an 'equalisation factor' which is chosen to reflect the average increase or decrease in land value in that particular municipality over a period of time, roughly since the last valuation was carried out.

Taxable land value ($)	Rate of tax
Below 225 000	Nil
225 000 to 539 999	$250 plus 0.2% for each $1 above $225 000

Taxable land value ($)	Rate of tax
540 000 to 899 999	$880 plus 0.5% for each $1 above $540 000
900 000 to 1 619 999	$2680 plus 0.8% for each $1 above $900 000
1 620 000 to 2 699 999	$8440 plus 1.3% for each $1 above $1 620 000
2 700 000 and above	$22 480 plus 2.5% for each $1 above $2 700 000

Source: State Revenue Office of Victoria

In Victoria a land tax surcharge applies now to trusts. The surcharge commences at 0.375 per cent for landholdings valued at $20 000 and starts to phase out for combined property exceeding $1.62 million at the rate of $55 for every $10 000 increase in value. The surcharge imposes an additional burden but it need not rule out the use of a trust in Victoria if the structure is useful for other reasons.

These figures and information were correct as at April 2007. Check for changes, exemptions and updated information at:

State Revenue Office
www.sro.vic.gov.au
Phone 13 21 61

Western Australia

Land tax is assessed on the total unimproved value of your assessable land holdings, including investment properties, as at midnight on 30 June each year.

Your principal place of residence is exempt from land tax. No land tax is payable on total land value up to $150 000.

Taxable land value ($)	Rate of tax
Below 150 000	Nil
150 000 to 390 000	0.15 cents per $1 above $150 000
390 000 to 875 000	$360 plus 0.45 cents per $1 above $390 000
875 000 to 2 000 000	$2542.50 plus 1.62 cents per $1 above $875 000
2 000 000 to 5 000 000	$20 767.50 plus 2.30 cents per $1 above $2 000 000
5 000 000 and above	$89 767.50 plus 2.50 cents per $1 above $5 000 000

Source: Office of State Revenue of Western Australia

In addition, there is a metropolitan region improvement tax (MRIT) levied on land in metropolitan regions which is subject to land tax. The tax raises funds to provide land for roads, open spaces, parks and similar public facilities.

These figures and information were correct as at April 2007. Check for changes, exemptions and updated information at:

Office of State Revenue
www.dtf.wa.gov.au
Phone (08) 9262 1200 or 1300 368 364

Table 8.1 presents an example for a property with unimproved land values of $300 000 and $600 000.

Minimising land tax

Part of your pre-purchase planning should include a thorough consideration of your land tax situation—even for a first property investment. In fact, you can amass a substantial portfolio of property without being liable for land tax.

Here are some common ways to escape or minimise land tax liability:

Table 8.1 How much land tax?

State/territory	UPV* $300 000	UPV $600 000
ACT	see page 122	
NSW	nil	$4 316
NT	nil	nil
Qld	nil	$1 200
SA	$570	$2 945
Tas	$1 563	$6 838
Vic	$400	$1 180
WA	$225	$1 305

*UPV = Unimproved Property Value

- Purchase property which has a land value below the tax threshold.
- If you aim to own more than one property, buy them in separate names: for example, you own one, your spouse owns another. Again, both properties should have land values below the tax threshold, where one applies.
- Purchase properties in different States/territories. Remember, land tax is a State tax—one State or territory has no authority across the border of another. This is one reason why many investors in cities such as Sydney and Melbourne will own an investment unit on Queensland's Gold Coast. It takes them across State borders.
- Buy in the Northern Territory, where, at least at present, there is no land tax.
- In the Australian Capital Territory and New South Wales family-style discretionary trusts don't get a tax-free threshold. In the Australian Capital Territory tax applies on a property-by-property basis. To summarise, the tax-free thresholds for trusts were zero in 2007 in the Australian Capital Territory and New South Wales

(compared with below $352 000 in New South Wales for individuals), below $20 000 in Victoria; up to and including $110 000 in South Australia, $24 999 in Tasmania and $150 000 in Western Australia; and below $300 000 in Queensland (below $500 000 for individuals). These figures are updated periodically.

The practicalities of the tax

- Land tax is assessed on your land holdings at different dates in the various States and territories (see above for details).
- It is an annual tax, assessed and paid annually (quarterly in the Australian Capital Territory).
- If you own investment property—or your home is liable for assessment—you should telephone the Land Tax Office in your State/territory each year to find out your current valuation for land tax purposes. In this way you will know if you should be preparing a land tax return for lodgement.
- You can appeal the assessment.
- Once you have paid tax for one year you will be contacted automatically in later years.

One more thing. The State/territory government wants you to pay your land tax liability and will not let you get away with avoiding it forever. Because it is up to you to initiate the process—that is, to recognise you have a land tax liability and to lodge your first tax return—it is possible to carry on for many years without even realising you are liable for this tax. Interest is charged on late tax, and you can end up owing thousands of dollars in back tax and interest.

An outstanding land tax liability can be a charge on the land itself and will pop up when you try to sell the property (or even change your finance arrangements). For this reason, a purchaser always gets a certificate from their State/territory land tax or revenue office confirming there is no land tax owing on the property.

How the expenses pile up

Ongoing expenses for 2006–07 financial year

Property: 6 Dundas Crescent, Goldmine Hill, Victoria

Price paid: $500 000 **Land value:** $250 000 **Rent:** $300 p.w.

Vacancy: Four weeks during the year

Managing agent

• commission (48 x $300 x 7.7%)	$1108
• reletting fee	$300
• document fee	$15
• sundries	$36
Total	**$1459**

Insurance

Landlord's combined policy premium

(House and contents, Workers' compensation, Public liability, Rent)

Total	**$550**

Rates

Council	$1200
Water	$1000
Land tax (Victoria)	$300
Total	**$2500**

Strata levies

not applicable

Maintenance

Clearing gutters	$200
Water damage to bathroom wall	$185
Cleaning carpet	$120
Replacing broken light switch	$99
Replacing stove element	$188
Total	**$792**

Pest inspection	**$300**
Total outgoings for year	**$5601**

One telling fact should be immediately apparent from this list: You are keeping a whole team of people employed! A second point emerges, too: This is not the rate of return the selling agent told you to expect on your investment!

A rule of thumb in a large city like Sydney is to expect a return on your investment of 2.5 per cent (although you can get up to double this in the best parts of the northern beaches and half this on high-value properties). The return is the ratio of rent income to the price you paid for the property.

In this example, the annual rent is 52 × \$300 = \$15 600
The price paid for the property was \$500 000.
The return is expressed as 15 600 ÷ 500 000 = 3.12%

This is a gross return. This means you have not taken into account your expenses, or the period of any vacancy when no rent is received.

If we assume the property was vacant for four weeks during the year (cost: 4 × \$300 = \$1200), the total rent actually received would be:

\$15 600 – \$1200 = \$14 400
Now, deduct the actual expenses (\$5601)

The net income for the property for the year was \$14 400 – \$5601 = \$8799

Therefore the net return was 8799 ÷ 500 000 = 1.76%

When assessing a potential investment, always calculate both the gross return and an estimate of the net return. This enables you to compare one deal against another. It also indicates how much of the rent is available for paying the mortgage.

SUMMARY

- Expenses don't stop when you complete the purchase of your investment.
- Ongoing costs include rates (council and water), levies (where the property is a unit in a larger development), insurance, pest inspections, gardening, repairs and maintenance, managing agent's fees and charges, and possible land tax.
- Do your sums when comparing potential investments, and discount the gross rental returns accordingly.
- Land tax can become a burden. Consider issues of ownership and locality if you wish to minimise its impact.

Section IV
YOUR MONEY

Chapter 9

A rate of considerable interest

When I sold my first home, I needed somewhere safe to keep the proceeds. I also wanted that money to earn some more money while it sat there, waiting until I spent it on buying my next home. I asked my bank what deposit rate it would pay me. When I looked at advertised interest rates in the newspaper, however, I realised I could do better by moving my money elsewhere while it was stuck within its holding pattern. On the off-chance, I thought I would see whether my bank would match one of the higher rates offered by its competitors.

My bank showed no interest in upgrading its interest rate! It was impossible to offer me one rate and everyone else a different rate, they said. It just wasn't done. Customers—especially small customers—are not able to get individual treatment.

But that wasn't the end of it. As it happened, I wanted to keep my money with my bank and did not really want to move it elsewhere. I was thinking about security. One of the basic rules of investment is 'the higher the reward, the greater the risk'. We were talking about my life's savings here—and I did not want to put them in jeopardy by jumping from one of the largest financial institutions in the country into the hands of a smaller, lesser known corporation. To me, the extra reward—around 0.5 per cent additional interest—did not make up for the higher risk. In effect, I was a captive customer, tied in by my own free choice. I would not be taking my money elsewhere.

Still, I was annoyed that my particular bank had chosen not to be competitive on deposit interest rates. There seemed to be no good reason why it should lag behind the field. Having met resistance at the branch level, I decided to phone head office. I said I wanted to discuss interest rates with someone and explained the situation to the person on the other end of the line. I told him how much money I wished to invest (some tens of thousands of dollars—nothing huge, but it was a big amount for me), and asked whether the bank could do better for me than their current advertised rate.

This person listened to my story and agreed with my criticism that the bank had fallen behind its competitors for deposits of my scale and type. While I waited on the phone, he got in contact with the bank's 'dealing room', where the bank's trading staff placed the bank's moneys out into the financial marketplace. When he returned, he said the bank's dealers could offer me that 0.5 per cent extra on my deposit. My money somehow happened to fit in with the bank's own strategies and dealings at the time.

I hadn't expected this response. I was used to thinking of banks as institutions set in stone, their ways inscrutable, their workings beyond my understanding. And that is often true at the branch level. Like a planet, the surface can be crusty and rigid, while everything becomes more fluid the closer you get to the core. The customer has to make his or her own journey to the centre, typically without a map.

The rewards for making the journey can be well worth the effort.

This was how I learned that deposit rates were negotiable if you had something to offer in return. They are not limited to the numbers that appear in black and white on the bank's brochures. Closer to the core, they must link into a moving marketplace.

A little while later, I found that interest rates for loans—your property mortgage—could also break out of rigid boundaries. As a solicitor, I had been involved in many large property deals where different loan interest rates were offered by a range of financial institutions. Each potential lender would look at the deal as a whole, its time frame, the degree of risk, the amount of money required, the track record of the developer, the potential profit to the developer and a host of other factors, and then offer a loan interest rate based on its assessment. Rarely did any two banks or financiers offer the same interest rate or deal.

I did not think the same situation would apply to the small investor. After all, those 'customised' deals involved millions of dollars. Why would a bank go out of its way to offer me a better interest rate than it did the general public? In fact, some financial institutions charge you a higher interest rate on an investment property than for a mortgage over your residence.

When I was about to make my first purchase of an investment property, I took a good look at the interest rates being charged by the various financial institutions. I immediately discounted those which applied an interest rate above that for a home mortgage. My own bank would charge the same rate, irrespective of whether the property was for me to live in or to rent out. And so I spoke to the loans officer and got some more particulars. The deal looked fine—although I noted that the bank would charge higher annual fees than for a home loan.

As this was my first big move out of the relative safety of a home mortgage, I thought I should check with another couple of lenders, and made the appointments. The next bank charged the same interest rate as my own bank, but its loans officer kept putting obstacles in my way. I would need more documents from my accountant, there would be extra forms to fill in and personal guarantees to deliver, they wanted the investment mortgage to be registered against my home as well as the property I was purchasing for investment . . . the list went on. Amazingly, every new document they requested was accompanied by its own set of fees.

I felt I was running a steeplechase! The second bank was throwing everything but the very desk and chairs in my path to financial well-being. And it was all so unnecessary. I knew I was a 'good proposition' for a lender, with an excellent track record for credit, a good income and a strong asset base. I knew my own bank didn't require half of what this new one wanted from me.

I pressed on to the next interview. Whereas my first bank was basically indifferent to my investment project, and the second bank was almost hostile, here I was to encounter a bank which actively sought me and my kind of investor.

The third bank, from its highest levels, had set itself the task of attracting the small property investor. I suspect its management realised that small investors were good, juicy business—highly motivated, goal-oriented, on the way to becoming medium-sized customers.

This was the first time I had encountered a lender which offered me a lower loan interest rate than the general public would receive. It had a list of criteria which defined the type of customer it wanted and I happened to fit the description. They didn't want to take a mortgage over my home in addition to the investment property; they didn't require personal guarantees; and they *offered* other valuable incentives—they weren't taking them away like some of the other financial institutions.

I was very pleased with the deal I was offered. Nevertheless, I had been a loyal customer of my existing bank for most of my life. I felt I owed it to them to tell them the details of the deal I had been offered elsewhere so that they had the opportunity to hang on to me. Initially the response was cool. My bankers were not even aware of the lower interest rate and deal being offered by their competitor. I couldn't actually blame them for this—I had never seen it publicised either. Still, I had the deal outlined in writing, and showed it to them. They were amazed, but unmoved. 'The bank cannot lower its interest rate for you,' I was informed. Nor would they waive various fees—although they might, just might, be able to get approval for a reduction in one of the fees.

After a couple of days, my original bank called me back in. 'Success!' they cried. 'We can reduce some fees for you, as a very special dispensation.' But I was more concerned with the interest rate, and on that they would not budge. As we played with the figures, however, it turned out that the reduction in fees (which included credit card annual fees) was valuable. On an ongoing basis, my potential saving on bank fees amounted to a reduction in the mortgage loan rate of 0.2 per cent. The bank was talking 'fees' not 'interest rates', but the net result was a lower cost of borrowing—a drop in the interest rate for me.

That's the end of the story. You *can* negotiate your interest rates. If you are an attractive customer with good prospects, or you have a large amount of money to deposit or borrow, the system is open to influence. But for a small investor to make a better deal, they must find their way past the road blocks at the branch level.

You don't have to be belligerent or annoying, but you must persevere and be prepared to walk away. Sooner or later, you will find someone who talks your language and who is prepared to refer your investment to a higher authority—someone closer to the molten core.

We don't get any training in this. At school no one teaches us how to negotiate with the finance world. If anything, we subconsciously pick up signals and images that establish the banks and other financial institutions as solid, conservative bureaucracies. Increasingly, the media presents the banks as fallen idols—money-grubbing corporations interested only in maximising dividends for shareholders through raising fees. A different image, it is true, but an image that still suggests an impersonal, imperious attitude and a lack of flexibility, just like in the old days.

In my property dealings I have found:

- If you want to be treated as an individual, you can be.
- If you want to get a better deal than the general public, you will find it.
- If you want a better interest rate, you will uncover it.
- If you are blocked on one road, you can usually find a concession down another.
- It is helpful to recognise that fees and loan costs can be equivalent to an interest rate hike or, when waived, a reduction.
- Sometimes the barriers to a better deal are nothing more than words.
- If you 'negotiate' in a belligerent manner, you will miss out on one of the premier benefits of the give-and-take process: finding a lender with whom you can communicate *now* and for the *future*.

The investor succeeds by putting together a top-notch support team. Having a reluctant banker on your team is worse than having a couldn't-care-less banker. Your task is to find a banker or other lender with whom you have good communication, then encourage them to dig out the concessions for you. They will do this either because they like you, or simply because you look like the type of customer who will come back time and time again over the years with more profitable deals for the bank to share in. This reflects very well on your banker/lender, as viewed from head office. But some wouldn't recognise a good customer—particularly one just starting out—if he or she jumped up and bit them.

INTEREST RATES: HOW THEY WORK AND WHERE THEY COME FROM

Starting with the obvious, when you borrow money you have the obligation to repay it. The amount you borrow is called the *principal* of the loan. A second obligation, in most cases, is to reward the lender for having lent you the money. When this reward takes the form of money, it is called *interest.*

The same word—interest—is used when you lend your money to the bank or other institution. Your savings or transaction account earns interest for you. This time you are on the receiving end. Of course, this is because you have lent your money to the bank in the first place. But there are other benefits for you in this situation: you get to put your money in a safe place until you want it, and you can withdraw your money whenever you want it. For these reasons, the interest you earn on your bank accounts is very small—particularly when compared with the interest you must pay when you are the borrower. There is a difference of around 7 to 8 per cent annually between a transaction account and a property loan.

If you put your savings into a term deposit, for example, the gap between the rates of interest you pay on your loan and earn on your deposit gets much smaller. The difference might only be 2 or 3 per cent. This is partly because you are giving up the freedom to withdraw your money from the bank whenever you want it. With a term deposit, you must leave your money (the principal) with the bank until the expiry of the term (the duration) of the deposit. This fixed term might be as little as 30 days or as much as five years. You get to choose how long you will tie up your money. The benefit usually is that you get a more favourable interest rate with a longer deposit term. Table 9.1 gives some examples.

Table 9.1 Term deposit rates as at March 2007

Term	Bank interest rates paid to you (% per annum) on $10 000 deposit
30 days	2.55
3 months	5.05
6 months	5.10
1 year	5.95
3 years	4.85
5 years	6.20

Source: Reserve Bank of Australia

When it comes to borrowing, there are still many different interest rates out there (see Table 9.2). The range is quite remarkable—highlighting the importance of checking with a number of lending institutions before locking in a deal. Interest rates change regularly. This table (with figures correct as at 4 April 2007) shows you how much variation there is between institutions. It also shows how a lender's rates can be uncompetitive for one type of deal but suddenly very competitive for a different term or product, and how some online lenders shave their rates even further. The fees, however, are also very important in determining the cost-effectiveness of the deal.

Table 9.2 Investment mortgage rates (%) on the sum of $250 000

Lender	Variable rate (basic)	Variable rate (standard)	1 year fixed	3 years fixed	5 years fixed
AIMS	6.22	7.93	7.89	7.86	7.83
AMP Banking	7.39	8.07	7.35	7.39	7.34
ANZ	7.37	8.07	7.45	7.45	7.45
Aussie Home Loans	7.49	7.95	7.49	7.49	7.39
Commonwealth Bank	6.44	8.07	7.35	7.35	7.35
Credit Union Australia	7.29	7.99	7.40	7.29	7.25
Heritage Building Society	6.82	7.35	7.20	7.30	7.30
Mortgage House of Australia	7.59	7.60	7.80	7.80	7.75
National Australia Bank	7.37	8.07	7.37	7.42	7.42
RAMS Mortgage Corporation	7.24	8.17	–	7.35	7.35
Rate Busters	6.90	7.17	7.29	7.26	7.22
Suncorp	7.49	8.07	6.90	7.19	7.20
Wizard	7.39	7.72	–	7.35	7.35

Source: Cannex Australia, 4 April 2007

Interest rates are determined by a mix of factors including:

- the cost to the financial institution of obtaining money;
- the amount of money you are investing or borrowing;
- the size of the bank's fees;
- the term of the deal;
- the restrictions placed on the borrower and lender;
- predictions and concerns about interest rate movements; and
- overheads.

These factors are relevant whether talking about lending or borrowing. One is the reflection of the other. Inserted in the middle is the bank's profit. You benefit from finding the deal where the gap closes, where the bank's nominal profit is smallest. This raises the important strategic question: how do I find the best interest rate for my investment loan?

CHOOSING THE RIGHT RATE

Interest can be paid at different intervals, on different components and in different ways, for example:

Different intervals:

- daily;
- weekly;
- fortnightly;
- monthly;
- quarterly (every three months); or
- yearly.

Different components:

- interest only; or
- interest plus a component of repayment of principal.

Different ways:

- in advance (e.g., the payment covers the month or even year ahead); or
- in arrears (e.g., the payment covers the month or year just past).

A typical investment property loan from a bank could be said to involve monthly repayments of interest plus a component of principal. But these days there is room for you to vary the factors and structure a deal that best suits you. In this regard, relevant personal factors might include:

- how frequently you are paid—whether you receive your income weekly, fortnightly, monthly or at irregular intervals;
- how quickly you want to repay the loan—the more you pay, and the more often you pay it, the faster the process will be;
- whether you want to repay principal as you go along, or leave it to the end;
- whether you want to make repayments well in advance, rather than in arrears, perhaps for reasons of income tax (discussed in Chapter 13); and
- whether you want to keep the loan rate variable or to fix it.

The interest rate is the most influential component on the overall long-term cost of a particular mortgage. A 'no frills' or basic loan will save you 0.5 to 1.0 per cent off your rate for the life of the loan. If you're eligible for an investor package deal you could save 0.5 to 0.8 per cent off the rate. Online mortgage lenders may have some restrictions on features and accessibility but could cut as much as 1.25 per cent off the rate charged by your conventional lender.

There is freedom to move here, to put together a loan contract that fits you. Sometimes there are good personal reasons for not accepting a loan package straight off the shelf. A good lending officer will assist you in designing the right deal. If you want to compare mortgage products which have different terms and interest rates, you can ask your lender to calculate some 'comparison rates'. For more on this, see Chapter 14.

WHAT IS THE RATE CHARGED ON?

When you borrow money, you know you have to repay the principal plus interest—but on what basis is the interest calculated? How does the lender calculate the interest you will pay? Here, too, you will find variation in the ways the various deals work. This can have important consequences for the effectiveness of your investment.

In the past, there were major differences in the way the interest rate was charged. For example, some loans applied the interest rate against:

- the highest loan balance over the course of the month just passed; or
- the loan balance at the last day of the month.

These methods of calculation were capable of distortion and did not always operate fairly. Now it is common for the rate to be applied against the loan balance each day.

Interest-only versus principal-reduction

Assume your interest rate is 8 per cent per annum and your loan principal is $100 000.

Loan #1

Interest-only loan (no repayment of principal), interest payable monthly in arrears, for a term of three years. At the end of three years you must make a lump sum repayment of $100 000.

Your repayment instalment at the end of the first month will be:

$$\$100\ 000 \times 8\% \div 12 \text{ months} = \$666.66$$

which is interest only. This will also be the instalment for each and every month of the three-year term. It will not increase or reduce.

Loan #2

Principal-reducing loan, with a variable interest rate payable monthly in arrears, for a term of 25 years, with zero principal remaining to be paid at the end of 25 years. Interest is calculated on a daily balance.

Your repayment instalment at the end of the first month will be $956, which includes approximately $666 as interest and $290 as repayment of principal.

The second month's instalment will look like this:

$$\$99\,710 \times 8\% \div 12 \text{ months} = \$664.73$$

as the principal used for the calculation has been reduced by the first month's repayment of $290 principal.

And on it goes for 25 years in this manner.

CHANGES TO INTEREST RATES

While there are no guaranteed methods of predicting future movement in interest rates, there are a few telltale signs that indicate when change is likely.

Reserve Bank meetings

In Australia, the Reserve Bank plays a major role in determining interest rates. The Reserve Bank of Australia is a statutory authority established by an Act of the Commonwealth Parliament, with a charter 'to ensure that the monetary and banking policy of the Bank is directed to the greatest advantage of the people of Australia'. This means aiming for stability of the currency, the maintenance of full employment and the economic prosperity and welfare of the people of Australia. Control of inflation is at the heart of the matter.

The Reserve Bank has set a target inflation rate of 2–3 per cent per annum. During the late 1990s and early-to-mid 2000s, inflation was within this target range, with growth in the output of the economy moving at 3–5 per cent.

The main tool for control is the overnight interest rate in the money market—the *official interest rate* or *cash rate*, which is the interest rate charged on overnight loans between institutions operating in the money market. The cash rate is the foundation on which all other interest rates in Australia operate.

To help keep interest rates focused on the Reserve Bank's cash rate, the Reserve Bank also exercises control over the supply of money into the economy, restricting or opening up the amount of money it makes available.

It is important to realise that the Commonwealth is the main provider of loan funds to Australian business. Even the banks raise no more than half their monetary needs from their own depositors—they must borrow extra funds (in huge amounts) from the Reserve Bank. So, when the Reserve Bank says 'this is the interest rate we want for our money', it carries weight.

The Commonwealth government has enormous financial resources to invest—including our taxes. It doesn't just put its money under the bed. It lends it out and earns interest on behalf of taxpayers.

For example, at a time when the official cash interest rate was 6.25 per cent per annum, the banks were lending money at around 8.07 per cent per annum for a standard mortgage—a margin of 1.82 per cent per annum. Lenders purchase money from the Reserve Bank (at the official interest rate) and lend it out after adding their profit margin. The size of that margin is determined by the type of loan—with its risk to the lender and contractual obligations. Table 9.3 (page 151) illustrates this with an example from a major bank.

As you can see, financial institutions are doing very well out of credit cards, with rates up to 11.50 per cent above the cost of funds to them. If you want to borrow a little money for two or three years, you are murdered by using a credit card or unsecured personal loan for the purchase, compared with a secured personal loan (generally secured over your home or other substantial asset).

This bank, like the others, was charging its customers as

little as 6.75 per cent for a variable-rate loan and as much as 17.75 per cent for a credit card—a range of 11 per cent. The highest rate is nearly three times the lowest rate being charged.

The aim for an investor is to get your loan at the cheapest rate for the type of deal you want. What Table 9.3 shows is that the banks and financial institutions are comfortable with the idea of offering their money at vastly different interest rates.

Clearly, to follow the direction of movement of interest rates in the Australian economy, you must look to the Reserve Bank.

The Reserve Bank has its regular meeting on the first Tuesday of the month. It is unlikely that official interest rates will change in the week or so leading up to a meeting. If there is to be a change in official interest rates, it is likely (though not always the case) that the Reserve Bank will announce the change on the day after its monthly meeting.

A change in official interest rates has its most obvious effect, for borrowers, on the variable loan interest rate. Longer-term, fixed interest rates move to a different rhythm (see below).

Table 9.3 The interest rate tower as at 4 April 2007

Type of loan	Interest rate charged (% per annum)	Margin charged above official RBA cash interest rate of 6.25 (% per annum)
Honeymoon rate (first year of variable-rate loan)	6.75	0.50
Variable investment rate for special investors (variable)	7.37	1.12

Type of loan	Interest rate charged (% per annum)	Margin charged above official RBA cash interest rate of 6.25 (% per annum)
Fixed interest rate mortgage		
• 1 year	7.45	1.20
• 3 years	7.45	1.20
• 5 years	7.45	1.20
• 10 years	7.55	1.30
Fixed rate mortgage (interest only)	7.15	0.90
• 3 years, interest paid in advance		
Variable home loan rate	8.07	
Investment mortgage rate	8.07	1.82
Home equity loan	8.57	2.32
Margin lending	9.10	2.85
Basic overdraft rate	13.17	6.92
Personal loan rate (variable, unsecured, $10 000 for 3 years)	14.22	7.97
Personal loan rate (fixed, unsecured, $10 000 for 3 years)	12.74	6.49
Credit card rates		
• low	12.49	6.24
• standard	17.49	11.24
• gold	17.75	11.50

International developments and the bond rate

For long-term interest rates (such as for a fixed-rate loan), look to international developments and the bond rate. Long-term interest rates take many of their cues from overseas economies. In part, this is because the Australian economy relies on overseas investors pumping money into our marketplace. To attract investors from other countries, our interest rates must be more attractive than those offered by the other countries, bearing in mind the local economies and their risks.

This means you can anticipate rate changes in Australia by keeping your ears open for changes in major economies such as those of the United States, Japan and Europe. If their interest rates go up (or down), there will be pressure on Australia's rates to follow suit. Interest rates for property mortgages here will begin to climb (or fall) on the basis of interest rate changes taking place on bank bills and bonds.

Speed and amount of rate change

Banks and other large lenders are big organisations with fairly standard patterns of response to interest rate triggers. For example, they are generally quick to raise interest rates following a lifting of official interest rates by the Reserve Bank. You can expect a change to variable rates on the day the Reserve Bank announces a rise, or within two or three days after that. Experience also tells us that banks are generally much slower to pass on a fall in official interest rates. And any new, lower rate will be offered first to new, potential customers, and only some days or weeks later to those customers with existing loans.

Another pattern is that a rise in official interest rates will prompt lenders to raise their variable rates by the same amount, but a fall in official interest rates will not necessarily be passed on fully to borrowers.

Lenders' habits

When raising or lowering long-term rates, lenders try to manage the situation by timing the release of the news. For this reason, such changes often take place over a weekend or after close of business. The first news many bank staff have of a change in rates is when they read it in the weekend newspapers or hear about it on the TV news.

In some cases, institutions notify their branch management of upcoming changes in long-term interest rates on the Friday afternoon before making an official announcement over the weekend.

HIGH INTEREST RATES CAN BE GOOD

A low interest rate seems such a good thing for everyone—at first glance. Why would the Reserve Bank want to raise interest rates and ruin a good thing? There are powerful reasons for doing just this.

Not everyone wins when interest rates are low. The most obvious group is investors who earn a substantial proportion of their income from fixed-interest investments such as term deposits. Retirees, who prefer capital-guaranteed or other 'safe' investments for their money, often find themselves in this position. A sustained period of low interest rates hurts them badly.

From another perspective, if inflation starts to increase there is the danger that our investment earnings—and indeed, our wages and salaries—will be devalued. Inflation makes today's dollar worth only, say, 96 cents in a year's time. Inflation eats into our savings, taking value away day by day. Shops put up their prices to cover money's loss in value. As the economy grows faster and faster, demand for goods and services escalates. Suppliers cannot meet the full demand and must ration their supplies, typically by increasing prices. Workers demand wage rises to help meet the higher cost of living, and a harmful spiral develops of ever-increasing wages and costs.

Low interest rates also discourage overseas investment in this country.

When the Reserve Bank raises interest rates, a number of things happen:

- We reassess how much money we will borrow—high debt becomes dangerous.
- We delay making some purchases—local demand slows.
- The value of Australia's dollar could rise. If this happens, imports become cheaper.

In fact, the whole process is now so well rehearsed that the Reserve Bank can start to apply the brakes to our economy without necessarily raising interest rates—it merely has to *suggest* that rates may rise. Like Pavlov's dogs, the economy will start to act out the chain of events in anticipation, delaying purchases and putting a hold on expensive plans for business expansion. (Of course, the markets can act perversely too.)

Interest rate movements are rarely one-off events. Where there is one rise (or fall) in rates, it can be assumed that more will follow. For example, interest rates fell gradually, one step after another, through the late 1990s, bottoming at 4.75 per cent per annum in December 1998. Eleven months later, in November 1999, came the first increase in five years, a mere 0.25 per cent. This was followed by further increases in the order of 0.25 per cent and 0.5 per cent each time. The rate then held steady for five months before rising once more. At this new level, rates remained steady until November 2003, when another rise of 0.25 per cent signalled another corner had been reached.

All investors must be aware of movements in the interest cycle and where the current phase fits into the broader scheme of things. It is impossible to pick accurately when the cycle will change direction, but the media will signal well in advance that a change of direction is coming; in fact, the media will almost froth at the mouth calling for a change in interest rates. We will all have plenty of notice.

Figure 9.1 Movements in the official cash rate, January 1990–November 2007

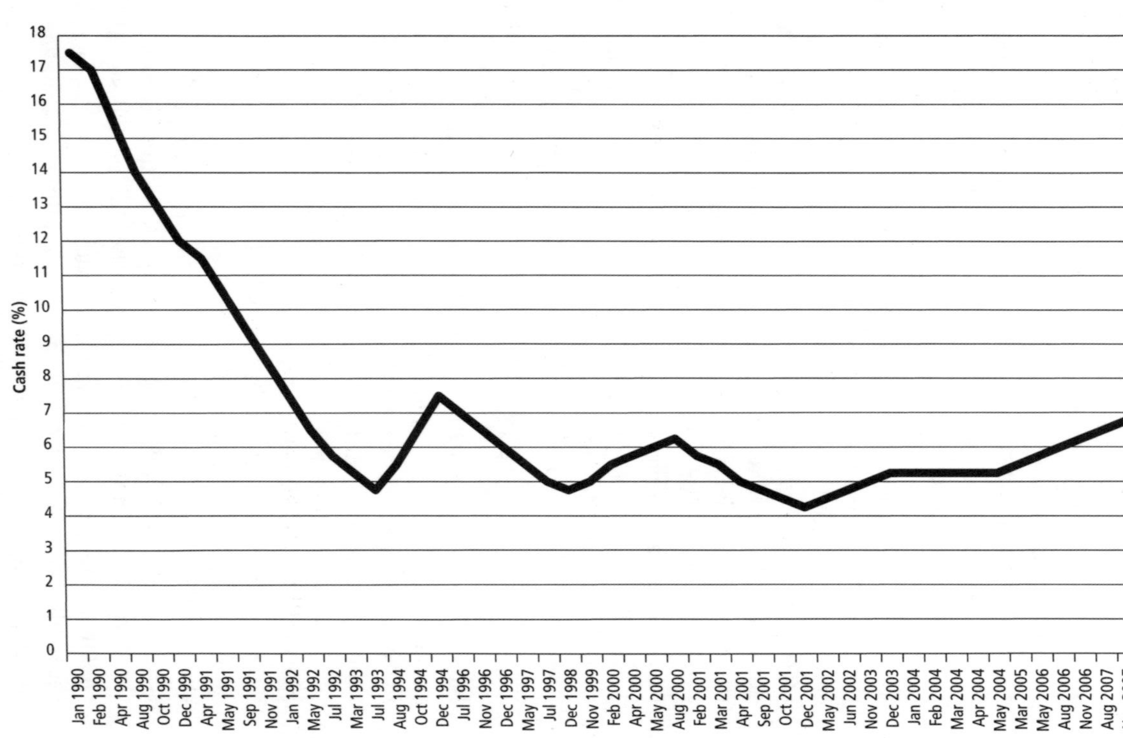

As Figure 9.1 shows, the cash rate rises and falls—it is not a constant. Let's not forget the high interest rates people paid in 1990–91. Now the rates are lower . . . but we borrow much more.

SUMMARY

- No matter what people tell you, interest rates are, ultimately, up for negotiation.
- You may have to leave your current bank or financial institution to get a better deal.
- You can be treated as an individual; you can get a better deal on interest rates. Send the loans officer into the fray with head office to negotiate concessions for you.
- A concession on fees or charges, or any other benefit of value to you, is equivalent to a change in interest rates when calculated over the term or likely term of the loan. Don't get hung up on the words—analyse the cost of the deal to you.
- If all else fails, contact the head office of the bank or lender; persist until you find someone who will listen to your story and then refer you to someone closer to the fluid core of the organisation.
- Your lender is part of your team—if your relationship is not working out, move on. Don't leave it until a crisis arises.
- Look to the Reserve Bank and finance media for indications of trends in interest rates.
- As recently as 1990, official interest rates were over 17 per cent. Could this happen again? You must look at the effect that rising interest rates would have on your ability to continue to pay your mortgage.

Chapter 10
A loan together

Choosing a loan involves starting a relationship which could last much longer than most other relationships in our personal lives. There are literally thousands of loan products out on the market—which one is right for you and your investment project?

The thousands boil down to ten basic types, and there are pros and cons for each:

- variable interest—standard and budget versions;
- fixed interest;
- mixed variable and fixed (split);
- capped;
- line of credit;
- all-in-one;
- split-purpose;
- low-documentation ('low-doc');
- shared equity; and
- terms contract—vendor finance.

As you look towards buying an investment property, you will already have faced many of the decisions you have to make when you bought your home, although the situation is not the same. When choosing an investment loan, some factors within the bundle increase in importance.

TAX IMPLICATIONS

You'll want to gain maximum taxation advantage by making deductions for interest and fees. You don't want to muddy the waters (and risk losing deductions while incurring penalties) by trying to do too much with the one loan product.

RISK

If you own your home, and perhaps have other significant debts, an investment loan starts to push you towards the limits of risk tolerance. Ways of controlling risk become more significant.

FEATURES

Many of the bells and whistles which lending institutions use to attract home borrowers are of less importance now. It's the long hard grind of the interest rate and accompanying fees which should be your focus.

VARIABLE-INTEREST LOAN

The word 'variable' refers here to the interest rate charged on the money you have borrowed. The interest rate can change as and when the lender wants, either increasing or decreasing. A change usually takes place in response to movements in interest rates within the wider economy.

You can set the length (term) of the loan for whatever duration you want. It could be one year, five, ten, thirteen, 25 or even 30 years. Each lending institution will have, as a matter of policy, a maximum and minimum term on offer. The longer the term, the lower your periodic repayments will be, but the greater the amount of interest you will pay over the term.

The common variable rate loan, whether for a home or an investment, requires repayments of both interest and principal (the capital amount borrowed); over time, the amount of the loan falls until it is all paid.

The variable-rate loan has two great advantages over the fixed-interest loan. First, if interest rates fall, the variable loan rate will also fall. Second, you can pay off the loan in full, or in part, as quickly as you like. If, for example, you take out a 25-year loan, you are free to pay it off in anything up to and including 25 years. If you come into some spare cash—a lottery win or an inheritance, for example—you can pay off the loan at once.

In many cases, there will be no financial penalty for doing this. However, some institutions charge a fee for ending a loan contract early which traditionally might have been in the region of 'an additional one month's mortgage repayment'. Now, however, lenders are rapidly expanding the fees/penalties they can extract in this way. Called an 'early termination fee', 'deferred establishment fee', 'settlement fee' or many other colourful terms, they may amount to several months' additional interest, typically dependent on how many years of the mortgage have been completed (especially in the first one to five years). Check the fine print.

Many lenders offer variations of their variable loans, which I'll call 'standard' and 'budget'. The standard product has all the features, while the budget loan sacrifices features and flexibility in order to give the borrower the lowest possible interest rate. For example:

- *standard variable loan*—redraw facility at nil or low cost per transaction; link to interest-offset accounts; link to line of credit; lower ongoing fees; and
- *budget variable loan*—interest rate around 0.5 per cent below the rate charged on the standard loan; redraw not permitted, or allowed at high cost or on a limited number of occasions; higher fees as soon as you want anything;

more difficult to link loan to other accounts and benefits.

A special type of variable loan is the 'honeymoon' or 'introductory rate' loan. This starts with a very low interest rate for the first year or two—designed to suck you in with its incredibly low figure—which defaults to a much higher rate for the rest of the term. Reality bites. Hence the title 'honeymoon'. The introductory rate may be fixed for the honeymoon period, or may be the type which can fall should rates move downwards.

The idea nonetheless has some merit. It means you can start your borrowing life at an artificially low cost. This might enable you to purchase a more expensive property. The justification is that, a year or two later, your salary might have increased and you can now handle the regular variable rate. It also allows borrowers to get over a short-term liquidity crisis—young children might now be old enough to go to childcare or kindergarten, for example, allowing a single-income family to regain a dual income.

It's also a way of getting in over your head. But don't the lending institutions just love sticking that low, low interest rate in big, big figures on their TV and magazine ads! Interestingly, since the introduction of a requirement for mandatory disclosure of a comparison rate in all advertising and promotion (1 July 2003), financial institutions have backed away from honeymoon rate deals. They no longer look as attractive as they once did.

FIXED-INTEREST LOAN

A fixed-interest loan locks three things into place:

- the interest rate;
- the amount of your repayments; and
- the term of the loan.

As we shall see, the lock is not necessarily absolute.

The term (duration) of the loan is typically one, two, three, five or ten years, although some degree of innovation has been shown recently, and it is possible to track down fixed deals of almost any term (though not necessarily from conservative institutions).

The great advantage of a fixed-interest loan is that borrowers are protected against any rise in interest rates. That means from day one to the last day you know exactly what your regular financial commitment will be, and you can budget accordingly.

On the other hand, should interest rates fall, you are contractually bound to keep paying the fixed rate—although there is something you can do about this (see below). If you are stuck with a fixed rate, you will suffer knowing you could be paying a lower instalment on a variable-rate loan.

Your regular instalment may be limited purely to interest—that is, you are not paying off any of the capital/principal—but it is common for the lender to incorporate a small amount of principal reduction in each instalment. You will only wipe a small percentage off the original principal, however, so don't think of this as a fast loan-reduction strategy.

You also lose flexibility in respect of the term of the loan. It, too, is fixed. If it is a five-year term, for example, you cannot pay out the loan earlier without incurring what might amount to a substantial penalty (a 'break cost').

Before you consider getting into a fixed-interest loan you must understand how the penalty system works. It is based on the idea that, when interest rates fall, the bank or lender will lose money by letting you repay the loan early and then lending it out to some other customer at the prevailing lower interest rate.

There is no standard formula which all lenders use to calculate the break costs on a fixed loan. It could be a mix of flat fees and percentage calculations. If the fixed interest rate increases (say, from 8 per cent to 8.5 per cent), the bank will come out ahead should you pay off your loan early. That is because the bank will be released from a deal where it is earning only 8 per cent per annum and be able to lend the money out at 8.5 per cent per annum. If rates rise beyond your fixed rate, it is sometimes bank policy to let you off without paying an 'economic' penalty. Remember that the term of the loan is fixed too—it's not just the interest rate. The lender is doing you a favour by letting you out early. At the very least there will be some administrative cost for changing your contractual arrangements, and it is only fair that the borrower should pay some sort of genuine fee.

If you are getting out of one loan and into another with the same lender, however, you should negotiate a reduction in fees payable. The lender is going to do quite nicely out of your business and should do their utmost to facilitate any restructuring of your loans and property.

Tip: It is nothing more than folklore and lender PR that says you cannot pay down your fixed loan over time. This will depend on the lender—many allow extra payments in reduction of the principal. It might be an annual or term limit (e.g., 'no more than $10 000 over the term of the loan') or monthly (e.g., 'up to an additional $1000 per month'). This is an area where change is subtle and rarely advertised, so you have to check with each lender you approach. You might find your periodic repayments also include an element of capital, up to 1 or 2 per cent.

How a penalty might be calculated

On 15 January 2005, John and Lisette borrow $100 000 at a fixed rate of 8 per cent per annum for a fixed term of five years, to assist with the purchase of a home unit. The loan is set to fall due for repayment in January 2010.

In January 2007, fixed interest rates have fallen to 7 per cent per annum and Lisette discovers she is pregnant. She and John decide to sell their unit and move to a larger home. Settlement of the sale takes place on 15 March 2007, at which point the loan is repaid to the bank (34 months early).

In addition to repayment of the outstanding principal of the loan, John and Lisette must pay a penalty to the bank for ending the loan early. The penalty is calculated by reference to what the bank has lost on the deal now that the relevant interest rate has fallen from 8 per cent to 7 per cent. The bank will look at the cost of its funds—the cash rate—which has probably fallen around 1 per cent too.

'Economic penalty' = the drop in the cash rate (1 per cent) expressed as a monthly figure (i.e. ÷ 12) × the principal of the loan ($100 000) × the outstanding portion of the contract term (15 March 2007 to 15 January 2010, being 34 months)

= 1% ÷ 12 × $100 000 × 34 months

= $2833.33

In addition, there might be an 'administration fee' of a couple of hundred dollars or so. It all adds up to quite a lot of money. Different financial institutions will have their own variant of this calculation, but this should give you an idea of what's at stake.

At the end of your fixed loan, you have a choice:

- You can repay all outstanding principal.
- You can 'roll over' the loan into another fixed term (at the applicable rate and deal available at that time—it is a fresh contract).
- You can convert the loan into another type of loan: variable or split, for example.

You might face a new round of fees—even a property valuation or fresh inquiry fees—when the term expires. You should bear these additional costs in mind when choosing the length of your fixed term. Convert these costs into what you have been paying on your instalments and you'll see your interest rate notch up a few points.

If you have a high income or two good incomes, you might be prepared to take the risk of not fixing your loan rate, even where rates are pointing upwards. A fixed rate will usually be higher than the variable rate. If, when the rate clouds gather, you voluntarily start paying the higher, fixed rate while maintaining the variable loan, you will pay off more and more principal. Your overall debt, even at a higher rate of interest, may be lower because the outstanding principal is now a smaller figure.

It's up to you, of course. It is a riskier strategy, as you are gambling that variable rates won't rise much beyond current fixed rates. By sticking with your variable-rate loan you also enjoy the opportunity to continue making extra payments in reduction of the principal.

MIXED OR SPLIT LOAN

You can hedge your bets to some degree by splitting your loan into a variable component and a fixed-rate component. This gives you some security in knowing that you have part of your loan protected against a possible rise in interest rates, but you can also benefit from a potential fall in interest rates. Such loans are called mixed, split or combination.

Just as importantly—particularly if you are the sort of person who is good at saving and paying off loans early—there is a part of your loan which you can work on paying out as quickly as you like. And there will be no penalty for doing this.

Potential benefits from a mixed loan

John and Lisette are buying an investment property. Interest rates have been steady for many months, but there is talk on the news that interest rates might soon rise. They need to borrow $200 000 to complete the purchase. They can afford to meet current interest rates of 8 per cent (variable) and 8.5 per cent (fixed for five years), but would be in real trouble if the variable rate rose by more than 2 per cent per annum. A rise of 2 per cent on a loan of $200 000 would mean monthly repayments would rise from $1544 to $1818, based on a 25-year term for the loan.

They would find it very hard to pull the extra $274 per month out of their pockets, even allowing for the eventual tax deduction on their interest payments.

John and Lisette believe interest rates will rise—if not immediately, then well within the first two years of the loan. By splitting their loan into two components—$100 000 variable and $100 000 fixed—they will gain some protection against the full burden of an increase in rates.

(For this calculation we will ignore the effect of reducing principal in the variable loan.)

Their repayments now will be:

$100 000 at 8 per cent p.a. variable over 25 years = $772 per month,

plus

$100 000 at 8.5 per cent p.a. fixed over 5 years = $810 per month (which includes a component of repayment of principal)

Total = $1582 per month.

And when interest rates rise by 2 per cent p.a.:

$100 000 at 10 per cent p.a. variable over 25 years = $909 per month,

plus

$100 000 at 8.5 per cent p.a. fixed over 5 years = $810 per month.

Total = $1719 per month.

This represents a saving on a fully variable-rate loan of $137 per month.

Bottom line: A fixed loan brings security, but at a price. At a 2 per cent rise in variable rates John and Lisette will enjoy only a modest benefit for having fixed half their loan. If interest rates continue their upward trend they will be glad they chose this tactic. And, of course, once rates begin rising, so do the fixed rates. It becomes harder and harder to make the decision to run for security and pay the higher fixed rate.

If variable interest rates get as high as they were in the late 1970s or early 1990s (over 17 per cent per annum), the savings become huge.

Table 10.1 Variable versus fixed loans

Variable		Fixed	
Advantages	**Disadvantages**	**Advantages**	**Disadvantages**
If interest rates fall, you gain	If interest rates rise, you lose—you are vulnerable	Security—if interest rates rise, you don't lose	If interest rates fall, you lose
	There is uncertainty over the precise amount of future instalments	You know exactly the amount of each instalment for the term of the contract	The instalment won't go down if interest rates fall
Term is not fixed—you can pay off the loan as soon as you like		Term is fixed—your deal is secure for the length of the term	Term is fixed
Increasingly there are new fees or penalties for early repayment of principal, especially in the first five years of the term			
Term can be as long as 30 years			
		There is lesser penalty for early repayment of principal if interest rate has risen	Penalties can be substantial for repayment of principal if interest rate has fallen
			Term is shorter than with a variable loan (five years is common, but you can find longer deals)
			At the end of the term you must either pay out the principal or renegotiate a fresh loan. This may have an unattractive interest rate (much higher than in your first term) and will have its own fees
You can redraw any equity in your loan			No redraw facility

CAPPED LOAN

Feel like hedging your bet, but don't want to go and fix your loan? Are you worried that interest rates will go up . . . but you couldn't live with yourself if, having fixed the loan, rates went down and you were stuck at a higher level?

An alternative to the split loan, though less well known, is the capped loan. A capped loan lets you set an upper limit to the interest rate you are prepared to pay. No matter how high interest rates rise under a capped loan, you will never (during the term of the cap) pay more than the capped rate.

However, unlike a fixed loan:

- you don't have to pay the higher, capped rate until rises in interest rates reach this level; and
- if interest rates fall, your rate goes down with them.

In other words, there's a ceiling, but no floor. You continue to enjoy the flexibility of a variable-rate loan, but you've hedged your upper risk.

Sounds good? Yes, but there is a price to pay. Competition between lending institutions may be fierce, but once you step outside the popular loan choices, the deals start to have fresh wrinkles. The cap is not given away for nothing. You can expect to pay a fee or a slightly higher interest rate, or a mixture of charges and rates which reflects the cost to the institution of giving you greater security. The lender is locking itself into a risky commitment and this will impact on the cost of the funds it is supplying.

Second, lenders don't like giving a cap for a lengthy period—a few months to a year is common. That doesn't mean you can't push for more. Long-term rates are known and it doesn't take a genius to work out a price for you.

When the capped period ends, the loan reverts to the current variable rate. Make sure you find out *which variable rate* your capped loan will turn into—lenders have a range of variable rates and products.

LINE OF CREDIT

Do you want to use your property loan for more than just the property? A line of credit, secured by a mortgage against the property, lets you dip into the lender's money—up to a predetermined limit—whenever you want to borrow extra cash. In this way, your property can secure the cost of your new car, the pool, the overseas holiday, the children's orthodontic treatment.

It sounds immediately attractive:

- You can borrow whenever you like.
- You don't need anyone's approval.
- You can spend the money on whatever you want.
- You are paying the lowest of all possible interest rates—the housing mortgage rate.
- You can get a much higher credit limit than on a credit card.

BUT this attractive, 'living' loan can turn into your very own portrait of Dorian Gray, rotten through and through:

- You are mixing your private and personal expenditure with your tax-deductible loan expenses and interest payments: there's room here for a taxation disaster.
- You are confusing two separate strategies: long-term wealth creation and lifestyle gratification.
- You risk turning a small saving into a long-term debt: instead of paying off a car loan in three or four years, you could be rolling it on for the full 30 years of your property loan. You'll still be paying off the old car by the time you need another vehicle (or two). You may need to lift your

repayment rate to prevent the debt blowing out and sucking up your remaining equity in the property.

For tax reasons, line-of-credit loans are arguably better suited to a home loan than to an investment loan. But in all cases they make a terrible master if they get out of control.

ALL-IN-ONE LOAN

All-in-one loans are a basket of goodies, combining the best features for maximum flexibility. Tax and lifestyle issues come together in potential harmony. They work like this:

- You have a single account for the loan and for daily transactions.
- You pay your salary direct into this account—get your paymaster to do this for you.
- Instead of earning a pitiful amount of interest on your transaction account savings, here your deposits earn no interest. And you therefore pay no tax on such non-existent income.
- Every dollar sitting in your account helps to lower your interest repayments on the loan. Interest repayments are calculated on the outstanding balance (daily, monthly, as per the contract), and every time a salary deposit is made it lowers that balance in your favour. While you are waiting to pay off your credit card balance, your money is reducing your loan instalment—it is a 100 per cent offset.
- Features abound: redraw, interest offset, cheque account, credit card.
- You can make additional repayments of principal, generally without attracting extra fees.

Convenience is a big factor here. But all of this takes the package out of the realm of the budget loan, so you can expect to be paying a higher 'standard' interest rate. Again, there are taxation problems if you start mixing personal and investment expenditure.

SPLIT-PURPOSE OR 'PORTFOLIO' LOAN

A split-purpose loan is a slippery creature to have confidence in. It dances a tango with the tax rules and is therefore always one step away from disaster. Using a single account, the investor runs two (or more) loans/mortgages for different purposes. One is for investment (such as to finance the acquisition of a rental property) while the second is for private purposes (the family home). By arrangement with your financier, you allow interest to build up on the investment mortgage (which is tax deductible), thereby capitalising the interest, while applying your loan repayments strictly to the private mortgage (which is not tax deductible).

The savings can be significant. But the Tax Office took the matter of these loans to court to strike them down. The Federal Court found them to be OK, but the Tax Office appealed to the High Court. The High Court's decision was to disallow deductibility for interest which does not relate directly to the investment part of the loan. Investors should therefore be very careful with their bookwork if they choose to use a portfolio or split-purpose loan product.

LOW-DOCUMENTATION LOAN

These are loans provided by specialist mortgage originators to borrowers who say they can afford the repayments even though they lack the traditional 'full' documentation (such as tax returns) which proves they have the net income to do so. Often these borrowers will be people who run their own business—and therefore have tax returns designed to show how *little* clear money they are making, rather than how strong their financial position is. Or they may be people with a poor credit history—a discharged bankrupt or someone who has just gone through a divorce/separation and whose financial position is asset-ravaged or up in the air. Some are simply looking for a very high loan-to-valuation ratio (LVR).

The loans are called 'low-doc' or 'non-conforming' (in reference to the borrowers who do not conform to traditional lending requirements). They first surfaced around 1997 and now account for something like 5 per cent of home loans. Some investors use them too.

Of course, there is a downside:

- The interest rate might be 0.5 per cent or more above a standard mortgage rate. With some lenders, the rate falls over a two- or three-year period, in steps or straight, until it hits the standard variable mortgage rate.
- The LVR could well be lower than the usual 80 per cent ceiling, so you might need to contribute a higher deposit.
- There can be high charges for exiting the loan in the first few years.

Bear in mind, if contemplating one of these loans, that borrowers are usually keen to refinance a non-conforming loan into a more traditional, cheaper mortgage as quickly as they can get their financial affairs into good shape, so 'break' fees and charges are a serious issue.

SHARED EQUITY

In 2007 this type of loan started getting the hard push, trying to establish a solid beachhead in the property finance area. Essentially, a loan is made more affordable by the borrower agreeing to forego part of the equity—and capital gain—for the benefit of the lender. They're now on offer from banks and even from some State/territory governments as an attempt to bridge the home affordability gulf.

For example, the lender provides you with a 25-year mortgage so you can purchase the property. The loan covers up to 20 per cent of the value of the property and it requires no repayments until the end of the term or you sell the property, whichever comes first. This supplies a substantial boost in the total amount you can borrow.

In return, although the borrower retains 100 per cent ownership of the property for the term of the deal, the lender takes as much as 40 per cent of any capital gain when the property is sold or refinanced. It's not an ideal product for the investor and is primarily marketed, at this stage, at desperate home buyers.

Shared equity loan illustration

Jessica buys an apartment in 2008 for $400 000.

She enters into a shared equity mortgage for 20% of this and borrows the remaining 80% at 8.32% p.a. (variable) over a 30-year term.

Her loan looks like this:

Loan principal $320 000 . . . monthly repayment $2420.
Shared equity component $80 000 . . . monthly repayment *nil* – a saving of $605 per month.

Six years later Jessica sells her apartment for $600 000.
Her loan principal has, by this time, fallen to $301 300.
Total equity in the property is $600 000 – $301 300
= $298 700

The provider of the shared equity finance gets 40% of this, or $119 480 plus their initial contribution (20% of $400 000), $80 000. This is a total of $199 480.

So Jessica gets to keep:

$600 000
– $199 480
– $301 300
= $99 220

> But, of course, she has not had to pay interest or repayments of principal on the borrowed sum of $80 000 which, for six years, would have amounted to $43 560.

TERMS CONTRACT—VENDOR FINANCE

This is an old-fashioned way of purchasing a property, rebadged and marketed to hungry investors and owner-occupiers. It works like this:

- A property is for sale.
- The vendor sells the property to purchaser number 1—a 'wrapper'—who usually finances the arrangement with an ordinary mortgage.
- The wrapper on-sells the property to purchaser number 2—the ultimate owner.
- The wrapper provides full vendor finance to the purchaser.
- The contract is very different from an ordinary contract for sale:
    - — payment is by instalments;
    - — the vendor retains legal title to the property until the last instalment is paid or the deal is refinanced;
    - — the purchaser, however, can renovate the property (at his or her own cost) and must pay rates, insurance and keep the place maintained;
    - — the contract contains a caveat: the wrapper cannot sell the property to someone else without the purchaser's consent—unless the purchaser is in default; and
    - — the loan principal to be repaid might be higher than the actual purchase price. This gives a capital gain to the wrapper—which might be as

much as an additional 25 per cent of the purchase price.

- The term can be for 25 to 30 years, depending on the wrapper, but the purchaser is encouraged to refinance within a couple or years or so. Some have high break costs if you get out too early.
- The interest rate is in the order of 2–2.5 per cent higher than a standard bank mortgage.
- Default will attract substantial extra costs—and the wrapper can repossess the house.
- You could also lose the value of any renovations you have made.

It's a disaster waiting to happen. In short, under one of these vendor-financed, instalment (or 'terms') contracts, the purchaser is in a highly vulnerable position with restricted rights (and, in all probability, lacks the financial means to enforce any rights). According to the Reserve Bank, anecdotal evidence in late 2003 suggested default rates on these deals as high as 10 per cent compared to a mainstream rate of 1 per cent. This compares unfavourably with another dangerous situation—where the LVR is above 100 per cent—which has a default rate of around 3 per cent.

Increasingly these types of finance are being made illegal by State and territory governments.

DEPOSIT BONDS

Investors have taken to new finance products, such as deposit bonds, with fervour. If you are unfamiliar with the product, it works like this:

- You want to purchase a property (perhaps it is up for auction) but you do not have the deposit money available at that moment.
- Or, you want to make a purchase but you don't want to

pull the deposit money away from somewhere else—perhaps it is caught up in the sale of a business, or a bonus that has not been paid, or a property sale which will not settle in time.

- Or, you are purchasing a property 'off the plan' which will not be complete and ready for settlement for many months—so why leave your deposit money sitting around doing little for you in the meantime?
- You can arrange for a financier to look after the deposit for you, guaranteeing to the vendor that you will pay the full deposit amount upon settlement.
- You pay the financier a fee for this deposit bond.
- The fee is assessed according to the amount, the time period to settlement (generally six, twelve, eighteen, up to 48 months) and prevailing interest rates. Different financiers have their own scales.
- The fee will be in the range of 1.25 per cent to 10 per cent of the deposit amount. For example, a \$60 000 bond for six months will cost around \$750, or \$2930 for eighteen months.
- The fee is not credited towards the purchase price of the property. It is nothing more than a fee.
- If you fail to complete the purchase contract, the financier pays the deposit to the vendor and comes looking to you for reimbursement.

The deposit bond is a powerful tool when used correctly. This generally means that the purchaser has got finance under control and intends to complete his or her acquisition of the property. However, in the excitement of the property boom people began purchasing multiple properties using deposit bonds, hoping the extreme leverage they provide would reap massive capital gains rewards when 'off the plan' contracts were on-sold before completion. This is just another example of a paper property empire—all greed and no substance.

LOAN PORTABILITY

The notion of loan portability resurfaces periodically. In recent times, as finance companies search high and low for new features to distinguish their loan products from those of the competition, the concept has re-emerged.

Is there any benefit in being able to move your loan from one property to another if you should sell the one you have now and buy another?

It won't save your conveyancing costs—you will still need all the usual government inquiry certificates and possibly a property survey or valuation too. And there will still be registration fees and mortgage stamp duty in States and territories where this tax is charged. The lender might waive a fresh loan application fee but, then again, there may be a 'transfer fee'.

Of course, if you go across the road to a different lending institution, it should offer you a sweetener for leaving your existing lender and taking out a loan with it. A little fee waiver isn't worth a lot these days.

A traditional problem with transferring a loan has been that the amount borrowed could not be increased—as that would turn it into a new loan. But these days, redraws and line-of-credit or all-in-one loans are much more common due to their popularity with customers. It is hard to see any theoretical benefit with loan portability—scratch the surface and you may as well start afresh.

In fact, once you have established a good track record as an investment borrower, you have a lot to offer any lender. You're a good risk and a good saver. See what the world can offer you.

STRATEGIES FOR SELECTING YOUR LOAN TYPE

There will be many factors at work behind your choice of interest rate for your investment property. Here are some sample strategies for consideration.

Who are you?

You are a good saver and work well when you are set a target—you are motivated to reduce that loan.

You could go in either of two directions. A fixed-interest loan will not let you make substantial extra repayments of principal. You might find this frustrating and limiting. If your risk profile leads you towards a fixed-interest loan, you should set yourself a target of setting aside money which will repay the principal of the loan when it falls due at the end of the term. You could do this by investing elsewhere—in shares or managed funds, for example.

Alternatively, you could go with a variable-rate loan—or part variable, part fixed—and take your chances on a rate rise. By pouring extra repayments of principal into the loan, you might find you are capable of reducing your risk exposure to an acceptable level fairly quickly.

You are a poor saver and lack the motivation to do more than you have to.

If you find you don't have spare money at the end of the month—somehow it has all been spent on high living or just mysteriously disappeared—you should think about fixing a large part of your investment loan. Where would you find the extra cash if interest rates rose? You don't have an established pattern of controlling your expenditure.

You have a high regular income and money left over each month—you find you don't even have to think about how much you are spending.

If you are in this fortunate category, you could probably handle a fair hike in interest rates. You can more confidently proceed with a variable-rate loan, perhaps with a smaller component that was fixed—this will take the edge off interest rate rises. They will still hurt you, but not quite as much as if your loan was fully variable.

You have a moderate regular income.

You are in a dangerous risk category. A fully variable investment loan is, in my opinion, a game for gamblers or those with high disposable incomes. Yet people with moderate incomes need to work their investments smarter and harder than those who are already wealthy or enjoying high incomes. It comes down to your skill and preparedness to keep a close eye on interest rates in the marketplace. You can squeeze a little extra juice by paying the variable rate for as long as you think it is either stable or more likely to go down and, when an undesirable upward change seems likely, convert your loan to a fully fixed or largely fixed interest rate deal.

You are worried about borrowing a lot of money.

You should be thinking about fixing part or all of the interest rate. You will sleep easier if you know you can afford to meet the repayments—even if, in so doing, you are paying higher instalments than a different deal would require.

You are a gambler by instinct and are prepared to take risks to save money.

Think about a variable interest rate for as long as you gamble on rates being steady or likely to fall.

You have a 'professional' occupation—lawyer, doctor, dentist, accountant or other traditional profession.

Don't fail to check out special offers to professionals—you may have to ask your lender about them. Weigh any saving against your risk exposure. Take account of any other benefits in the package.

You have very uneven income from one year to the next.

With some loan types, it is possible to pay a whole year's interest either in advance or in arrears. This lets you plan your income (rent) and greatest expense (the mortgage repayments) to maximise your tax benefits. There are rules to this, so discuss the idea with your accountant. Not all loan products will let you do this—generally only certain types of fixed-rate loans, not variable ones—so it is best to sort this out when applying for the loan. You might be offered different interest rates, although the margin may be little more than 0.2 per cent for paying interest in arrears compared with payment made twelve months in advance.

Your income is strong but your paperwork is patchy.

Just divorced? Your business tax returns are running two years in arrears? Low-documentation loans, despite their drawbacks, at least offer the opportunity to buy property before you have all the normal formalities in place. Ensure your income is secure and adequate. Find a deal you can refinance out of with minimal penalties.

SUMMARY

- There are ten basic types of loans: variable interest (standard and budget versions); fixed interest; mixed variable and fixed (split); capped; line of credit; all-in-one; split-purpose; low-documentation; shared equity; and terms contract-vendor finance.
- Understand their differences, paying particular attention to: security and risk ('Can the interest rate go up? Can it go down?'); fees; being locked into a fixed rate or fixed term; and penalties for early repayment.
- Don't ignore the tax implications of taking a type of loan with a redraw facility for a line of credit—you don't want to be mixing private expenditure with investment tax deductibility.
- Fixing the interest rate comes at quite a cost—unless variable interest rates rise by at least a couple of percentage points.

Chapter 11

Raiders of the home equity

Unless you come into an inheritance or borrow from your parents, the easiest way of making that first property investment is to use the equity in your home. Equity is the value of the property less all moneys owing on it.

CALCULATING EQUITY

Equity = valuation minus loans

Say, for example, that you have owned your home for five years. You bought it in 2002 for $350 000 and borrowed $230 000 to do it.

Purchase price ('valuation'): $350 000

Original mortgage principal: $230 000

Ratio of loan to valuation: 230 000 ÷ 350 000 = 66%

Your 'equity' in the property, in 2002, was $120 000.

Over the five years, you have diligently paid your monthly or fortnightly instalments, and have made substantial extra repayments whenever savings permitted. Now the outstanding principal of the loan has been whittled down to $90 000.

2007 mortgage balance: $90 000

And, after five years, the property is now worth $450 000.

2007 property valuation: $450 000

Your equity in the property is:

$450 000 – $90 000 = $360 000

Ratio of loan to valuation: 90 000 ÷ 450 000 = 20%

Your equity is now equal to 80 per cent of the value of the property.

With a debt of only 20 per cent of the valuation, you can apply to your lending institution to borrow against your equity, pushing the debt level back up to as much as 80 per cent of valuation, or beyond (if you are willing to pay mortgage insurance and are prepared to move into much riskier territory).

At an LVR of 80 per cent, you can work out how much of a debt you can secure:

Total potential debt: 80% of $450 000 = $360 000

Now, deduct the amount you still owe on your home, and you get the figure you can borrow to put to use in purchasing an investment property:

2007 potential additional borrowings:

$360 000 – $90 000 = $270 000

Of course, you still have to meet the lender's loan requirements, including having sufficient income (on its tests) to pay back the new, higher loan.

The next step is to find an investment property. You've got up to $270 000 in your bag. But that's not all. You can borrow up to 80 per cent of the purchase price of the investment property (or more if you are prepared to pay mortgage insurance—even up to 95 per cent of valuation). For example, if the place you want is selling for $250 000:

Purchase price of investment: $250 000

You can borrow 80% of $250 000 = $200 000 secured by first mortgage against the investment property.

Your shortfall on the purchase price is $50 000, plus costs and expenses of, say, $15 000.

This makes a total needed of $65 000. For this you reach into your home equity bag.

And that's how it works when you borrow 100 per cent of the value of the investment property.

Alternatively . . .

Of course, with the potential to borrow $270 000 based on your home equity, you really don't need to borrow extra against the investment property. You can get the cash together without a second loan.

But it is simpler and better to put the maximum loan on the investment property and top it up, if necessary, from your home equity.

This leaves your home equity in good shape, able to be used in the future for any private purpose such as putting in a pool or building an extension. It's good to have that equity up your sleeve.

AND HERE WE GO AGAIN . . . HOW TO USE YOUR HOME EQUITY TO PROVIDE THE DEPOSIT FOR YOUR INVESTMENT

Many investors do this shuffle more than once. Every few years they get their properties revalued, then use any increase in equity to provide the 20 per cent deposit on the purchase of a new investment property (plus an 80 per cent borrowing against the purchase price). People rave about this as the strategy for wealth creation.

Yes, it can work. But it worked better in the past, particularly before the introduction of capital gains tax and reduced personal tax rates. It's a strategy that relies on continual, real capital gain. Most of the time, all you've got is a pile of debt which, by the way, attracts enormous outgoings in rates, maintenance and necessary upgrades.

Without equity you've got nothing. You're just making a lot of other people wealthy—agents, gardeners, local councils, solicitors, State/territory governments, plumbers and lending institutions. Your risk multiplies. You are highly vulnerable to any fall in property values—as much as 20 or even 30 per cent in certain developments in late 2003 to 2007. If circumstances force you to sell during a property downturn, all your hard work and stress will deliver you a big, fat zero.

Second, if you use this as your prime investment strategy, you are almost certainly breaking the most fundamental rules of good investment:

- You are skewing your portfolio to property at the expense of balance between the classes of property, shares and cash-based or fixed-interest investments.
- If you buy all your properties in the same town or selection of suburbs, you are increasing your exposure to outside events beyond your control. (What if a Grand Prix racetrack is proposed? Or an incinerator? Or a flight path?)
- Your debt-to-valuation ratio is dangerous. What's OK when you have only one investment property, plus your home, starts to become over-exposed when you seek to apply the same principles and rates to a second or third investment property.

If you didn't see a licensed investment adviser when you bought your first investment property, you certainly should when considering the second one. As your level of debt increases, you need to upgrade your use of quality experts.

A revenue-neutral stance

Raoul and Cathy looked at their finances, looked at the heated Sydney market, and decided they could not afford to purchase an investment property in their own city.

Actually, that is not completely correct. They could borrow the necessary money and use their home equity to provide the rest, but they realised it was all too hard.

'When we sat down and did the figures—the potential rent, the rates, levies, insurance, managing agent's commission and the rest—we saw that although we could meet the bank's lending rules we would be creating a rod for our backs. The repayments month by month would cut into our lives. We would have to stop taking any but the simplest, cheapest holidays. We would have to eat out less and cut our expenses by around $200 per week. And then, in only 10 or 15 years, we could return to normal!

'It just wasn't for us at this stage of our lives. But we were still keen on property as a limb of our investment strategy. So we started looking in other cities and towns. Eventually we found a helpful estate agent who put us onto a block of flats in a rural city. Vacancy rates were low, there was a good history of tenancy, it was affordable and well-located, and produced a gross return of 12 per cent. We were able to borrow 80 per cent of the money and come out of it revenue-neutral. In fact we earn a bit out of the property over and above what it costs us to run.

'We are quite aware, however, that there is little room for capital gain or rent increases in the short term. But one of the reasons we chose this site was its size and location within the town. It has the potential to become a more modern townhouse site sometime later. If that goes ahead we will make a tidy capital gain.

'As it is, we have used this investment to help fund a second property investment. The first one had increased in value, enabling us to borrow against the equity to provide the deposit on another. We're not in a hurry, but property gives you a good base to work from.

'Our tip is to live with a level of risk with which you are comfortable. Others will get richer than you, but will they be happier? They'll own a car with expensive European roofracks instead of the ones you got from Kmart. You're not on this planet just to maintain an aggressive investment strategy!'

SUMMARY

- Many investors repeat their success, buying additional properties and borrowing 100 per cent of the necessary funds, relying on the equity in their home and other investment properties.
- This strategy is founded upon updating property valuations and healthy capital gains on your existing portfolio.
- This strategy works well up to a point—push it too far and you never actually get ahead. If you had to sell the lot, would you have any genuine equity left over? Are the valuations genuine?
- You can amass a pile of real estate—along with a pile of debt.
- Don't neglect the rest of your investment portfolio: strive for balance.

Section V

IT'S TAX THAT LUBRICATES THE MACHINE

Chapter 12

What the taxman giveth

All the rent you earn from your investment property will be assessable for income tax. Other benefits might also be assessable, such as in circumstances where you are entitled to keep a tenant's bond or an insurance payout compensates you for lost rent.

Fortunately, there is a generous scheme of tax deductions which reduce your overall tax burden and make it easier for you to own your investment property. In fact, it is the kindness of other taxpayers—that is, all Australian taxpayers—chipping in a few dollars that makes you wealthier. Let's be clear on how these tax deductions work and what can be done to make your financial load lighter.

TAX DEDUCTIONS

It all comes back to the basic principle of tax deductibility: when the federal government taxes you on the money you earn (including rent), it also lets you deduct the expenses you incur in earning that assessable income. Some expenses can be deducted in one hit and in full, but they must have been incurred in earning assessable income. Examples relevant to investment property are shown in Table 12.1. Some will be apportioned between strictly private use and use related to the investment (e.g., phone line rental). When you include these items in your tax return, you will receive the benefit when your overall annual tax is calculated. The deduction is not spread over a number of years.

Table 12.1 Tax-deductible expenses—some examples

Managing agent's commission and charges	Advertising to find tenants Light bulbs
Plug for the kitchen sink	Loan fees and charges
Fresh paint for the ceiling	Electricity
Cleaning	Mortgage interest
Gas	Landlord's insurance
Government taxes on your loan account	Land tax Legal expenses
Travel expenses—such as the use of your car—to carry out inspections at the property, collect rent or perform maintenance	Pest inspections and treatments Strata/unit levies Security patrols Telephone calls and line rental
Rates—council and water	Bank fees on account where rent is banked
Repairs/maintenance (for wear and tear)	Initial borrowing costs (see below)
Bookkeeping fees	

Capital works deductions

Your tax deductions are aimed at compensating you for the expenses of running a business or earning income—the Tax Office is not attempting to prop up your capital gain. So you cannot generally claim a tax deduction for matters which are characterised as capital.

If you replace all or most of a fence, the roof or the floor, these are capital expenses and are not immediately deductible; however, if you repair or replace a small part of the fence, roof or floor, you can claim a tax deduction. Defining something as 'repair' or 'maintenance' can lead to differences of interpretation—though I would back the Tax Office to win that argument.

There is no blanket tax deductibility for repairs and maintenance, even where only a part of a structure is being fixed. The problem area concerns faults which were part of the property when you purchased it, as opposed to faults which emerge while you are running the place. Tax rules take the view that in fixing a problem which came with the property you are really making a capital payment—in fact, a belated adjustment to the purchase price of the property. After all, if everything had been in good order and condition, you probably would have had to pay more for the place. Watch out for money you spend on fixing problems like this—don't rely on getting the immediate tax deduction you hoped for. As a rule of thumb, allowable repairs and maintenance are generally related to wear and tear or damage which occurred as a result of renting out your property: a storm, a tree falling, abuse by a tenant, and so on.

If you do more than repair, maintain or fix a fault—that is, actually *improve* the property with your work, then it could be regarded as a capital expense—for example, if you use brick in place of timber, marble in place of ceramic tile. The question to ask yourself and which will also be asked by the ATO is: will your efforts restore the property to its original condition or make it *better* than its original condition?

Your accountant should advise you on these matters, but seek clarification if you have any doubts—*before* you launch into serious repairs or upgrading.

Some capital expenses can be depreciated during your period of ownership under the capital works or 'building allowance' deductions rules, and are finally included in the calculation of the asset's 'cost base' for capital gains tax purposes.

Capital works deductions include such things as:

- *alterations*—reconfiguring the layout of the property;
- *extensions*—adding a new master bedroom off to the side or into the roof cavity;
- *new buildings*—such as a garage; and
- *structural improvements*—carport, sealed driveway, retaining wall, fence, pergola.

The rate of deduction depends on the date construction started and the type of construction (see Table 12.2).

Table 12.2 Rates for capital works (building allowance) deductions

Date construction commenced	Allowable rate of deduction (p.a.)
Before 18 July 1985	none
18 July 1985 to 15 September 1987	4.0%
16 September 1987 and onwards	2.5%

At a rate of 2.5 per cent, you enjoy 40 years of deductions (2.5% × 40 = 100%); at 4.0 per cent the benefit lasts up to 25 years.

Trap: Don't assume that you are ahead with a new unit because of the high building depreciation benefit. Some new developments will go from strength to strength, with unit values never sagging. Other developments carry a price premium simply for being new (a lot of people want to live in brand-new housing) and this premium drops away as soon as the first occupant moves in. It will take some serious inquiry and a definite gamble to determine whether you are better off buying the new property with its high depreciation benefit, or the 'used' unit without the premium price.

This is an area you must discuss with your accountant and, if buying a new property or one 'off the plan', you should seek information from the developer.

Trap: The Tax Office says that 'a reasonable period of time' must pass between acquisition and doing renovation/maintenance if you are to avoid it being treated as capital works. The ATO looks at your intention when you purchased—was it to renovate?

Mortgage interest and fees

The fundamental tax saving enjoyed by the property investor is that interest paid on the mortgage, plus fees and charges, is tax deductible. But you must be careful not to muddy the waters here—mistakes can be made.

- You can only claim a tax deduction for the interest you are paying, not for any repayments of principal which might be a component of your instalments.
- The property must be rented or available for this purpose in the financial year where you are claiming a tax deduction. Just because you own it and it is not your main home doesn't make the interest a deductible expense! This is the flaw behind many 'holiday home' investments.
- If you stop renting out the property and make it unavailable, you are no longer entitled to claim ongoing interest expenses.

- If you borrow money for repairs or renovations, or to purchase items for the property, interest on that loan is deductible too.
- Initial borrowing costs are deductible over five years or the term of the loan, whichever is the lesser.

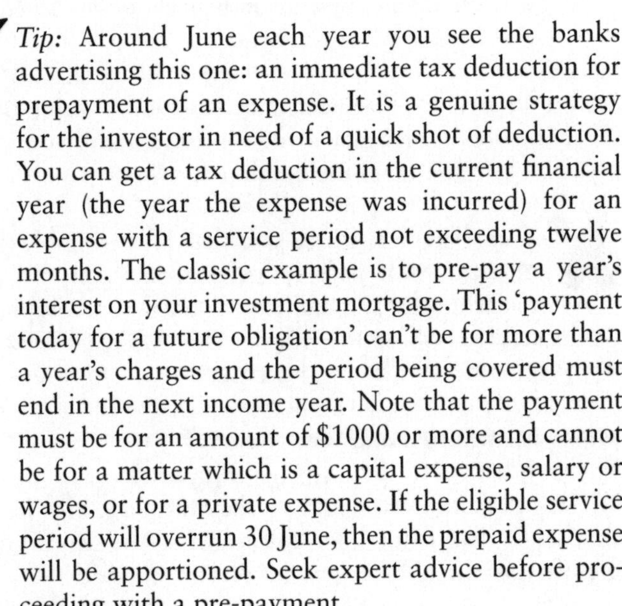

Tip: Around June each year you see the banks advertising this one: an immediate tax deduction for prepayment of an expense. It is a genuine strategy for the investor in need of a quick shot of deduction. You can get a tax deduction in the current financial year (the year the expense was incurred) for an expense with a service period not exceeding twelve months. The classic example is to pre-pay a year's interest on your investment mortgage. This 'payment today for a future obligation' can't be for more than a year's charges and the period being covered must end in the next income year. Note that the payment must be for an amount of $1000 or more and cannot be for a matter which is a capital expense, salary or wages, or for a private expense. If the eligible service period will overrun 30 June, then the prepaid expense will be apportioned. Seek expert advice before proceeding with a pre-payment.

DEPRECIATION

What happens when something you buy for your property has a lifespan lasting several years? Examples include crockery, an air-conditioning unit or heater, curtains, the hot water service and even the building itself. As you might expect, you can't claim a 100 per cent tax deduction all at once. Depreciation is about writing off the cost of capital assets over a period of time as a tax deduction. These capital assets must, of course, be used in producing assessable income (such as rent).

Effective life

For fittings and chattels, you must work out the effective life of each asset. Up until September 1999, the Tax Commissioner published tables of depreciation rates for various items which taxpayers were obliged to follow. From 21 September 1999, however, the system changed. Now depreciation rates must be fixed by reference to the effective life of each asset—how long you expect it to be of value for producing income if it is maintained in good order and condition and subject only to normal wear and tear.

You have the option of using the Commissioner's published guide to effective lives (available from the Tax Office), or you can decide on the appropriate rate of depreciation based on your own view of the effective life of the item. You must be in a position to back up your estimates if required to do so by the Commissioner, so you should base your decisions on things such as the manufacturer's specifications for the product or past experience by users of similar items. As with the rest of this chapter, these are matters to discuss with your accountant.

There are two methods for calculating depreciation. For newly acquired capital items, you can choose whether you want to use the *prime cost* method or the *diminishing value* method. Each has its advantages.

Prime cost

This method lets you write off the same number of dollars each year. For example, if the new item cost $2000 and the (prime cost) depreciation rate was 20 per cent, you could claim a tax deduction of $2000 @ 20% = $400 each year for five years.

Diminishing value

This method gives you a longer run from your tax deduction. Each year you write off a smaller sum than the year before, by applying a depreciation rate against the written-down value of the item from the previous year. Rates used under the diminishing value method are one-and-a-half times the rate used for the same thing under the prime cost method for eligible assets acquired up to 9 May 2006. For example, a $2000 capital item with a (diminishing value) depreciation rate of 30 per cent would give you a tax deduction of $2000 @ 30% = $600 in the first year, but ($2000 – $600) @ 30% = $420 in the second year.

The diminishing value rate has risen now to be twice the rate used for the same thing under prime cost calculations. For example, if you acquired that $2000 capital item after 9 May 2006, the diminishing value rate would rise to 40 per cent or a deduction of $800 in the first year followed by ($2000 – $800) × 40% = $480 in the second year, and so on.

Tip: The diminishing value method provides a higher tax deduction than the prime cost method in the first year or two. This can be valuable if money is tight for you. Towards the end of the effective life of the item, the prime cost method produces the higher annual tax deduction.

Except for the 'pooling' option outlined later, if a capital item is purchased part-way through the financial year, you must apportion a full year's depreciation accordingly.

Depreciation example

On 1 March 2007, Jenny purchases a new electric heater for her investment flat for $800. As it is an item of capital or 'plant', she cannot deduct it fully in the 2006/07 financial year.

The effective life for this item set out in the guidelines is ten years. This equates to a depreciation rate of 10 per cent per year if using the prime cost method or 20 per cent using the diminishing value method.

In the first year, however, Jenny could claim a deduction only for the number of days in the financial year for which she owned the heater. That was 122 days out of 365.

Prime cost method

Depreciation rate of 10%
Depreciation deduction for Year 1: $800 × 10% × (122 ÷ 365) = $26.74, rounded down to $26
Remaining undeducted cost of $800 – $26 = $774

Year 2: $800 × 10% = $80
Remaining undeducted cost = $774 – $80 = $694

Year 3: $800 × 10% = $80
Remaining undeducted cost = $614

Year 4: $800 × 10% = $80
Remaining undeducted cost = $534

Year 5: $800 × 10% = $80
Remaining undeducted cost = $454

And so on through the years.

Diminishing value method

Depreciation rate of 20%
Depreciation deduction for Year 1: $800 × 20% × (122 ÷ 365) = $53.48, rounded down to $53
Remaining undeducted cost of $800 – $53 = $747

Year 2: $747 × 20% = $149
Remaining undeducted cost = $747 – $149 = $598

Year 3: $598 × 20% = $119
Remaining undeducted cost = $479

Year 4: $479 × 20% = $95
Remaining undeducted cost = $384

Year 5: $384 × 20% = $76
Remaining undeducted cost = $308

You can see that after the fifth year the diminishing value method plunges below the prime cost method in terms of the annual tax deduction for this item.

Tip: You are not limited to using the same method of calculating depreciation across the board. You can approach your depreciation on an item-by-item basis. So, for example, you might use the prime cost method for the carpet but the diminishing value method for the above-ground swimming pool.

Trap: Once you have chosen one method of depreciating an item, you are not allowed to change to the other method for that item. You must continue with the method previously used.

Table 12.3 Comparing the two depreciation methods

Prime cost	Diminishing value
Applies the depreciation rate against the cost of the item each year	Applies the depreciation rate against the written-down value of the item each year
Uses a lower depreciation rate than the diminishing value method: Z%	Uses a higher depreciation rate than the prime cost method: Z% x 2
Tax deduction remains the same each year	Tax deduction is highest in initial years, but becomes much smaller in final years

Table 12.4 offers some guidelines about which items are depreciable and which items are not.

Table 12.4 What can I depreciate?

You can depreciate	You cannot depreciate
Refrigerator	Garage roller door
Washing machine	Floor tiles
Hot water service	Wall tiles
Heater	Clothes hoist
Stove	Non-portable shed
TV antenna	Security doors and screens
TV	Bath
Video recorder	Sinks
Lawnmower	Laundry tub
Air-conditioning	Toilet bowls
Most floor coverings	Gas fittings
Radio	Driveways
Rainwater tank	Paths
Microwave oven	Skylight
Solar water heater	Electrical wiring
Above-ground swimming pool	Kitchen cupboards (built-in)
Swimming pool filter	In-ground swimming pool
Swimming pool cleaning equipment	Spas
Furniture—beds, chairs, tables, etc.	Fences
Blinds	

Here are some examples of effective life from the ATO.

Table 12.5 Effective life

Depreciable asset	Effective life (years)
Furniture (freestanding)	13 1/3
Electric heater (not fixed)	15

Depreciable asset	Effective life (years)
Carpet	10
Garbage bin	10
Cook top	12
Cutlery	5
Smoke alarm	6
Bathroom exhaust fan (with light/heating)	10
Shower curtain (excluding rod)	2

IMMEDIATE DEDUCTIONS

For rental properties (where you are not carrying on a property business but are merely an investor), there is an immediate deduction for depreciable assets costing $300 or less—crockery, toaster, linen, etc. You should be aware that if you purchase what amounts to a 'set' of individual pieces over the course of a tax year, the rules might mean their individual values are added. If the total exceeds $300, you will not get an immediate tax deduction for them—for example, if you buy two dining chairs in May at $100 each and another two in June at $100 each.

The pool alternative

Since 1 July 2000, there has been an alternative way of deducting small expenses. It is called pooling. You can choose between the general depreciation system (*prime cost* or *diminishing value*) or the new pool system, under which you can put a number of items with different effective lifespans into a pool and claim a write-off against the lot. There are several conditions:

- A particular benefit is that you do not have to apportion the period of use of an item if it was not owned for the entire twelve months of the tax year, unless there was some private use. In that case, the value of the item would be reduced by the relevant percentage before it was put in the pool. You get a full year's write-off on the pool irrespective of when the individual items were acquired.

- The value of each pooled asset must be less than $1000. There is no limit on the size of the pool.
- The depreciation rate is 18.75 per cent (new assets) for the first year and an annual diminishing value rate of 37.5 per cent for subsequent years.
- Any existing assets valued at less than $1000 brought into the pool can be depreciated at 37.5 per cent.

Tip: When you purchase a property for investment, either have tax-deductible items priced in the contract of sale or engage a professional to produce a tax depreciation report straightaway—before you start renovating or purchasing. Your accountant may be able to prepare the report for you, or will arrange for an expert to do so. This will stand you in good stead when you seek to claim the related tax deductions and depreciation.

The pool

Illustration

Two assets in your low-value 'property investment' pool are from the 2007 financial year—a heater written down to $500 and a table written down to $400. This gives a closing value for the pool of $900.

In the 2008 financial year you buy a lounge chair for $700 and a mower for $800 with an average 'taxable use percentage' (that is, the proportion of investment use to personal/domestic use of the mower) of 40 per cent. This is called a low-cost asset.

You also decide to throw into the pool a small portable air-conditioning unit purchased in 2005 and depreciated since then using the diminishing value method. Its opening adjustable value for 2008 is $950. This is called a low-value asset.

What is your pool worth for depreciation purposes?

Start with the new low-cost assets (chair and mower):

These are depreciated using the pool's first-year rate of 18.75 per cent.

($700 × 18.75%) + ($800 × 40% × 18.75%) = $191.25

Add the low-value asset (air conditioner) pooled for this year:

$950 × 37.5% = $356.25

Add the pool's closing balance carried over from the previous year (heater and table):

$900 × 37.5% = $337.50

Total decline in value = $191.25
$356.25
+ $337.50
= $885.00.

I'm sure you can use the money for something and would like to get it sooner rather than later—so get your depreciation running faster through the use of a low-value pool.

Tip: Do you own your rental property with a partner? If so you can use the pool for items which cost more than $1000. For example, if you are 50:50 owners, that $1500 washing machine is actually $750 in your hands and $750 for your partner to deal with. As your share is under the $1000 cut-off mark you can add it to your pool.

The personal touch

One day you decide to go down to the shops and buy a lawnmower so you can tend the gardens at your investment property . . . and save precious dollars currently chewed up by that lazy, overcharging gardening service! The lawnmower is a tax-deductible item which you intend to write off against the rent income. However, you also want to use the shiny, new mower to do the lawns at home. Can you do this?

Yes, you can. But you will be mixing the use of the item between business and personal categories. You cannot claim a tax deduction for the whole of the cost of the mower, but must apportion the cost according to the percentage of private and business use. This will be reflected in the depreciation schedule to your tax return.

OK, maybe the Tax Office won't know you are using the mower in two places. But they will have a fair idea of what's going on if they carry out an audit and find that you have only one lawnmower. In any event, where do you draw the line? Once you start merging personal and business matters while seeking maximum tax benefits you are on a slippery slope.

Trap: Have you sold an item that you were using at your investment property? If you were depreciating it, you will have to make a balancing adjustment on the depreciation schedule of your next tax return. For example, if the written-down value of a TV was $240 and you sold it for $300, you would have to make an adjustment for the $60 'profit'.

Tip: Has something broken down and is not worth repairing? Don't just keep depreciating it for the next few years—you can write it down to zero value if it fails early. Bring such things to the attention of your accountant.

GETTING RID OF NEGATIVE GEARING?

There have been various government investigations into how to make housing more affordable. While the federal government said it will not move to close down negative gearing (as happened in 1985), there is no doubt that many in the community consider this tax break to be unfair and counter-productive for our economy. After the 1985 removal of negative gearing benefits—which were reinstated just two years later—there appeared to be a sudden collapse in the availability of properties for rent. With hindsight, it appears that Sydney was worst affected, but commentators and experts remain divided about the circumstances that led to this problem. Certainly negative gearing was not the only relevant economic condition exerting pressure at that time.

The experts can and will go on arguing about this. What is most relevant for any investor thinking that they will be able to rely upon negative gearing is that the issue has freshened during the recent property boom. Truly, it is fair to ask whether negative gearing is the best use of the considerable amount of money involved in granting and maintaining a tax concession. It ensures that we pour vast amounts of cash into residential housing as opposed to more productive pursuits. Yet would it be fair to deny negative gearing to one category of investment while retaining it for shares, for example? Or stamp collections, or managed funds?

Investors should keep an eye on developments in public policy over negative gearing. Some thoughts being tossed around include:

- denying investors the opportunity to use their home as security for a negatively geared property investment. (After all, the home is a tax shelter—why give tax benefits twice for the same property?);

- requiring investors to put a higher proportion of equity into property investment;
- increasing stamp duty on property investment purchases; and
- changing the rules on depreciation for property investment.

PROBLEMS WITH JOINT OWNERSHIP

Trap: If two people own an investment property jointly—and are not carrying on a business but merely running a small investment—they must divide the expenses equally between them, even if one of the two owners is contributing more money than the other.

So much to do with your investment works its way back to your original decision about how you will own it—in whose names and in what form of ownership. It is a mistake to think that if one of you puts more money into the deal that person can enjoy the benefits of a higher proportion of any tax deductions which flow from the property.

Ownership as joint tenants

Pedro and Linda want to buy an investment property for $400 000. Pedro earns $60 000 per year and Linda earns $170 000. They decide to own the investment in the same way that they own their home—equally, as joint tenants. This is a reflection of their relationship, with equality in all things. However, the financial reality is that the majority of the funds used to purchase the investment will come from Linda's higher income. In an ongoing sense, too, Linda's remuneration is bankrolling the expenses.

When it comes to tax time, Pedro and Linda have agreed to give the lion's share of the tax deductions to Linda. After all, it is her money which is supporting the investment, and her marginal income tax rate is 45 per cent compared with Pedro's more modest 30 per cent. Every dollar of deductions will be more powerful in Linda's tax return than in Pedro's. They think that, as Linda contributed 75 per cent of the purchase price and met 75 per cent of the ongoing expenses, she should add 75 per cent of the net loss generated by the investment to her tax return; Pedro gets 25 per cent to handle.

But this cannot happen. If you own an investment property as joint tenants, the income and expenses are divided equally between the owners. The tax situation will not change even if you prepare a legal agreement which says the two of you own the property in unequal shares.

Tip: Pedro and Linda's problem in the above example lies in their being joint tenants. If they owned the property as tenants-in-common, however, they could allocate proportions—80:20, 60:40, however they liked, adding up to 100 per cent. The same holds true where there are more than two owners. If the property will be running at a loss for many years, you may wish to purchase it as tenants-in-common. This is a matter to discuss with your advisers. That you want to invest as a 'family unit', or that you want complete equality within the relationship, is not necessarily the best principle for maximising the financial effectiveness of your investment.

Obviously, as with anything owned in clear proportions, a wrong decision can come back to haunt you later. For example, if you pay down the loan and the property generates a net income each year, this will benefit the partner with the higher proportional ownership more than the lesser partner. And at this point the marginal income tax rates will cut back the family's net result.

Many investors working together will believe they are in some form of legal partnership, even if they have never arranged for a solicitor or accountant to prepare a formal legal document. Generally speaking, however, the title deeds for the property or properties will show whether they are owned as joint tenants or tenants-in-common, and much flows from this.

It may be possible to split the income and expenses arising from property in unequal proportions even though you own the properties in equal shares (whether as joint tenants or tenants-in-common). A salary could be paid to the 'working' partner and justified for tax purposes on an arm's length, commercial basis. Usually this would be a situation where a number of properties are involved and where the owners approach their investment as a business, devoting substantial attention, involvement, organisation and time to their properties. This can still apply if managing agents are appointed to run the properties.

This solution is certainly a fair way down the track for the first-time investor, so the tax benefits of becoming a property investment business are not available. Yet I believe it is useful to have an understanding of the importance of the ownership decision now and for the future. If your investments turn into a business there will be other tax benefits and obligations affecting you beyond those discussed here.

Tip: You can always change the way you own a property—it is not a decision which can never be reviewed. If you find that ownership of the investment in equal shares is not effective financially—it may even become unviable if one partner in the relationship is not working or earning—you can change it. In most cases, stamp duty will have to be paid on the value of any property interest transferred. It is not a move to be made because a short-term problem has arisen. Bear in mind that today's highly paid executive might be tomorrow's over-aged and unemployed restructuring casualty! Again, seek specific advice while keeping your eye on the long-term consequences.

Tip: Many of the issues of equality within a relationship, tax performance and asset ownership can be sorted out if you intend owning more than one substantial asset. For example, each of you can own one of the properties. Plan for the long term.

Trap: Don't ignore the effect of your ownership decision should one of you die. A property owned as joint tenants will not pass through the owner's will. The dead owner's share of ownership passes directly to the surviving joint tenant (or joint tenants if there were more than two owners). This might be what you intend to happen, but it might not always be the best solution for your surviving family. It's a matter to sort out when you prepare or update your will.

Ownership is discussed further in Chapter 16.

TAX PROBLEM SCENARIOS

As you can appreciate, the tax system's rewards require that you follow the rules. Dinner parties are full of loose talk about taxation and investment properties, and this is where people can run into trouble. Below are three typical 'problem' scenarios.

The old home/new home switcheroo

Most of us seem to start out with our home. When the loan is under control—usually when it has been substantially paid off—we turn our eyes to property investment. But we don't want to sell the current property. (Think of the agent's commission and conveyancing fees.) We want to move out, buy a new home, turn the old one into an investment, and claim a tax deduction for the loan interest and expenses.

The Tax Office won't let you claim a tax deduction for interest on a loan used to buy a non-income-producing new home. This is the case even where that loan is secured against your old home. However, if the old home still carries a mortgage, you will be able to claim a deduction for interest incurred on that loan once the property is available for rent.

I have heard of a number of supposed ways to get around this, but they could land you in trouble. Keep the clear principles in mind when discussing any tax scheme with your advisers. The intent of the rules here is quite plain.

The holiday home getaway

People talk about renting out their holiday home on the Gold Coast or wherever, claiming a tax deduction for the expenses and still using it for their own holidays. What's more, they claim a tax deduction for travelling to the holiday home (airfares, etc.) as the costs of 'necessary inspections'. Can this be right? Will the Tax Office pay for your 'holiday' in the sun?

This desirable-sounding rort can work to a degree, but not if you push it too far. Expenses are tax deductible in the usual manner—meaning you must disclose and exclude periods where the property is being used by you and apportion the costs accordingly. As for travel expenses, they are allowed as a deduction only where the *sole* purpose of the trip relates to the property (collecting rent, inspecting, repairing or maintaining).

If the main purpose of the trip is a private holiday, you cannot claim your travel costs—even if you do in fact carry out some repairs, maintenance or inspection of the property while you are on holiday. The Tax Office may, however, allow you to claim local expenses directly related to the property inspection or work, such as local travel (e.g., taxi fares, car hire or petrol) and a proportion of any accommodation costs incurred.

Holiday homes are not all that rare—8.4 per cent of Australian households own a holiday home (BIS Shrapnel, *The Holiday Home Market in Australia: Outlook to 2009*). According to the survey, the youngest households (18–34 year olds) made least use of their holiday home, with a mean use of 5.5 weeks per year. If the family had children under five, this already low use dropped to 3.4 weeks.

This means you must either have some spare cash put aside or you intend putting the property on the holiday rental market to help meet upkeep expenses. Be aware of the traps with holiday homes and the Tax Office:

- Apportion the costs—if you use the place yourself, or allow your friends to use it, deduct this period from your calculations.
- Charge a commercial rent—or the Tax Office might ignore both your deductions claim and the small amount of income from the property.
- Don't claim the full cost of an inspection visit when part of your trip was for personal reasons.

The fast-and-loose redraw

Financial institutions have pushed hard the concept of all-in-one or line-of-credit loans, partly because they deliver tax savings. However, the investor needs to tread carefully when using the features offered by these loans. It is a very different position from your home loan. In particular, it is best not to mix private expenses with loan moneys. This can easily happen if you are getting your salary paid directly into the loan account and then using the redraw facility when you want to buy something for private use. The loan balance fluctuates, but how much is due to the mortgage?

You must keep strict records of what goes into and out of a mixed-use account. When preparing your tax return, you must also apportion the interest bill between private purposes and the investment mortgage.

Tip: You must keep records of what you earn from the property and what expenses you pay out on it for five years from the date you lodge your tax return. When it comes to capital gains tax, you will need to keep your records for five years after you sell or otherwise dispose of the property or item.

SUMMARY

- You can claim a tax deduction for expenses incurred in earning assessable income from your investment property.
- Some of these expenses can be deducted in the year they were incurred; others, of a capital nature, are depreciated or added to the cost base for capital gains tax calculations.
- Repayments of loan principal are not a tax deduction.

- You can choose which method of depreciation you want to use: prime cost or diminishing value. Each has its own benefits for your tax planning.
- One alternative is to pool a number of items.
- You cannot claim a full tax deduction for items which were used partly for the investment and partly for your private life, but your investment and private usage can be apportioned.
- Your choice of legal method of joint ownership of a property—joint tenants or tenants-in-common—has ramifications for the way you run the tax deductions and income from the property.

Chapter 13

What the taxman taketh

As an investor, you have to deal with taxes left, right and centre. We have looked at how the tax system helps the property investor, through tax deductions and depreciations. Here is the other side of the coin: your tax obligations. These include income tax, Pay As You Go (PAYG) and the instalment activity statement (IAS); the goods and services tax (GST), and capital gains tax (CGT).

INCOME TAX

A major component of the year 2000 tax reform package was a raft of income tax cuts. In most income categories, the fall in rates was useful though not earth-shattering. But for those earning $38 001 to $50 000 the fall was dramatic, with marginal personal income tax rates dropping from 43 per cent to 30 per cent (plus the Medicare Levy of 1.5 per cent). Further tax cuts followed; the changes are summarised in Table 13.1.

These cuts must be taken into account when an investor plans his or her strategies. For example:

- 'Income splitting' remains attractive. Income splitting is perhaps a misnomer, for it really is a matter of determining which partner in the relationship will own each income-producing asset. The year 2000 increase in the tax-free threshold (from $5400 to $6000) and the various drops in tax rates mean there is more value to be gained from income derived by the lower-earning partner.
- Tax deductions have lost a little sparkle. Look at your marginal tax rate before you go out and buy a tax-deductible item on a whim. As the tax rate falls, so does the degree of benefit you gain from the tax system for your deductible expenses. It cuts both ways. Negative gearing—the situation where a property's expenses exceed its income, resulting in a tax loss on the investment—has become less attractive than it used to be.
- Superannuation has become much more exciting of late, since the 2006 Budget removed Reasonable Benefits Limits and enabled those aged 60 or over to withdraw their super without extra tax. Generous deductions for voluntary deposits into super have also meant that superannuation is undergoing a resurgence in interest as a tax management vehicle.

PAY AS YOU GO (PAYG)

Before 1 July 2000, it was common for investors to be required to pay provisional tax as well as income tax. Provisional tax was an assessment of income tax for the year ahead, and was paid in advance along with an 'uplift factor' which assumed that you would earn more money in the next year than in the past year. It was not a popular tax with investors.

The year 2000 tax reform package removed the provisional tax system, leaving in its place an obligation under the Pay As You Go (PAYG) scheme. PAYG picks up the

Table 13.1 How income tax rates have changed

Pre–1 July 2000		1 July 2000		1 July 2007	
Income ($)	Tax rate (%)	Income ($)	Tax rate (%)	Income ($)	Tax rate (%)
0–5 400	0	0–6 000	0	0–6 000	0
5 401–20 700	20	6 001–21 600	17	6 001–30 000	15
20 701–38 000	34	21 601–52 000	30	30 001–75 000	30
38 001–50 000	43	52 001–62 500	42	75 001–151 000	40
50 001 +	47	62 501 +	47	151 001+	45
Company tax rate	36	Company tax rate	30	Company tax rate	30

Note: These rates are for Australian residents.

situation where a person earns more than $2000 by way of business or investment income (including rent income) and where the debt on the person's income tax assessment is more than $500. Importantly for investors, you now have a choice: to pay income tax on what you might earn or on what you actually earned.

The tradeoff is that you might be required to pay the tax into government coffers more regularly. Your instalments of PAYG tax are worked out by applying an 'instalment rate' (which the Tax Office will determine from your tax returns and assessment) against your income. Alternatively, you have the choice of paying a precise quarterly amount of tax, which the Tax Office will calculate from your last annual income tax return, adjusted by a GDP factor.

As an investor or business person, you will receive notification from the Tax Office that you will be required to meet the PAYG obligations. This could come in one of two forms:

- the requirement to prepare and lodge a Business Activity Statement (BAS) in full or part (based on estimated figures). This is the tax reporting form used by businesses and the self-employed (it also includes a GST return) and investors receiving commercial rent above $75 000 per year; a BAS is lodged quarterly or, if you choose to accept the Tax Office's instalment amount, just after the first quarter; or
- if you are not running a business, but have investment income above the threshold, you might have to prepare and lodge an instalment activity statement (IAS). There is no GST component to this. You can also report any fringe benefits tax obligation here.

The IAS is really about picking up those people who paid provisional tax under the previous system and who would still be paying provisional tax if that system remained. Not everyone is caught by one of these obligations—it will depend on your own income and tax situation.

Along with the completed form—whichever one is appropriate for your situation—you have to pay any tax for which you are liable.

Quarterly instalments of PAYG are due on the 28th day of October, February, April and July. If you are an 'annual' taxpayer, your PAYG is due on 21 October each year. Those special people who fall into the twice-yearly category will pay 75 per cent of their annual PAYG by 28 April and the remaining 25 per cent by 28 July.

The investor's life has become a little more complicated and it is recommended that you discuss the ramifications of complying with the BAS or IAS requirements with your accountant or whoever assists you in the preparation of your tax returns.

One of the great problems to be confronted in buying your property is that you don't get the benefit of your tax deductions until you lodge your first tax return. This means you are carrying the cost of such things as mortgage interest, rates, levies, insurance, managing agent's commission, and so on.

You can apply to the ATO for a **PAYG withholding variation** in the tax instalments deducted from your wage by your employer. This reduction will be based on an estimate of your tax refund. If the property is negatively geared, it is obvious you will be dipping into the tax otherwise payable on your salary.

It seems to me, however, that if you are so strapped for cash that you need to take advantage of this tax procedure you are probably out of your depth financially and should reassess your purchase and finance strategy. Nevertheless, you can find out more at the ATO website—www.ato.gov.au—and you can either download an income tax withholding variation form or contact the ATO on the relevant information line, 1300 360 221. Importantly, your employer doesn't have to see or approve your application. When your form is lodged, the Tax Office will assess your application and, if your situation complies with the requirements, write to you and to your employer advising them of your new tax rate. From that point, your salary or wage should be adjusted by your employer.

It is a fairly speedy process. To set up the variation will take about 28 days (from receipt of your form at the ATO in Brisbane) if you send it by mail, or around half this if you apply online via the ATO website.

THE GOODS AND SERVICES TAX (GST)

Income tax is called direct taxation—it comes straight out of our pay packet. Other taxes are less obvious, applying at the time we spend our money or otherwise behind the scenes. These are the indirect taxes. The GST, now a regular part of our lives, impacts on property investors in a number of important ways.

Buying a property

A property purchaser's costs went up when the GST was introduced. The 10 per cent GST applies where indirect taxation has never gone before—on the fees charged by conveyancers, pest inspection and building inspection companies, valuers and surveyors. Mortgage interest rates and application fees have not increased.

However, if you get your loan through certain types of intermediary (as opposed to direct from a lender), and that intermediary charges a fee for its service, you could find a GST component on this fee. Watch out for this trap. State/territory stamp duty on the loan and purchase documentation has not increased. There is no GST on the price of an established property—although GST is added to the price

'It's a matter of intelligent observation'

'I stumbled into property investment by accident rather than design,' says Maurice. 'Otherwise I would have my savings in managed funds. The big disadvantage with having your money in property is the lack of liquidity.

'What I've found is that I've been able to invest because of the huge equity I have in my principal residence. If you've got the cash flow to support it, you should borrow as much as you can for growth assets using your home as equity.

'By applying to the Tax Office you can have your salary tax-adjusted [varied to reflect your estimated tax refund]. This helps you afford the mortgage by giving you the cash flow now.

'Now I might look for a further property investment or move into managed funds, I'm not sure. It's very hard to identify which managed funds will perform above average, but it's not too hard to identify which suburbs and areas are undervalued: it's a matter of intelligent observation.

'I'm sure there are an awful lot of people out there sitting on paid-off or almost-paid-off homes and dithering about what to do with their investments.'

of a new construction. Stamp duty is payable on the purchase price including GST—that's a tax on a tax.

The Commonwealth government will provide a once-only cash bonus of $7000 to anyone buying their first home in a bid to offset the full impact of the GST on first-home buyers. The allowance is not means tested (that is, your income is not a relevant condition). It can be used for the purchase of a brand-new construction or an existing property, but not a property purchased for rental. The grant is administered by State and territory governments, not by the Commonwealth.

Victoria now offers an extra $3000 bonus on established homes up to $500 000 to first-home buyers (this rises to $5000 for new homes), and all States and territories have a range of concessions on State/territory duties to assist first-home buyers. Check with your State/territory revenue office (see 'Contacts, websites and further research'). Go to www.firsthome.gov.au.

Selling a property

A vendor's costs have increased under the GST, with 10 per cent tax being added to conveyancing costs, advertising and estate agent's commission.

The tenant

The GST passes private tenants by. A residential tenant does not pay GST on top of rent; nor is there GST on residential leases. The GST does apply to most commercial leases.

The landlord

The landlord is in a tricky position. Residential rent is 'input taxed'—which means the landlord pays out GST on most of the services and goods they buy for the property but cannot claim it back and must not charge GST to the tenant on rent. The managing agent's fee, gardening, maintenance and repairs, unit levies and insurances all carry GST. Council and water rates do not include GST.

The government designed the tax in this manner so as not to give an advantage to property investors over home owners. Both home owners and investors must pay for repairs and maintenance—costs that are increased thanks to the GST—and it would be unfair if investors were entitled to relief from the GST when home owners were not.

As a property investor, you don't have to register for GST

and an Australian Business Number (ABN) if you only invest in residential property. However, you should seek advice on registering if you invest in commercial property such as a shop, or a shop with a residence. GST is added to commercial rent, so registration allows the landlord to claim back any input credits (GST charged on goods and services).

Trap: When getting work done on your investment property by tradespeople, make sure you ask whether they have an ABN. If they have an ABN and are registered for GST, they will add GST to their invoice. If they do not have an ABN, you must withhold 46.5 per cent of the invoice total, paying the tradesperson only 53.5 per cent. What you are withholding is income tax. You don't need your own ABN to do this. The money you withhold must be passed to the Australian Taxation Office, usually on your activity statement form.

Tip: If an invoice for goods or services is $50 or less, you do not have to withhold part of your payment and the provider of the goods or services does not have to give you their ABN.

Tip: A landlord is not required to quote an ABN to a residential tenant since GST is not added to their rent. However, commercial landlords will supply their ABN to their tenants.

Tip: Don't immediately assume you must register for GST and get an ABN where there is mixed use of your investment property. Under the GST rules, a property investment is to be treated as residential even if there is some minor business use of the premises by the tenant. Seek professional advice.

CAPITAL GAINS TAX

Since 20 September 1985, we have had capital gains tax in Australia (although not on our home). The tax applied at the time a property owner sold, gave away or otherwise disposed of their interest in the property. In essence, it was calculated by looking at the real capital cost of the property over time, not merely at the nominal or face value of the gain. And the tax was only paid *after* the asset was sold or disposed of.

So, for example, if you purchased an investment property in 2000 for \$200 000 and sold it in 2007 for \$220 000, your gain for tax purposes was not assessed simply as the \$20 000 difference. The price, over time, was adjusted for increases in the cost of living—the effect of inflation on the value of money. Twenty thousand dollars today will not have the same value as \$20 000 in five years' time.

In addition, expenses of a capital nature—such as a new kitchen or roof for the property, as well as the expenses of actually purchasing the property (conveyancing, stamp duty, etc.)—were added to the base price, increasing it from \$200 000. The net capital gain was then added to the owner's income for tax assessment purposes.

These were attempts to bring the tax process in line with investment reality. It was a complex process, requiring good record-keeping by the owner and necessitating fresh calculations each time capital works or asset purchases were added to the property.

For assets purchased or acquired after 11.45 a.m. (AEST time) on 21 September 1999, a different method of calculation applies. This second method simply taxes 50 per cent of the net capital gain. This means that the maximum rate of CGT anyone will have to pay is 23.25 per cent—that is, half of the highest marginal tax rate of 46.5 per cent (including the Medicare levy).

To work out how much CGT you will pay, you first have to calculate the CGT 'cost base' of the asset. For a rental property, this is likely to include:

- the money you paid for it;
- expenses related to the purchase or acquisition such as stamp duty on the transfer, conveyancing and solicitor's fees, accountancy fees, surveyor's fees, and valuation report;
- expenses related to the sale or disposal such as agent's commission, advertising, conveyancing and solicitor's fees, accountancy fees, and valuation report; and
- capital expenditure such as initial repairs when you acquired the property or major structural repairs.

Then deduct the following:

- any amount for depreciating assets (e.g., furniture) included in the *purchase* price you paid for the property;
- any amount attributable to depreciating assets included in the *sale* price for the property; and
- any capital works deductions (building or improvements write-off) you have claimed or were entitled to claim—such as that extra bedroom you added.

Nothing in the cost base is indexed for inflation. There are quite a number of relevant dates and exceptions to this brief outline, so be sure to discuss the issue of CGT with your tax adviser.

Land is an asset for CGT purposes, as are some improvements (such as buildings) put on it. You should ask your accountant whether your property involves more than one CGT asset as, upon sale or disposal, there might need to be separate CGT calculations for each asset. One of the most obvious effects of the new regime is to encourage investors to weight their investment decisions towards high-growth assets ahead of high income–producing assets—you pay tax on half your capital gains but 100 per cent of your income (rent, dividends, interest, etc.).

Trap: To be eligible to use the second method of CGT calculation, you must have owned the property for a minimum of twelve months. Sell within the first twelve months and you must calculate your CGT liability without the 50 per cent discount.

Trap: You can lose the CGT 50 per cent discount! The Tax Office looks at the purpose for which you acquired the property. If it was acquired as an income-producing investment for the long term, then (provided you have owned the property for twelve months or more) you will pay CGT on half of any gain. But if your purpose all along was to buy a place to fix up and sell at a profit, then it could become a profit-making scheme and you will fall outside the terms of the 50 per cent concession.

Investors can choose which method of calculation of CGT they want to use, provided the asset was purchased or acquired on or after 20 September 1985 and before 21 September 1999 and was owned for at least twelve months. The cash difference in your property can be significant. This means you should give thought to this issue even before you commence action to sell a property. Timing could be important.

If you choose the old method, you should note that indexation has been frozen at 30 September 1999. No matter how long you hold a property after that date, no further inflation will be taken into account. The indexation adjustment applied to your sale price will be that of the

September 1999 quarter. Another principle, the averaging of capital gains over a number of years, ceased in the 1999/2000 financial year and is not relevant for those planning their first property investment now.

If you have a number of asset sales within the same tax year, some with capital gains and others with capital losses, the capital losses can be applied against the capital gains in whichever order will deliver you the greatest benefit. Clearly this is a matter to discuss with your accountant at the earliest opportunity. A capital loss must be offset against a capital gain before you apply the CGT discount in your calculation of tax payable.

Trap: Companies do not enjoy the 50 per cent discount on capital gains for CGT. This is yet another reason why a company structure can be a poor choice of investment vehicle for the small investor.

CONTACTING THE TAX OFFICE FOR INFORMATION

www.ato.gov.au
Business Tax Information Line 13 28 66
Income tax withholding variation 1300 360 221
Personal Tax Information Line 13 28 61
Translating and Interpreting Service 13 14 50
Commonwealth Treasury at www.treasury.gov.au

SUMMARY

- The tax obligations facing the property investor include income tax, PAYG and the Instalment Activity Statement (IAS), the goods and services tax (GST) and capital gains tax (CGT).
- You should seek expert advice on how best to structure your investment before you purchase it.
- The CGT regime has shifted attention away from the income generated by the investment to the potential for strong capital gain. Take this into account when planning your strategy.

Section VI

PREPARING TO BUY

Chapter 14

Choosing a lender

When the time comes to choose a financial institution for your loan, what are the key factors to bear in mind? I'd suggest they should be communication, convenience and comparing the deals.

COMMUNICATION

Communication is the linchpin of the whole endeavour. You need a lender whose representatives are keen to get your business and to make you happy. They display this by the speed with which they return your calls and the willingness with which they seek concessions from head office on your behalf.

The lender's loans officer should be good with figures, and able to quickly reset the computer to give you printouts of various loan scenarios. They should be able to answer questions about their loan products and how they can be incorporated with various accounts to give you the best way of managing your financial affairs at the lowest cost in terms of fees and charges. They should actively advise you how to minimise their own fees.

CONVENIENCE

The second important factor is convenience. For some borrowers, the internet provides the ultimate convenience, so those financial institutions with the best websites—good information, ease of use, speed of use, credibility and helpfulness—score highly. Many lenders now operate primarily on the web.

Some things to bear in mind when searching the web for a loan are:

- You can get your loan approved without ever seeing a person face to face.
- To get the best out of a web mortgage, you need to keep your options simple and standard. The more a process is automated, the less room there is for individual solutions. Flexibility is lost.
- However, some sites are gaining a reputation for speedy action, which can be important if you suddenly find you miscalculated your needs and settlement is looming. You can find some attractive interest rates on the internet, but watch out for the fees and charges. Always get the full story and take the details to somewhere like the Cannex website (www.cannex.com.au) where you can program a calculator to give you a comparison rate incorporating the effect of fees in the nominal interest rate (see the section on comparing deals, below).
- Right from the start, try to get the name of a person who will handle your application. You don't want to get lost in anonymity—that could cost you precious time and certainty if, for example, you are heading to auction.
- Paper documents must still be signed by you. This means using couriers or, where time permits, post. It is not a paperless system and time must be allowed for the necessary steps to occur.
- If you are under time pressures and do not yet have a loan approved, it can be prudent to have a 'virtual loan' under consideration as well as a back-up loan where you are dealing with another institution face to face.

You can't shout at your computer with any expectation of a civil response or contrition.

Also, a trend towards mobile lenders—they come to your home or workplace and sit down with the papers—has made the process easier for many borrowers. Don't settle for a lender who won't deal in a way that is convenient for you. And don't forget, that whichever method you use, you will have to spend time comparing the various deals.

COMPARING DEALS

- 'Our application fee is zero.'
- 'Introductory rate of only 7.05% p.a.* (*for first year).'
- 'No-frills mortgage—7.59% p.a.'

Are these loans really different? Which is the cheapest? It's a tricky matter to compare deals in a meaningful way. Honeymoon rates which crash to earth a year later; a 'no-frills' loan rate, with high annual or monthly fees equivalent to what you might have saved on the rate . . . confusion is rife when you sit down to work out which deal is the best—or simply the cheapest. That's because 'rates aren't rates'—there's a lot of fudging going on to attract your attention.

For many years now, there have been calls for a standard way of measuring the true costs of a loan. If there was a standard method of bundling all the costs together—up-front fees, ongoing fees, introductory 'special' rates and ongoing interest rates—comparison of various deals would be simplified.

Such a system does exist and it's known as the compulsory comparison rate (CCR). This is the rate prescribed by the CCR legislation which took effect nationally from 1 July 2003 under the Consumer Credit Code. This law requires financial institutions to specify the 'comparison rate' in their fixed-term consumer credit advertising and promotions (that is, it excludes 'indefinite' credit products such as credit cards and line-of-credit loans). The comparison rate is based on the interest rate of the loan (including any cheaper rate during the initial period) plus fees and charges, and is designed to calculate an all-up cost of the loan over a set period. The scheme will be reviewed.

The calculation is based on a mortgage of $150 000 over a term of 25 years, with monthly repayments of principal and (variable) interest, and fees and charges connected with the loan—application and ongoing fees. Importantly, government fees and charges, including stamp duty, are excluded, as are fees which cannot be ascertained at the start of the loan, such as charges for missing a payment or for 'breaking' the loan and terminating early.

A previous, voluntary comparative scheme was the AAPR, or average annualised percentage rate, though the term is still in use. Always check the terms of the comparison so that you are comparing apples with apples. Lenders are required to provide you, the borrower, with CCR figures based on the details of your prospective loan, such as the term, interest rate, fees, etc.

Here's an example of a comparison rate in action: in March 2007, Collins Securities advertised a 'Lo Doc' home loan with an initial two-year variable rate of 7.79 per cent and a post two-year variable rate of 7.64 cent as having a comparison rate of 7.70 per cent based on a $150 000 loan for a 25-year term.

If you have the details of a particular loan—fees, rate, term—you can find out its comparison rate by using the calculator found at the Cannex website. As you are free to insert the variables relevant to the type of deal you want (e.g., a 25-year term), you can create a set of figures for different loans and institutions in a way that makes fair comparison possible. Your prospective lender should be willing to help you to make these comparisons.

WHO ARE THE LENDERS?

Who are the lenders and where can they be found? Getting a loan is no longer restricted to a call to the local bank, building society or credit union. New entrants to the mortgage arena have had to compete hard for business and have found great success. Today, many of them are offering benefits and features which the banks won't be offering until next year. Even if you intend to borrow the money from your bank, you owe it to yourself to find out what the newer lenders are putting in their deals.

Consider these possible lenders:

- banks;
- building societies;
- credit unions;
- superannuation funds;
- other financial institutions;
- mortgage managers;
- solicitors;
- your family; and
- finance companies offering low-doc or non-conforming loans.

Banks and building societies

Banks and building societies have been forced to catch up to the innovators. In some cases, their packages are very attractive. Don't neglect to consider the smaller institutions which have been quite successful in attracting a loyal following. This category includes:

- ANZ Banking Group: www.anz.com.au
- Bendigo Bank: www.benbank.com.au

- Citibank: www.citibank.com.au
- Commonwealth Bank: www.commbank.com.au
- National Australia Bank: www.national.com.au
- St George Bank: www.stgeorge.com.au
- Westpac Bank: www.westpac.com.au
- The Rock Building Society: www.therock.com.au

When banks were much tougher, credit unions were one of the few ways ordinary working men and women could get a substantial property loan. Times have changed but much of the previously generated loyalty remains. Credit union customers are often fiercely supportive. If you're having a hard time with the banks, give the credit unions a call. They include, for example:

- Credit Union Australia: www.cua.com.au
- Sydney Credit Union: www.sydneycu.com.au

Superannuation funds

If you are an employee, you will know how your superannuation is mounting up, out of reach until your preservation age (55+, depending on when you were born). The superannuation funds are now lending some of this money by way of property mortgage through organisations such as MembersEquity Bank (www.smhl.com.au); check with your superannuation fund.

Other financial institutions

Finance companies, insurance companies and a whole range of established players are now competing strongly in the mortgage market. With some, such as insurers, there could be valuable tie-ins between your investment loan and other products or services. They include:

- AMP Banking: www.amp.com.au/banking
- Morgan Brooks Direct: www.morganbrooks.com.au
- Ratebusters: www.ratebusters.com.au

Trap: In times of financial uncertainty—and particularly when there are issues of oversupply of certain property types or within identified locations—there is a greater imperative than ever to shop around for the right financial institution to finance your investment. Watch out for low LVRs, early thresholds for lender's mortgage insurance, a reluctance to lend on studios and one-bedroom apartments and attempts to hit you with suspicious-looking fees.

Tip: Is your regular financial institution showing some reluctance to offer you the same generous mortgage terms and conditions which you might have expected a year or so ago on a city apartment? Take a drive into the country and speak to loans officers or mortgage brokers who operate in regional Australia—they may have a less jaded view about the ups and downs of city property values and can be keen to get some city properties on their mortgage books. In particular, ask whether they make their own decisions at branch level.

Mortgage managers

One of the truly remarkable changes in property finance has been the emergence of the 'mortgage managers'. Colourful advertising campaigns, often based on consumer hostility to the high-fee banks ('We'll save you!' screams the boss of Aussie Home Loans), have sucked a huge hole in bank mortgage portfolios.

These are the ones who really kicked off the service idea of 'We come to you'. They will meet you at your home or workplace; their representatives do much of their work out of their cars. Now that they have established a healthy customer base, they are expanding into credit cards and a range of other financial services. They include:

- Aussie Home Loans: www.eaussie.com.au
- RAMS Home Loans: www.rams.com.au
- Wizard Mortgage Corporation: www.wizard.com.au

Solicitors

Solicitors are often entrusted with funds from clients seeking slightly higher returns than are available from other basic investments such as term deposits and debentures. In the past, solicitors did a healthy trade in top-up mortgages and bridging finance. If you find you are running short of what you need, discuss this with your solicitor.

Your family

Certain cultural groups have this one down to a fine art in Australia. One by one, each family member is supported by the rest of the family, until all own a home.

If you intend calling on your family for substantial financial help in acquiring a property—that is, more than a few thousand dollars—you should get a solicitor to prepare a proper, legally binding mortgage to cover the situation. Do this when everyone is happy and cooperating nicely. The time for putting things down on paper is not when something has gone wrong.

Trap: Seek advice on the impact of a formal family loan on any participant's social welfare eligibility, or you may find they risk losing part or all of their pension or other benefit. Assets and income, even if thought of as 'private' within the family, must be declared by those on or applying for government financial assistance.

Family loans can give a lot of satisfaction. Parents take pride in seeing their offspring advance financially in life; they get the opportunity to give generously while they are alive and around to enjoy it, rather than holding everything back until they have died and the inheritance comes into effect. But watch out for the guilt factor—it is better to walk away from a family loan that brings too much baggage with it.

Finance companies offering 'low-doc' and non-conforming loans

These products are discussed in Chapter 10. Generally only those with a poor credit history or who have difficulty fulfilling the traditional criteria required by banks and similar financial institutions will bother with these mortgage products. However, if you want to pursue these loans, here are some providers: EZYMortgage, eChoice, Morgan Brooks Direct, Advantage Finance, Collins Home Loans, AIMS, Loan Australia and Royal Guardian. Even some of the banks are now getting in on the act.

MORTGAGE BROKERS

They're not after your savings for a deposit account and there's no free moneybox. Mortgage brokers will look at your personal situation and then recommend the best lender and deal. As they are paid by the institution that ultimately wins your loan, their services are at no cost to the borrower. They don't put up the money themselves, but refer you to those who do.

As business has expanded in this field, mortgage brokers have established well-organised operations across Australia. Some have offices, but it is common to arrange for a representative to visit you at your home or workplace.

If you get in touch with a mortgage broker, inquire at length about the basis on which they make their evaluation and recommendations:

- Do they consider *all* the major banks and lenders?
- Do they evaluate several loan products from each institution, including 'budget' and 'premium' loans?
- How do they calculate the impact of fees?
- Do they apply weightings to various parts of the deal? If so, what features are regarded most highly and what features are treated as being of little or no value to the hypothetical borrower?
- And this last important question: does the broker's commission vary according to which loan he or she recommends?

Examples of mortgage brokers include:

- Aussie Mortgage Broker: www.aussie.com.au
- eChoice: www.echoice.com.au
- Loanmart: www.loanmart.com.au
- Mortgage Choice: www.mortgagechoice.com.au
- The Mortgage Bureau: www.tmb.com.au

SUMMARY

- There are many alternatives beyond the traditional banks and building societies.
- Think in terms of communication, convenience and how they compare on the deals.
- The internet is a powerful research tool for finding the best deal.
- Many of the newer lenders are innovators—you can find different features here.
- A mortgage broker will do the searching for you—and will be paid by the lender that gets your business following the broker's recommendation. You must still be on your guard, however.

Chapter 15

Putting a team together

You can do it all on your own. But it can be much more rewarding to form good relationships with those who are involved in making your property investment work. Let's face it, you're going to be spending a lot of hard-earned money owning and running an investment property. You might as well get some ancillary benefits from the process. I think of it as 'putting together your property investment team'. It's quite a crowd. Here are the players you'll be dealing with:

- the estate agent who sells you the property;
- the agent who manages the property for you;
- an insurance broker;
- your loans officer;
- a gardener;
- the secretary of the body corporate or unit council (where relevant);
- a plumber;
- an electrician; and
- a handyperson for the odd jobs.

You can either think of them as just ships in the night, passing without any interaction, or you can seek to form meaningful professional relationships. Don't just let the managing agent handle the 'team' for you. While it's convenient if the agent does the general running around and chasing up, the system works best if the tradespeople know who *you* are. In that way, some of the goodwill from all the money you will spend on repairs, maintenance and insurance will attach to you (not just to the managing agent's business).

This comes in handy in various ways. The insurance broker who values and insures your investment property will be prepared to answer your questions about your other private insurance matters. The electrician will respond more quickly to your needs once he or she knows you have a couple of properties providing work.

If you are purchasing a unit in an apartment block or a managed estate, it is vital to have a strong contact/informant in the development. If that person is the company secretary or treasurer—so much the better. At the very least, you should form a genuine friendship with a resident owner who will tell you what went on at any meeting you missed. Clearly you should value anyone who helps you in this way—certainly with a Christmas 'thankyou' card and a bottle of bubbly.

Tip: Think of yourself as creating a team. If you don't take the time to get to know the people who do the work on your property, you will be letting the managing agent get all the goodwill arising from the spending of your money. When it's time for a favour, who will the tradesman remember? You are building a business, not just owning a small investment property! Let everyone know that you're the one paying the bills, you're the one with the money, you're the one to whom they owe their allegiance and support.

The same applies down at the bank or wherever you source your mortgage. If you spend time getting to know your loans officer, you will find it easier to sort out any problems which arise later on. In addition, should you reach the point of wanting to restructure your finances (such as moving from a variable to a fixed-rate loan) or borrow for a second investment property, you will find a ready ally. Again, you are running a business and the loans officer and manager should see you as a businessperson, not just a one-off domestic customer with a modest loan.

You are going to make money for them! Let them know it, let them value your business and, hopefully, value you too.

And when you find a good estate agent—and have given them some work and income because you purchased the investment property from them—you have made a contact who will, with some degree of loyalty, help you with hard-to-get information and local gossip about other potential investment purchases.

It's fashionable to say bad things about real estate agents—'sharks', 'dishonest', 'only interested in a sale'. Real estate agents come close to the bottom on many community surveys of job credibility, lying somewhere near lawyers and used-car salesmen.

In my own experience, in many cases this bad reputation is deserved. Who can blame them? The system puts pressure on estate agents in ways which lead to desperation. For a start, their prime remuneration comes from commissions on sales—an agent can do a lot of work on the marketing of a property and, at the last gasp, miss the sale. This means no cash coming in the door. It is an all-or-nothing job. Hence the temptation to stretch the truth.

- 'The property will sell in the low $200 000s' . . . and it ends up selling for $280 000.
- 'This flat will rent easily for $270 per week' . . . and then you find out there are three vacant units in the block.

A second problem with the industry is that some people seem to drift into it after making a mess of their earlier careers—failed lawyers and accountants among them. It is a career where, if you are successful, you can make large amounts of money without having high-level academic qualifications.

Third, in many areas there are just too many estate agents. Competition is fierce and there can be long, lean periods.

In response to such concerns, new laws targeting auction situations have been enacted in New South Wales and Victoria.

Since 1 September 2003 in New South Wales (for New South Wales residential and rural property only), there has been a more elaborate procedure for bidders at auction. You must first give the selling agent your name, address and proof of identity, which will be written into the Bidders' Record. As a bidder, you will be given a bidder's number. Note that registering as a bidder does not mean you *must* bid—it merely gives you the *right* to bid. Don't neglect to register!

If buying in joint names, only one of you needs to register, but if you are representing joint owners you must show the agent a letter of authority from the other joint owner(s). Ditto if taking instructions over the phone or otherwise bidding on behalf of someone else. You can register at any time before the auction, but be aware that at the auction itself you must show the auctioneer 'proof of identity' (for example, a driver's licence, passport, ATM card, birth certificate or Medicare card) and your address (proven by a rate notice or electricity invoice, for example). You can combine two documents to show your name and address.

If you arrive late and have not registered, you should put up your hand and announce that you intend to make a bid once you are registered. Immediately go to the vendor's agent, register and get your bidder's number.

Another important change affects what's known as making a 'vendor bid'. This is a bid made during the auction by or on behalf of the vendor, typically to push the price up or to indicate to other bidders that they are still short of the reserve price. There have been issues about the number of times the vendor can jump into the heated auction process in this manner, as well as whether genuine bidders have the right to know where these key bids are coming from. In response, the New South Wales government has enacted provisions which mean that the vendor can reserve and make a single bid—by the vendor or on the vendor's behalf. Importantly, there must be a letter of authority for a bid made by someone acting for the vendor—ensure that you, as vendor, comply, or make the appropriate inquiry if you are a disgruntled bidder who suspects a dodgy intervention took place. The auctioneer must announce whether the vendor has reserved the right to make a bid and must announce when this bid is made (if used). Dummy bids are also illegal and fines are substantial.

Since 1 February 2004, estate agents in Victoria have had to make their assessment of a property's potential sales price more realistic—both to the vendor and purchasers. If they state a range of prices, the upper limit must not exceed the lower limit by more than 10 per cent of the lower figure. Estimates given to prospective purchasers must not fall below the lower limit given to the vendor as part of the signed agency authority agreement. When it comes to the auction itself, only the auctioneer can make a vendor bid—and must declare such a bid when made.

In the Australian Capital Territory, since 1 July 2004, laws have limited vendor bids, required registration of bidders and sought to stop dummy bids and dishonest representations of the selling price. In Queensland, dummy bids are outlawed and vendor bids must be disclosed. Similar new laws were passed by South Australia's parliament in 2007.

Check with estate agents in your State or territory to see whether changes to the rules will affect your planned sale or purchase. If you know the rules, you can play them to your advantage—or at least to counter any suspected disadvantage.

ARE REAL ESTATE AGENTS INVESTMENT ADVISERS?

Real estate agents are in a position to influence consumers to make good decisions or poor decisions. The point, really, is that the agent finds himself or herself at a critical spot where the consumer is about to spend very large amounts of money.

Fortunately, in Australia there are layers of consumer protection for the landlord, including licensing schemes and fair trading laws. But this is only part of the picture. For the investor, the estate agent is more than just a person who finds a property and a tenant. The agent also assists in finding a suitable investment and, on occasion, can recommend financiers, potential partners in the venture and suitable research tools to determine affordability.

Putting it in other words, is your real estate agent acting as some kind of investment adviser? This has implications in a society where investment advisers are required by law to have a special licence and to have undertaken a particular regime of study. These requirements exist because it is recognised that consumers are placing their life savings in the hands of their investment advisers. We demand that the investor has undertaken a serious course of study to demonstrate their competence to give advice and to place a person's money in sound investments within a professionally prepared financial plan. We demand that there is a national licensing scheme which consumers can recognise and in which they can place their trust—shonks will be found out and turfed out.

'Money can be lost'

Jim and Linda owned a small flat in suburban London. When Linda's job was transferred temporarily to Europe, they looked for an estate agent to handle the letting of their home. Once satisfied with their choice of agent—he had proved his worth by quickly finding and signing up a tenant—Jim and Linda set forth.

Initially the rent flowed across to Jim and Linda smoothly. After six months or so, however, there was a hold-up with the rent. Jim telephoned their agent, who said the tenant had not paid; he would chase him about it. A month passed—the agent said not to panic as there were rights which could be exercised against the tenant under the terms of the lease. The tenant could always be traced, through the references provided earlier, and made to pay.

A second month passed without rent. Jim and Linda began to get really worried. Still, their agent was professional—all would be sorted out in time. However, Jim and Linda's bank was starting to make demands of its own.

After a third month without rent, Jim and Linda decided that one of them would have to fly to London and have words with the wayward tenant. The tenant was now putting their loan in serious jeopardy! Clearly the estate agent was not able to drive the message home. In fact, the agent was no longer returning Linda's phone calls.

Jim bought an air ticket and headed for London. On arrival, he received disastrous news: the tenant had been paying his rent all along. It was the agent who had taken the rent money and who had now disappeared. Further, it turned out the agent wasn't properly licensed and there was no indemnity fund from which Jim and Linda could recover their lost rent. It was a disaster.

There have been attempts to bring real estate agents into line with the licensing, education and professional regulation applying to investment advisers. Would such a move be good for consumers and good for the industry? Or is it just more red tape?

In its major review of the financial system in Australia during the late 1990s, the Wallis Inquiry noted: 'The existing regulation of real estate agents should be reviewed. Real estate agents providing investment advice should be required to hold a financial advisory licence unless the review clearly establishes the adequacy of existing regulation'. (Go to www.treasury.gov.au and search under 'Wallis' for more information.)

Following this inquiry, the Australian Securities and Investments Commission (ASIC) undertook a review of the situation. In its interim report, delivered late in 1999, ASIC said: 'The regulatory regime applying to real estate agents was not designed for the purpose of regulating the provision of financial advice by real estate agents, particularly individually tailored financial advice . . . consumers do not appear to have the full range of safeguards which are available to them when they receive investment advice about securities'. (For more information, go to www.asic.gov.au)

An estate agent advising a potential property investor may be asked many questions by that investor when looking at a property. The agent could find himself or herself discussing matters of income tax, tax deductions, the application of capital gains tax, issues of risk, affordability, negative gearing, finance options and how a proposed investment might fit within the overall structure of a client's portfolio of investments and loans. These are weighty matters and a casual word from an inadequately trained agent could lead the investor down a financially dangerous path.

If real estate agents who are providing advice to potential investors were required to come under the same or similar system of regulation as currently applies to financial advisers, consumers would have much to gain, including these benefits and protections:

- All benefits, moneys, commissions and the like must be disclosed to the consumer.
- The agent must be able to show that his or her recommendations had a reasonable basis to them, particularly given the aims of the investor and their attitude to taking risks.
- The agent must warn customers about any limits applying to his or her advice.
- An agent would have to comply with education, competency and experience requirements before he or she could provide investment advice.
- A national system of regulation would apply, not a State-by-State variation of consumer protections.

At some stage, it seems quite likely that real estate agents who advise investors may have to come into line with financial advisers and securities dealers (who provide advice on shares and the like). After all, from the consumer's perspective they are all 'investment advisers'—what should it matter that one adviser has come from a different origin and professional background from another? The consumer protections should be equally powerful.

SUMMARY

- You can get a number of ancillary benefits from putting together your 'property investment team'.
- These can include preferential treatment, understanding of your problems and obtaining useful information for other deals.
- Think of the people you deal with as partners in creating wealth.
- Put time and effort into finding the right members of your team, then work on the relationships. It will pay dividends.

Chapter 16

In whose name?

In all the excitement about searching for a property and then doing the deal, it is easy to overlook one of the most fundamental concerns of all: who will own it? It's not as sexy as interest rates and haggling over the purchase price, but the wrong choice on the issue of ownership will surely come back to haunt you.

There are legal, taxation and control consequences which follow from who is on the legal title to the property. You can take action at this point which will minimise the tax you pay or which will actually actively maximise it; you can look ahead to your relationships or you can blindly assume that nothing will change. You can share control or you can seize control.

Will the title deed carry your name alone, or will a partner/spouse have his/her name there too? Should you use a family company or a discretionary trust? What does it mean if you buy the property in the names of a number of friends who banded together to make the investment?

Let's look at the choices: sole name; joint names; company and family trust; and partnership or syndicate. And the issues: Who has control? What is the tax position? What are the associated costs?

SOLE NAME

This is the easiest of the lot and the most straightforward. There's no costly scheme to set up, only a small additional expense for the extra work on your personal tax return and no ongoing government fees. You are the boss and are answerable to no one. Personal marginal tax rates apply and you get the benefit of the full capital gains tax concession when you sell. However, there is no opportunity to split the income costs or share the tax deductions.

JOINT NAMES

If you are buying with another person or persons, you must decide whether to own the property as joint tenants or as tenants-in-common. Joint tenants own the property in equal shares. If a joint tenant dies, their share automatically goes to the surviving joint tenants. Tenants-in-common can own the property in any proportions they like, provided the shares add up to 100 per cent. When one dies, their share passes according to the person's will—not necessarily to the surviving partners. Tenancy in common is therefore often more suited to the situation where friends (or a syndicate) are buying the property rather than two people in a relationship.

Where partners buy in their own names there are no ongoing costs or government fees. Control becomes more of an issue as decision-making is shared. Income and expenses are allocated according to the partners' shares, so there is room for income splitting and tax deductions all round. The partners also get the benefit of the full CGT concession when they come to sell. But things get messy and may have to be untangled if the friendship or relationship breaks up and you can no longer work together.

SYNDICATES AND PARTNERSHIPS

There's no doubt that some people get a thrill from making money. Perhaps the next step is to share that excitement with others. That's where a syndicate comes into the picture. When a number of people get together to pursue a course of investment in common, the benefits are obvious:

- You can aim for a greater spread of properties than any one person could buy on their own—crossing several suburbs or cities, some fashionable, some conservative and reliable.
- Alternatively, you can purchase a more substantial property than a single investor could afford—the grand home, the block of flats.
- One syndicate member might have good contacts for cheaper finance.
- One might be a solicitor, providing the group with cost savings on conveyancing and sussing out the legal issues.
- One might be a real estate agent, with a finger on the pulse and an ability to act quickly on upcoming properties.
- Those with less cash to contribute can add value to the group in non-cash ways—bookkeeping, inspecting properties, managing rents and properties.
- One might be a good and fearless negotiator.
- Regular group meetings will keep you all on top of things—there will be more than one head available to deal with a crisis.
- As a group you can be more powerful than the individuals on their own. You can also pursue a higher return on your investment through more aggressive strategies.

It all sounds very attractive. But, as with any relationship, there can be a downside:

- If you don't set it up properly you might find messy tax and personal liability problems.
- How do you get out of the syndicate when you need your money back?

When two or more people get together for a common business purpose, they might, as a matter of law, become a partnership. The word 'partnership', in general speech, is a mostly positive thing. But at law it has a dark side: personal liability for the actions and omissions of your partners. If one incurs a debt in the partnership name, all are liable to pay it. In fact, a creditor can sue any one of the partners. This is called 'joint and several' liability. And you may achieve this undesirable status even if you've never heard of the term or thought about the consequences. Can you imagine the trouble that might be caused in a property syndicate when individuals are engaging contractors (gardening, maintenance, building repairs or extension), giving instruction to managing agents, entering contracts and attending auctions without referring to the others? Partners also should consider the preparation and lodgement of a partnership tax return in addition to their individual tax returns. To fail to do so can be another way of getting into trouble.

The first rule of syndicates and partnerships, therefore, is to have a solicitor draw up an agreement before the cash starts flying around. Second, and of possibly greater importance, is the issue of getting out of the syndicate or partnership. When people are just starting a venture, it can be hard to focus on ending it. But it will end. It might end with a bang—when everyone in the room determines they hate each other and a general bust-up takes place—or, more likely, when one member of the group needs their cash back.

To work well, a general rule of property investment is that it is a long-term proposition. This means at the very least a five-year term, and probably closer to ten years, before the value really starts to show itself.

How many important financial decisions will you make over a five- to ten-year period? Such a decision might be brought about by having frail, elderly parents, or a serious illness in the family; someone might lose their job and income; you might want to move to another country or simply travel over an extended period; someone might get married and want to set up their home. And you might be walking down the street one day and suddenly see the home of your dreams—and you've just got to have it. You could start your own business. Or you might decide to leave the rat race and drop out.

If you have only one major financial decision to make each year, try multiplying that by ten years and then again by, say, five syndicate participants. The bonds that bind the syndicate will be tested time and time again.

But getting your money out of the syndicate is not easy. For a start, it might require the sale of a property. This could be necessary at a time when the market has fallen and prices are below their long-term value. The syndicate might be in the middle of renovating a property, and to sell it now would be financial suicide. Yet it would be heartless for the syndicate members to deny cash to someone who, for example, has a seriously ill spouse or child. An investment syndicate formed with friends is neither purely business nor purely pleasure. It is both. It is emotional, and the full strength and weakness of people's personalities will direct its course. A good solicitor will ensure that your syndicate agreement has a fair, workable 'get out' clause.

On balance, property investment syndicates are for people who are confident, can handle emotional conflict and can afford to tie up their money for the long haul. They are best entered into by those who lead stable lives, who have a fair bit of cash to spare, a good regular income and who can't wait to get their teeth more seriously into the investment game. If you can't handle even the idea of attending a body corporate meeting, for example, you are not cut out for syndicate life.

The syndicate agreement

The agreement should cover matters such as:

- shares (proportions) of ownership;
- whether you will be tenants-in-common;
- how to get out of the syndicate—a process, including period of notice, should be detailed in practical, fair steps;
- a procedure for one person to sell their share in the syndicate. For example, should their share be valued and offered to the other members of the syndicate before being offered outside the syndicate?
- how to end the syndicate for everyone—when it is time to close the whole thing down;
- the aim of the syndicate;
- the properties you will target;
- how decisions are to be made. (For example, one-person-one-vote, majority decisions? Or will voting be in proportion to capital contribution to the assets purchased?);
- what debt:asset ratio will bind the syndicate; and
- how to call a meeting of the syndicate.

COMPANY AND FAMILY TRUST

A company and family trust structure has the benefit of allowing income splitting among a range of beneficiaries (such as the wider family), although there are a number of limitations on this which must be discussed thoroughly with your accountant before you head down this road. As it is a structure which can continue after the death of the people who set it up, requiring no change of ownership, it can be a good way of controlling a portfolio of properties and other investments for the ongoing long-term benefit of the family.

It will cost you around $2000 to $3000 to set up the trust and buy the company, and there are ongoing fees of the order of several hundred dollars for extra accountancy services and the preparation and lodgement of various documents (including an additional tax return).

Choosing a company structure gives greater flexibility in tax arrangements for things such as superannuation, income tax, fringe benefits tax and the transfer of losses, but you miss out on valuable CGT and, in some States and territories, land tax concessions. That is a very significant loss.

Finally, trusts offer some protection for your assets against creditors seeking to make a claim. You should be aware, however, that the law places a raft of burdens on those running a company or trust and you can fall foul of your responsibilities if you treat the assets and income as merely a private matter.

SUMMARY

- Before you buy a property, you should consider in whose name it is to be purchased: sole name, joint names, syndicate, or a company or family trust.
- Issues revolve around income tax, land tax, capital gains tax, control, liability, establishment costs and ongoing costs.
- It can be expensive to change ownership later on.

Section VII
STRATEGIES

Chapter 17

Alternatives to meat-and-three-veg investing

Sometimes an investor just really doesn't want the hassles of being a landlord, put off perhaps by the financial uncertainties which come with owning an investment property. Five useful strategies for getting into property investment without the traditional buying and renting of a residential property are: property trusts; professional property syndicates; buying a better home; buying a car space; and the 'safer option' of buying defence housing, a retirement village unit or an apartment in a managed hotel.

PROPERTY TRUSTS

Will you have trouble obtaining the amount of finance you will need to purchase your own investment property? Do you lack a deposit? Is there no equity left in your home, or do you not want to use it as security for an investment loan? Don't despair—if you have even as little as $1000 to invest you can still enter the property market via a managed fund.

A managed fund is a way for investors with less money to get into an investment, without shouldering the full management burden themselves. This is particularly attractive now that property is so expensive and it can seem almost impossible to get started. The fund could be concerned with shares (equities), mortgages, fixed-interest or property—the idea remains the same. With property in particular, the small investor has the opportunity to expand beyond the residential and small commercial fields and into major commercial, industrial and other potentially more rewarding areas. Here's how it works.

Let's assume a promoter wants to put together a fund for the purchase of a suburban shopping centre. The promoter wants to get in contact with individual investors—people like yourself—as well as superannuation funds and large organisations with money to invest. By pooling the smaller investment amounts from a number of participants, the promoter is able to make a substantial purchase.

The fund will be divided into units. For example, the purchase of a $10 million shopping centre might involve the issue of 10 million units, each of which initially is worth $1. Someone who invested $10 000 would be issued with ownership of 10 000 units in the trust. The price of a unit in the trust fund will rise or fall according to the value of the fund (principally its net assets, but also according to market conditions).

There are two types of property trust: listed and unlisted. A 'listed' trust is one listed on the Australian Stock Exchange (ASX). As with shares, units in a listed trust are bought and sold on the ASX. Because they are handled in this way they have taken on some of the characteristics of shares: when the sharemarket goes up or down, listed property trusts may move with it. This means that as an investment, they can be as volatile as shares.

Unlisted trusts—and most property trusts fall into this category—behave differently. You buy units using a form attached to a document called a Product Disclosure Statement (PDS) and sell the units back to the fund (this is called 'redemption'). A PDS must comply with a whole host of legal requirements designed essentially to ensure that potential investors understand what they are getting into and that government regulations are complied with. The aims of the trust and its management must be stated. The PDS must say how many units will be offered to the public, how the project will unfold, whether there are restrictions on borrowing and debt, the amount of cash available to cover redemptions and much more. The PDS for a listed fund must be lodged with the corporate watchdog, the Australian Securities and Investments Commission (ASIC).

The PDS is advertised widely and made available through financial planners, financial institutions and individuals such as stockbrokers, who show it to their clients. You can get a PDS by telephoning the company or, in many cases, online at the company website.

The PDS should outline circumstances where the fund management must buy your units from you if you want to sell them. For example, the management will give you the value of the units within X weeks of receipt of a notice of redemption. Generally the notice period reflects the nature and liquidity of the underlying assets owned by the fund. Fund managers endeavour to give investors their money back well within the time stated as the full notice period.

You should think of these trusts as a long-term investment. Plan on keeping your money there for at least five years so that you can ride out any low points of the cycle and get a return on your investment which more than covers the fees and expenses incurred along the way.

You can make money out of a property trust in a number of ways:

- *Capital gain.* If the value of the units increases, you will make a capital gain. You will pay CGT on this. Of course the value of units can also fall. You might also receive potential capital gains if the fund sells a property asset.

- *Income.* The properties held by the fund should earn rent income. You will pay income tax on this.
- *Tax deductions.* You get the benefit of property-related tax deductions, such as building depreciation.

As an investor, you will receive one or more distributions from the fund each year. Capital and income gains must form part of your personal tax return. Fortunately the fund will summarise the gains and other relevant figures for you, simplifying the process and minimising the paperwork. When considering purchasing units in a property trust, discuss the fund with your financial adviser to ensure you get the mix which best suits your tax position.

How does an investment in an unlisted property trust compare with making a direct investment in real estate? The advantages and disadvantages are summarised in the following table.

Table 17.1 Unlisted property trusts: Advantages and disadvantages compared with direct investment in property

Trust advantages	Trust disadvantages	No difference
You can start small—$500 or $1000 will do for many funds; some require much more.		Benefit of capital gains when property values rise. Suffer capital losses when property values fall. You can borrow money to finance your investment. Interest and expenses are generally tax deductions.

Trust advantages	Trust disadvantages	No difference
You spread your risk because the fund generally invests in more than one property. Although fees are high, you can minimise them by choosing a discount broker.	You will probably never actually inspect the properties yourself—you literally take it on trust. High entry (purchase) and/or sometimes exit (sale) fees: around 3–5 per cent of the value of your investment.	Buying real estate is expensive too.
Good fund management will help minimise ongoing expenses (such as losing tenants, and timely maintenance).	In reality, you will have little information to provide an understanding of just how good or poor the fund management is. Every year, there are more fees to pay to management.	There are significant maintenance and other costs both ways. A managing agent of a direct investment in property charges ongoing fees too. Both are long-term investments of at least five years' duration.

Fees

Unlisted managed funds contain many layers of fees. Not all funds will charge the same types or amounts/proportions of fees. The ones to take into account are:

- *entry fees*—a proportion of the money you invest when buying units;
- *exit fees*—a proportion of the money you sell your units for when you leave the fund (in whole or part);

- *ongoing fees*—a fee for year-to-year management of the fund and trail commissions to any financial planner. The average is 0.4 per cent of your total investment, year after year.

Tip: You can avoid paying entry fees by choosing to purchase units through a discount broker. On the downside, you can't expect much from a discount broker in the way of personal advice about a particular fund and whether it is right for you and your portfolio. A good alternative is to seek advice from a financial planner who charges an hourly rate in place of taking the commission from selling the units.

Comparing fund units

Property also turns up in many funds which do not contain the word 'property' in their name. These might be 'balanced funds', 'superannuation funds' or 'multi-sector funds', to name a few examples, where property forms only one category of investment purchased by the fund.

In the performance tables published in newspapers and finance magazines, you can find information such as:

- the price per unit;
- the percentage charged as an entry fee or exit fee;
- cash returns to investors paid by the fund;
- the size of the fund (its market capitalisation);
- various rankings—for example, a 'quartile' number for each three-month period of the preceding year, showing whether the fund was ranked in the top 25 per cent of similar funds, or the second, third or fourth quartile;
- highlighting of top-performing funds in each category, perhaps in separate listings. It is common to show the best performers over one year, three years and five years. Look for names which appear regularly at the top, and

ask your financial adviser about them (as well as any others that catch your attention);

- other analysis tools. One example is a 'volatility' rating, which attempts to give an idea of how widely a fund has moved from its performance trend line over time. Some funds have very high volatility ratings, while others operate more smoothly; and
- MER—management expense ratios. This is a tool for comparing the ongoing costs of various funds.

When you turn to published tables showing prices and performance of unit trusts, there are some tricks to be aware of:

- You can't compare the unit prices between funds because the funds have different commencement dates, along with different mechanisms for determining the price of their units.
- Check whether all fees have been included in the figures. The figures might include ongoing fees but exclude entry and exit fees. This might be most important when comparing units against the return on other investments, such as shares or direct purchase of real estate.
- Tables are based on past performance of the funds—*and past performance is no guarantee of future performance.* Every year there is turnover of staff in the managed funds industry. A good team of managers could be split up, or leave *en masse* for another employer. Market moves could slaughter a previously good fund strategy.
- No matter how closely you look at performance tables, and how thorough your analysis, there is no substitute for discussing your investment decision with an experienced financial planner who, you hope, will have had dealings with the funds before and will be able to flesh out the figures to reveal their true, sometimes hidden, meaning.

Tip: You can get into managed funds online. A number of online sharebrokers and securities dealers, such as E*TRADE Australia, Direct Access and InvestorWeb, have added this facility to their websites. You can compare funds, do your research, buy and supervise your investment online. Additionally, look for lower or nil entry/exit fees and lower management fees.

BORROWING FOR FUNDS

If you don't have the money to invest in a property trust, you can borrow it. You won't necessarily be negotiating quite the same deal, however.

There are two basic ways of borrowing for this purpose: a loan secured against your home or an investment property; or a loan secured against the units in the property trust or trusts you want to purchase.

If you have some spare equity in your home or an investment property, you can either use an existing redraw facility to get hold of some cash (provided you are ahead with your loan), or you can approach the lender and seek to increase the amount of your total loan.

The second option is a loan specifically for the purchase of shares or units in a managed property trust and secured against them. This is called a *margin loan.* It is an altogether different beast and should not be thought of in the same league as your regular home loan. A home loan or direct residential property investment loan is an old tabby cat of a loan, which likes a quiet life. It likes it best if you don't trouble it—in return it won't want to trouble you. Just keep paying what's due and it will be content.

A margin loan, on the other hand, is more like the wolf lurking at the kitchen door. A margin loan keeps a closer eye on the deal. It knows with some precision the value of the security you have given (that is, the units in the trust). And it knows these values day by day, with all their ups and downs. If the value of the shares or units falls below a prearranged level (commonly a 5 to 10 per cent drop), upsetting the LVR established by the loan contract, you can expect the lender to get in touch with you and require that you put in more money (or additional equity as security) to return to the approved LVR.

This is known as a *margin call.* In a falling market, several margin calls might be made during the term of the loan. And you will have to come up with the money rapidly, generally within 24 hours of the call. Needless to say, this can be traumatic.

Still, margin lending is popular. Over the two years to June 2007 the amount of money borrowed by way of margin loans more than doubled in Australia, to something like $36 billion. Depending on the risk attached to the fund, you can expect to be able to borrow from 50 to 70 per cent of valuation.

What to look for in a margin loan

If you decide to finance your investment in managed property funds with a margin loan, don't assume all loans are the same. There are more than 100 different margin loan products out in the marketplace and their conditions vary considerably. Here are some important factors to consider when making your choice:

- *interest rate*—the lower the better;
- *approved fund*—the lender will have a list of approved funds; ensure the funds you want to invest in are on that list;
- *speed*—inquire about the time taken for loan approval and when the loan money will be available for use;

- *margin call conditions*—at what threshold will you be required to top up your equity?
- *penalties*—for failing to meet a margin call on time, or for wanting to end the contract early;
- *type of loan*—you should be able to choose from a range of types, including variable or fixed interest rates, and repayments which are interest-only or principal and interest;
- *fees*—is there an application fee? Are there ongoing fees? Are they payable monthly or at some other interval?
- *minimum*—is there a minimum loan? What happens if you pay the loan down below the minimum level?

Look in investment magazines and publications for comparisons of margin loans (e.g., research house Cannex produces a star rating system for comparing these loans).

PROFESSIONAL PROPERTY SYNDICATES

Many investors have quibbles about getting into managed funds. When literally thousands of individual investors are involved and the portfolio of underlying assets (properties) is great, the management and supervision costs can also be huge.

An alternative as old as the hills but making a fashionable return to prominence is the professionally managed property syndicate. This is an alternative to the private property syndicate put together by a group of friends or acquaintances that we covered in Chapter 16.

These syndicates have many of the hallmarks of property trusts—a registered prospectus, pooling funds from many individuals, the use of trusts—but there are a number of key differences or defining attributes:

- The minimum investment is much higher—$10 000, $20 000 or more.
- The syndicate will usually look to purchase a single

property—such as a shopping mall—although there may be a number of properties involved.
- The investment has a fixed term—it will be planned to sell the property and wind up the fund at the end of the stated term, which is commonly in the range of five to ten years.
- It can be a direct property investment in your name, or via a unit trust.
- Your investment will increase or decrease in value according to the strength of the property asset itself and the economy (e.g., interest rate levels), not simply because of factors more obviously connected to the stockmarket.
- Unlike a listed property trust, you cannot sell your units on the Australian Stock Exchange; and unlike an unlisted property trust, there is no obligation on the fund to buy back your units (redemption). The syndicate managers (called the 'responsible entity') will endeavour to find a buyer for your investment if you want to get out, but there is no guarantee.
- Syndicates often borrow money to finance the purchase of the asset.
- The fee structure can be quite different from that of ordinary property trusts. For example, there might be no entry fee.

Syndicate investors are looking for an investment vehicle which can be pushed harder and with a tighter focus than a property trust. They expect better returns on their investment. And the risks can be higher too, particularly where the syndicate has pinned all its hopes on a single property. For example, a shopping mall can lose a major tenant or suddenly become tired and unfashionable.

When investigating a property syndicate, look for a management company with a track record of taking a syndicate to completion. Read the registered prospectus carefully, compare the fee structure and ensure you can live with the minimum investment level and the term/wind-up date. If the property is already occupied by tenants it will be important to find out all you can about the tenancies. What is the vacancy rate? Are any tenants in arrears of rent? Is there a fight going on between tenants and management over critical issues of repairs and maintenance? If possible, inspect the property yourself.

BUYING A BETTER HOME

I began this book by saying that if you owned your home you were already a property investor. If you're in a mood to expand your property horizons, why not simply buy a better home rather than a property for rental purposes? If it has worked well for you already, maybe you should consider sticking with the successful formula. Borrow a bit more money and upgrade to a more desirable home.

Look at the advantages of this strategy:

- you will be living in a better house, perhaps with major lifestyle improvements such as extra bedrooms, views or a pool;
- no CGT. A better property has the potential for even greater capital gains;
- no problem tenants to supervise;
- less risk of high repair bills caused by failure to notice that a small maintenance job needed doing; and
- no fees to pay, no managing agent to support.

On the downside:

- your expenses are not tax deductible. A bigger or better home generally comes with a raft of increased costs, from higher mortgage instalments to costlier council and water rates, levies, insurance and so on; and

- there is no rental income to help you pay the additional mortgage and potentially higher expenses.

The rub is that, in order to turn our investment into useable cash, we have to sell it. If we leave this too late we become fatally attached to our homes and can't live without them. And then we have become paupers in palaces.

BUYING A CAR SPACE

How many car-parking spaces come with a typical two-bedroom unit or apartment? One. How many cars does a typical household have these days? More than one.

It's not often talked about, but there is a healthy property market in owning and leasing car spaces. Car spaces in many buildings are not tied up with any particular unit or apartment, but have their own separate certificate of title. In fact, in some developments they are designed to be traded.

What's a small slab of space on a concrete block worth? Would you be surprised to learn that in Sydney's CBD they are selling for $60 000 to $90 000, sometimes even $100 000? That's for one space. At the expensive end of the scale, you can expect the space to be in a great location or well-known building and/or to have its own walls and garage door. Even in suburban Sydney a lock-up garage will add $20 000 to $60 000 to a unit's value.

Central city estate agents should be able to direct you to buildings where car spaces are traded and give you details of the levies payable for the space (unit levies, council rates and possibly water rates too). You'll save a little on insurance premiums as well.

When checking out this type of investment, bear these issues in mind:

- Is the space on its own certificate of title?
- Does the strata/unit plan place restrictions on ownership or conditions on use of the space?
- Is it truly private and lockable, or open?
- What is security like in the car-parking area?
- Is there a pillar or other inconvenience adjacent to the space?
- Is there room for a full-size car or 4WD?
- Will people have to squeeze past or brush against any car parked in this space?
- How much are the levies?
- Does the space carry voting rights in the body corporate or unit company?
- Is the space suited to being enclosed (put up a wall and a garage door)?
- Is the space close to a range of potential tenants—residential and office workers?

This type of property investment is free of tenants complaining that the carpet needs cleaning or that the dishwasher keeps breaking down, and the emotional issues surrounding eviction are less painful—after all, it's only a car you'll be putting out on the street. However, if the space is part of a commercial car park, you will be in strife if the management company collapses or is fired, leaving you without income and an asset in limbo that will be hard to sell.

The market in car spaces reminds us of the fundamentals of property investment: land (space) in a desirable location is a limited commodity and people will pay extra for convenience.

'SAFER' OPTIONS

One of the big uncertainties for property investors is continuity of rental income. In the private market, there will almost always be periods where no rent is forthcoming, either because the property is vacant or because a tenant is being troublesome.

If it's greater certainty you are after, there are several schemes where you are given a rent guarantee or can see a waiting list for tenants. Here are the pros and cons of defence housing, the retirement village and the apartment in a managed hotel.

Defence housing

One way to avoid the risks of vacancy is to rent your property to Defence Housing Australia (DHA), the residential property leasing arm of Australia's military. They take long-term leases which guarantee the rent to you. It would be hard to find a more risk-free investment. This is how it works:

- You can't just purchase any property you like. You must purchase a property which the DHA wants to rent. You can use one of your existing properties if it fits their criteria—but check first.
- DHA pays rent monthly in advance.
- DHA guarantees the rent for up to twelve years, depending on the particular deal. Terms may be for three, six, nine or twelve years, with a three-year option.
- The lease allows for annual rent reviews—which can increase or decrease the rent, depending on prevailing economic conditions.
- There is no vacancy factor—rent will be paid for 52 weeks of the year.
- There is no gap between tenancies.
- There are no letting fees or advertising expenses to pay.
- DHA looks after maintenance and any tenant damage —so there are no surprises. However, you pay for it— management fees, which come out of the rent, are

16.5 per cent (including GST) for a house and 12–14 per cent for a unit or townhouse where there is a body corporate.

- DHA pays for the property to be repainted (inside and out) and recarpeted at the end of a nine-year lease (unless these are handled by a body corporate). After a six-year lease, it will repaint inside.
- DHA has locations in some capital cities as well as regional areas across the nation, so it should be possible to find one that is affordable (particularly for the investor with less money to invest) or one that is within reach of where you live.
- Another benefit of this arrangement is that if a tenant is causing trouble, you have someone to complain to. It's the same advantage you have when leasing a property to a major corporation for one of its employees. This adds a layer of extra security for the landlord.

Perhaps the investor's greatest area of concern about taking on a DHA property is whether it will benefit from the same capital gain as the better properties in the area. Will the house suffer from some sort of stigma as an 'army home', for example? This will depend on the local community and the location. My only comment is that the DHA properties I have seen tend to be stock-standard houses; they lack the eccentric architectural details which people fall in love with. This will have an effect when you come to sell it—in particular, your property might not attract the auction 'craziness' factor which comes from a home with emotional pull.

A second issue is whether the owner will have to refurbish the home from time to time to reach a required standard. DHA pays for repainting and recarpeting after a nine-year period, but there is so much more to keeping a property attractive to tenants—for example, updating kitchen cupboards and surfaces and daggy tiles in the bathroom.

You can get the DHA property guide by phoning 1800 813 621; or going to http://invest.dha.gov.au/dha. DHA manages around 19 000 homes across Australia.

Retirement village

While many retirement villages are owned by a single entity, from church to charity to private investment company, some developers put an expensive village together by selling the units to investors like yourself rather than to the occupants.

More opportunities to invest in aged and retirement properties are emerging. The private sector is the key to meeting the need, in particular through pooled funds such as unit trusts. Another opening will be provided by private property syndicates. The yield provided by well-managed, high-class aged care and retirement properties can be significantly higher than you would get from other types of residential property, and demand is set to continue its upward movement. It's one area of property where the customer base is expanding quite naturally.

Although there might not be a rental guarantee, there is the prospect of a waiting list and a strong demand for the units. Other features include:

- a stable government-funded income in many cases;
- automatic rental increases in line with six-monthly pension increases;
- an on-site manager to look after maintenance and tenants' needs;
- quieter tenants; and
- today's investment can become tomorrow's retirement unit for a member of your family or a friend.

On the other hand, retirement villages are prone to increases in ongoing costs. Apart from the manager's salary, there are significant gardening, energy, water rate and maintenance expenses to ensure the village continues to look good. And if the village acquires a bad reputation, you may find it hard to sell your investment.

Nevertheless, the benefits are unusual and attractive. Contact local estate agents to find out if one of these schemes is operating in your area.

Apartment in a managed hotel

Like the retirement village unit, another option is to purchase an apartment in a hotel development. The hotel might be a full building or might comprise just a number of floors in, for example, a refurbished historic office building in the heart of the city. A hotel management company runs the show and pays income to you.

The deal offers a rental guarantee which is usually highly competitive against a private rental proposition. Other benefits include:

- on-site management;
- great location—often right where the action is;
- a beautiful foyer area—and sometimes an historic building;
- you may get certain use rights to occupy your unit (or another) from time to time; and
- net yield is roughly 5–7 per cent and management fees from 10 to 15 per cent.

This kind of development suffers from the same downsides as the retirement village unit. Regular refurbishment can become a serious issue for a property which might potentially have hundreds of people moving through it each year. What does a hotel room look like when you move out?

Without superb management the value of your investment can fail. You might also find that some lenders and mortgage insurers will not touch these properties, so check carefully before you buy. They are seen not so much as a residential property investment but as commercial businesses.

SUMMARY

- If you don't have the money, time or confidence to get into direct property investment, there are four worthwhile alternative strategies: property trusts; property syndicates; buying a better home; and buying a car space.
- A further category of alternatives provides guaranteed rental returns or more attractive management. These include: defence housing; a retirement village unit; and an apartment in a managed hotel.
- You can finance your investment in managed property funds through a normal bank mortgage or a margin loan. Margin loans are very different from the property loan with which you may be familiar, so take special care to understand their demands. Be prepared to handle a margin call.
- Property trusts can be listed (on the ASX) or unlisted (with buy-back provisions from the fund).
- You can save on fees by buying through a discount broker; however, you should still seek expert advice on the right acquisition for your portfolio.
- Property trusts and property syndicates are not identical.
- Don't ignore the alternative strategy of selling your existing home and buying a better one. It, too, is an attractive form of property investment which comes with a real lifestyle payoff.

Chapter 18

Designing your strategy

There is no single way of conducting a property investment. Everyone you speak to will have their favourite method, so it is not the most reliable practice merely to imitate what a friend or media guru has done. After all, anyone talking about past success is actually talking about a world that no longer exists. Inflation, interest rates, access to loans, wages growth, property cycles, consumer optimism or pessimism, rising and falling markets . . . today is not the same as yesterday.

There are many strategies for investment success. We will run through a number of them shortly. But first, what makes a 'strategy'? A strategy is not just a gut feeling of which way to go; nor is it a hotch-potch of what one picks up from TV programmes, reading the odd magazine article or book, or asking friends what they do. That may be research, but it is not a plan.

A property investment strategy will have:

- an understanding of your needs and wishes;
- an aim;
- a timeframe;
- a way of measuring success and failure at several stages: a plan and timetable for reviewing and monitoring your investment;

- an understanding of how each individual investment fits within your overall financial plan: a budget and a vision for the total picture;
- a plan for controlling risk; and
- a plan for recruiting and dealing with your property team (managing agent, banker, insurance broker, and so on).

AN UNDERSTANDING OF YOUR NEEDS AND WISHES

Right at the start, before you allocate a single dollar to any investment above and beyond a bet on a horse race, you should establish a sound understanding of what you want out of life and what you can afford. Perhaps the best way to do this is to go to a licensed financial planner who will prepare a needs analysis with you.

This is not a magic document. It is a learning process and, as such, it seems to work better if an outsider is involved. How much money do you make? Will your job change in the next few years? Are you planning on having children or travelling extensively? How much money do you want in retirement? Where does the pursuit of money fit in your overall priorities?

And the vital question: do your partner's needs and wishes accord with your own? Joint property investment, like having a baby, is not a tactic best entered into when a relationship is shaky.

AN AIM

Property investment does not only have the one aim. Perhaps your major property investment—buying a home—can serve multiple aims:

- security now;
- security for old age;

- a savings plan—to prevent your wage frittering away;
- to take advantage of Australia's great capital gains exemption;
- to provide a stable place to nurture a family;
- to meet 'residence' criteria—for social security benefits, citizenship or to advance political aspirations;
- to balance an investment portfolio weak in the property sector;
- to live near your parents;
- to facilitate a lifestyle decision ahead of a financial one (for example, to live near the beach or on a rural property); or
- just to make money, pure and simple.

What is your aim *now*, at *this* moment as you read *this* page of *this* book? It might be something altogether different from anything in the above list.

Do you think your aim has changed since you first opened this book, or has it remained constant? Without a clear aim, not only will you wander but you might end up with other bits of the picture in conflict, such as your finance arrangements and the type of property you purchase.

A TIMEFRAME

Are you looking for a quick profit, to buy and sell in rapid succession? Property is generally not suited to a short timeframe—maybe you should put your money elsewhere. Anything less than five years would be an unusually ambitious timeframe.

'The long term' is not much help either. If you say 'My investment timeframe is the long term', do you mean:

- a specific term—ten years, for example;
- until I retire;

- until my partner retires;
- until I die;
- until my partner dies;
- until my children leave home;
- this property is so good I want to pass it on to my children intact;
- until planning laws change and I can subdivide or develop it further;
- until the market improves;
- I will hold it as an investment for many years, eventually turning it from an investment to my residence; or
- until I have amassed enough money from a range of investments to enable me to purchase a more expensive and more desirable asset, irrespective of whether this is one year or fifteen.

An understanding of your investment timeframe will help you with a host of planning decisions. For example, you might wish to have the property free of debt by the time you retire. Accordingly, you would select a mortgage repayment level which would ensure you meet this goal.

What is the timeframe for the property investment you are planning now?

MEASURING SUCCESS AND FAILURE

Are you an aggressive or a passive investor? Some people accept the cards life deals them, while others want to play three hands at once. And it is not necessarily a case of greed—many investors enjoy the thrill of the deal more than the actual spending of the proceeds.

How will you know whether your investment is making you money or draining your coffers with little hope of a good return? You may wish to involve a professional, such as an accountant, in regular reviews of your investment.

You can also use your own measures by which to assess how things are going:

- Keep in touch with local property prices in the papers and in estate agency windows.
- Ask agents who know the property—it may not be the agent who sold you the place, but others will also know the building.
- Read the loan statements from your lender—what is the outstanding principal now, compared with twelve months ago? How much money did you pay in interest last year? How much principal is included in each repayment?
- Every year or two you should discuss progress with the lender. Ask questions such as: 'What difference would it make if I paid more each time? How many years would it take off the term of the loan if I made a lump-sum repayment of capital?' You might choose to accelerate the process by restructuring your loan.
- Discuss the property expenses with the managing agent (if you have one) and whoever prepares your tax return. Are expenses rising while rent stays steady? Are vacancy periods extending? What benefit would come from improving the property—sanding the wooden floors, adding an extra bedroom, knocking through a wall to create a new window and bring more light inside, replacing old kitchen benches, updating the bathroom? Is your property costing more to run and maintain than comparable properties? What can be done to stem the leaks?

Tip: Your accountant can prepare a summary of your progress. It may be as simple as adding the amount of capital paid off last year, the net rent received (if any) after expenses or the net tax effect of your 'losses' and any potential capital gains. Deduct any significant and unusual pending expenses, such as a complete repaint or a new roof. This is the creation of your own personal investment 'index'—a measure which encapsulates what the property is doing for you financially.

There are different ways of doing the same thing, but the essence is to measure the progress. In the absence of a genuine attempt to quantify or measure what is going on, your decision-making can stray substantially off target. Don't just drift! Create your own review timetable—it might look something like the example in Table 18.1.

UNDERSTANDING HOW EACH INVESTMENT FITS INTO YOUR FINANCIAL PLAN

Your strategy obviously should include such basics as the name of the lender, the amount you are borrowing, the interest rate, term, amount and regularity of repayments and whether the rate is variable, fixed or mixed. But there's more to it than this. You need to have a budget for and a vision of the total picture.

It is one thing to know how much you can afford to pay to purchase and then run a particular property investment. But it adds a whole extra dimension when you try to fit this budget within the framework of your total household budget, including other investment plans.

As discussed earlier, we all need balance across the spectrum of investment categories. In my opinion, superannuation, equities—even preserving the value of your home through appropriate and timely maintenance—must not be neglected for too long. You might be able to afford the $200 each week you have to throw into the pot to cover the net loss arising from a property investment, but how will this impact on your wider plans? Don't lose sight of the big picture. A proper investment strategy makes you a field commander, not a foot soldier.

Table 18.1 A sample review timetable

Monthly	Yearly	Occasionally
Check rent is up-to-date	Meet your lender and review loan structure, rate, term, etc.	Inspect your property—a walk outside or, when vacant, a look inside. Is maintenance required (e.g. painting)? Is anything broken? Is there rubbish to be cleared? Should your tenant be notified of anything (e.g. mess, noise, damage)?
Check bank statement(s) for errors	Review insurances	
	Meet your managing agent and discuss maintenance or improvements to keep the property attractive to tenants	
	Should I keep the same managing agent or find a new one?	Look at comparable property prices and rents: newspaper and estate agency window displays
	Meet your accountant and discuss tax planning	
	Ask your accountant to determine if your investment is progressing satisfactorily	
	Is the gardener (and other tradespeople) doing a good job?	

CONTROLLING RISK

What type of person are you when it comes to facing risk? You have to know yourself before you can assess your attitude to carrying risk and the level of risk with which you are reasonably comfortable. Clearly this risk analysis has a place in your strategy.

Those with high disposable incomes can afford to carry substantial amounts of risk in terms of:

- the total amount borrowed;
- the level of repayments;
- the frequency of repayments;
- any gamble on rezoning or other potential capital gains windfall—or capital collapse due to such things as losing a view or the appearance of an unattractive neighbouring development;
- rising interest rates;
- your job security;
- your health;
- potential for accident or serious illness;
- family demands;
- the failure of any of your other investments;
- substantial necessary property repairs;
- the amount and nature of insurance cover you take out; and
- unforeseen changes to tax laws or building safety regulations.

In your strategy, try to put your attitude to risk into a couple of sentences. Turn something airy-fairy into a concrete statement. What are the risks that you fear most? Are they likely to happen? Use these categories of risk to guide your thinking:

- *government*—where governments change the rules, from tax to zoning to building safety regulation;
- *marketplace*—supply and demand for property in your chosen area; interest rate and inflation trends; consumer confidence levels and fears about the economy or social unrest;
- *personal*—your relationships, job security and mental/ emotional strength; over-confidence or lack of confidence; and
- *planning*—refusing to get independent expert advice in planning your moves; alternatively, obtaining advice from ill-prepared or lazy advisers; failing to plan for a spread of investments across a range of categories including property, shares and cash-based.

Once you have identified the risks, you can make plans to minimise them. Create your risk management strategy, which might include:

- fixing the interest rate on part or all of the loan;
- aiming to pay out the loan faster;
- selling one of your investments or assets so as to reduce your overall debt burden;
- increasing the ratio of net equity to debt in the property;
- reviewing the proportion and nature of your investments in equities;
- increasing or expanding the types of your insurance cover;
- deciding whether the property you are about to purchase should be the type which can be sold fast in a crisis, or whether you can ride out the down periods; and
- resolving any serious problems in your personal and workplace relationships.

Do you think you can carry the identified risks yourself, relying on your good health and salary income? If not, you should decide your tactics for controlling and reducing the various risks your investment will bring with it.

RECRUITING AND DEALING WITH YOUR PROPERTY TEAM

As discussed in Chapter 15, successful property investment is a team project. Your investment strategy should identify the individual members of your team and spell out how you will encourage them to give you their best attention.

For example, when you complete the purchase of a property, don't cut off contact with the estate agent. If you got on well with that agent, keep in touch with a call from time to time. Don't let the managing agents think of you as an absent landlord—let them know you are actively scrutinising their decisions and their service quality. Contact the gardener directly if you are not pleased with the way he or she is mowing the lawns.

How do you intend to foster the relationship and keep all members reporting to you with enthusiasm for your property, for your wealth creation and for your well-being?

STRATEGY EXAMPLES

We don't all get into property investment the same way. Informed by the thoughts and queries of your strategy document, a direction should present itself. Your friends will also be quick to tell you of their success stories and how they did it. New products and angles are emerging all the time, so the key is to find a lender you can talk to and who you feel is right on top of the game. Here are some examples of generic strategies which might give you food for thought as you discuss the issues with your advisers.

'Just another home loan'

If you've already been through the process of buying a home and have been happily making the loan repayments for a couple of years or so, you might well be very comfortable with the whole process. In fact, you might be keen to get into it once again—this time strictly as an investment. Your strategy might involve these aspects:

- Variable interest rate loan. If you have a high income or incomes, there is less pressure to fix the rate of the mortgage, even where rates are more likely to move up than down. Fixed rates are generally higher than variable rates (though not always—as occurred in mid-2003 and 2007, for instance), so instead of paying an extra 1 per cent or so, you could use the extra money to reduce the principal of your loan.
- Consider a term of less than fifteen years' duration—because you feel confident about your income and enjoy the challenge of paying off the mortgage quickly.
- If you have dependants, take out income protection insurance and term life cover for at least the amount of the loan.
- You might be prepared to borrow a larger percentage of the value of the property—as much as 100 per cent, secured in part against your home equity. Again, this is because of your positive existing experience and strong financial position.

'I hate risk'

If you can't deal with high risk, or you simply can't afford it, think in these terms:

- Fix the rate of your loan or borrow using a split loan (part fixed, part variable); you can ask your lender for a loan 'cap', which puts a ceiling limit on interest rate rises for your variable loan. Of course, you will pay a bit extra to get this feature.

- Don't borrow more than 50–60 per cent of valuation.
- If you have dependants, take out income protection insurance and term life cover for at least the amount of the loan.
- Choose a home unit rather than a house.
- Get a managing agent.
- Discuss with an accountant how you will be able to afford the repayments and other expenses, particularly in the period from purchase until you see the benefits of any tax deductions.

'I can't afford to buy in Sydney or Melbourne, so why bother?'

Sydney and, to a degree, Melbourne were major areas of high capital gain through the late 1990s and into 2004. In 2006–07 Perth took off in similar fashion. Property prices are now out of reach in these cities for all but those with existing assets, an inheritance and/or high incomes. Even if you do not fall within these parameters, don't give up hope of becoming a property investor. There are a number of strategies which you can use:

- Buy a property in a market which enjoys good capital growth but where property prices are lower than in Sydney and Melbourne. The hot spots vary from year to year, but Brisbane, Perth, Darwin and Canberra have been popular on occasion. Even Melbourne fell out of favour in recent years, before experiencing a resurgence of both population and redevelopment. The city has come back to life.
- Don't buy on your own. Find a partner and put your arrangement in contract form.
- Get Mum or Dad to help with the cash. Although it is common in some communities, I would never recommend that Mum or Dad help their child to the extent of

going guarantor or offering their own home as security for a loan. Too many of these deals turn sour—and you don't just lose the investment property.
- Buy something less than a home but still in high demand—investigate strata title car spaces in the central business district, for example.
- There are bargains to be found on the new fringes of capital cities, but one must question their investment potential.

'I don't want all the emotional hassles'

Maybe you've got enough emotional trauma going on in your life already without purchasing a whole lot more and having to handle tenants. If so:

- Consider investing in one or more property trusts rather than a direct investment in property or even, if you have at least $10 000 to invest, in a professional property syndicate (see Chapter 17).
- Consider buying a strata title car space instead of a unit or house.
- Consider putting more money into your superannuation fund and altering the proportions to weigh more heavily in property rather than equities.
- If you still want to invest directly in property, consider purchasing in partnership with a property professional, such as a builder (who can handle all the maintenance issues), or even with a friendly estate agent. Let them shield you.

'I'm prepared to wait . . . but I want to make big money out of this'

There is no room in property for the impatient investor, but there is a place for the big thinker. Here are some strategies:

- Select your property not for what it is now but for what it might become. A poorly maintained house in a good location might be a demolition prospect; a home on a large block of land might be suitable for subdivision; a large building could be turned into units. Can you see the future? How much extra is the property worth now because of its potential? It is a gamble, but your research effort can hopefully make it an informed one. [See *Smarter Property Improvement* (Allen & Unwin, 2004).]
- Borrow for investment purposes against the equity in your home (see Chapter 11).
- Aim to amass a larger deposit by putting your deposit to work in the stockmarket rather than more conservative bank or money market products. Seek expert advice first.
- Use newer financial products—such as a deposit bond—to enable you to hold a property at minimum cost over a lengthy settlement period (see Chapter 10).

While deposit bonds are most clearly useful in a rapidly rising market and with an 'off the plan' purchase, there is no particular reason why you cannot put a deposit bond to use in other more straightforward property deals where you are prepared to pay a fee for someone else to cover your financial obligation over the short term. Sometimes convenience is a simple enough justification—provided you have (or will have) the money available to meet your commitments when they fall due! Deposit bonds have been hyped in property seminars to the point where they have fuelled imprudent investment strategies based on speculation. The leverage or gearing these things provide is awesome—and of course it cuts both ways. Like many so-called 'secret tips of the wealthy investor that we can all use', they are best suited to the rich precisely because they already have the money to get themselves out of trouble.

These are high-risk strategies, however. Inevitably there will be losers among those who head into this territory.

By now you should feel more confident about getting out there and finding a good investment. You've read about the experiences of a number of first-time investors and have had the opportunity to reflect on the strategies and issues. Heed the warnings, seek out professional financial advice and get your money ready.

SUMMARY

- Investment starts with choosing your strategy. We don't all do it the same way, so don't worry just because you are charting a different course from your friends. It is wise to seek expert financial planning advice as you construct your investment and property strategies. This is the time to move beyond general information (such as that contained in this book) to a point where you are obtaining precise financial advice tailored to your personal situation, your hopes and your desires.
- A strategy incorporates an aim, a timeframe, a way of measuring success and failure at several stages (review and monitor), an understanding of how each individual investment fits within your overall financial plan, a budget, a plan for controlling risk and a plan for recruiting and dealing with your property team.
- Your strategy will include the type of loan you want (e.g., fixed or variable interest rate), its term, insurance issues (income protection, life, trauma, house and contents, landlord's insurance) and emotional/family concerns.

- You and your spouse or partner must be in agreement about the strategy.
- You might decide on a strategy which avoids direct investment in property, preferring instead to use property trusts, syndicates or even your superannuation.
- Now get out there and plan your investment strategy!

CONTACTS, WEBSITES AND FURTHER RESEARCH

CONSUMER PROTECTION AGENCIES AND ASSOCIATIONS

Australian Competition and Consumer Commission This independent statutory authority of the Commonwealth government administers the *Trade Practices Act*, *Prices Surveillance Act* and many other pieces of legislation. Phone 1300 302 502; www.accc.gov.au

Australian Securities and Investments Commission (ASIC) Information phoneline 1300 300 630; www.asic.gov.au and see ASIC's consumer and investor website called fido, at www.fido.asic.gov.au

Commonwealth Ombudsman The Ombudsman investigates complaints about Commonwealth government departments, agencies and officers. Phone 1300 362 072; www.comb.gov.au

Consumers Online This is the Commonwealth government's consumer protection site; www.consumersonline.gov.au

Department of the Treasury, Consumer Affairs Division This division looks after product safety recalls and some elements of consumer protection education and policy; www.treasury.gov.au see also www.consumer.gov.au

Australian Capital Territory Consumer Affairs Bureau Phone (02) 6207 0400; www.fairtrading.act.gov.au
New South Wales Office of Fair Trading Phone 13 32 20, www.fairtrading.nsw.gov.au
Northern Territory Office of Fair Trading Phone (08) 8999 1999; www.justice.nt.gov.au
Queensland Office of Fair Trading Phone 13 13 04; www.fairtrading.qld.gov.au
South Australian Office of Consumer and Business Affairs Phone 13 18 82; www.ocba.sa.gov.au
Tasmanian Office of Consumer Affairs and Fair Trading Phone 1300 654 499; www.justice.tas.gov.au/ca
Victorian Office of Fair Trading–Consumer Affairs Victoria Phone 1300 558 181; www.consumer.vic.gov.au
Western Australian Department of Consumer and Employment Protection. Consumer Protection Division Phone 1300 304 054; www.docep.wa.gov.au
CHOICE This is an independent, non-party political consumer organisation which publishes *CHOICE* magazine and lobbies for consumer protection and policy development. Phone (02) 9577 3333; www.choice.com.au

LAND TITLES OFFICES

These are where to find information about land titles, registration and title conversion, and to search property registers.
Australian Capital Territory: Land Titles, phone (02) 6207 0455; www.rgo.act.gov.au
New South Wales: Land and Property Information, phone 1300 052 637; www.lands.nsw.gov.au
Northern Territory: Land Titles Office, phone (08) 8999 6520; www.nt.gov.au/justice
Queensland: Department of Natural Resources and Water, phone (07) 3405 6900; www.nrm.qld.gov.au/property/titles

South Australia: Lands Services, phone (08) 8226 3983; www.landservices.sa.gov.au
Tasmania: Land Titles Office, phone (03) 6233 2618; www.dpiwe.tas.gov.au
Victoria: Land Registry, phone (03) 8636 2010; www.land.vic.gov.au
Western Australia: Landgate, phone (08) 9273 7373; www.dola.wa.gov.au

INDUSTRY ASSOCIATIONS

Real estate

The Real Estate Institute There is a national office and a separate office for each State and territory.
Real Estate Institute of Australia: www.reia.com.au
Real Estate Institute of the Australian Capital Territory: www.reiact.com.au
Real Estate Institute of New South Wales: www.reinsw.com.au
Real Estate Institute of Northern Territory Inc.: www.reint.com.au
Real Estate Institute of Queensland: www.reiq.com.au
Real Estate Institute of South Australia: www.reisa.com.au
Real Estate Institute of Tasmania: www.reit.com.au
Real Estate Institute of Victoria: www.reiv.com.au
Real Estate Institute of Western Australia: www.reiwa.com.au
The Property Council of Australia Phone (02) 9033 1900 www.propertyoz.com.au
Property Owners Association of Australia An information and lobby group for landlords/small business operators; www.poaa.asn.au
Property Investors Association of Australia Inc. (PIAA) Phone (02) 9499 9499, www.piaa.asn.au

Architects

The Royal Australian Institute of Architects is the principal industry association.

For building inspection reports carried out by an architect, contact an architect direct or for a referral go to Archicentre at www.archicentre.com.au or phone 1300 134 513. Archicentre is the Building Advisory Service of the Royal Australian Institute of Architects. It is the largest supplier of design and pre-purchase home inspections in Australia. Its other services include running seminars, an architects' advice line, renovation reports, advice on building contracts and advice on dealing with councils.

Surveyors

Surveyors have a number of professional organisations promoting their interests. For a referral to a surveyor, try phoning (02) 6285 3104 or go to www.isaust.org.au which is the site of the Institution of Surveyors. The address is National Surveyors House, 27–29 Napier Close, Deakin ACT 2600.

Engineers

The Association of Consulting Engineers Australia This association will help you find the engineer you need. You can search its website for issues of application to engineers, such as indemnity insurance.

Phone (02) 9922 4711; www.acea.com

Registered property valuers

For a referral to a valuer or to find out about their code of conduct, contact the Australian Property Institute.

There are individual State bodies but the national secretariat is at 6 Campion Street, Deakin ACT 2600, phone (02) 6282 2411. Its national website is www.propertyinstitute.com.au

Financial planning

Financial Planning Association of Australia
Phone 1800 337 301, or for referral to a financial planner 1800 626 393; www.fpa.asn.au

Tenancy advice

Tenancy Information Centre of Australia www.tica.com.au. This is a site very much for landlords, looking at how to check on prospective tenants.

LAW SOCIETIES

Do you need to find a solicitor? The local lawyers' society or institute will direct you.
The Law Society of the Australian Capital Territory Phone (02) 6247 5700; www.lawsociety.com.au
Law Society of New South Wales Phone (02) 9926 0333; www.lawsociety.com.au
The Law Society of the Northern Territory Phone (08) 8981 5104; www.lawsocnt.asn.au
Queensland Law Society Phone (07) 3842 5842; www.qls.com.au
Law Society of South Australia Phone (08) 8229 0222; www.lawsocietysa.asn.au
The Law Society of Tasmania Phone (03) 6234 4133; www.taslawsociety.asn.au
Law Institute of Victoria Phone (03) 9607 9311; www.liv.asn.au
The Law Society of Western Australia Phone (08) 9322 7877; www.lawsocietywa.asn.au

INDUSTRY COMPLAINTS HANDLING SCHEMES

Banking and Financial Services Ombudsman The Ombudsman handles disputes involving member banks and can make an award in the consumer's favour up to an amount less than $280 000. There is no charge for this service. Phone 1300 780 808; www.abio.org.au

Credit unions and building societies

Complaints and disputes are handled by more than one potential agency. You may have to contact a couple of agencies before you find the right one for your particular financial institution.

The Financial Co-operative Dispute Resolution Scheme (FCDRS) deals with complaints from consumers about credit unions and building societies which are members of the scheme—issues such as ATM, eftpos and credit card disputes. Phone 1300 139 220; www.fcdrs.org.au. This scheme does not replace an earlier dispute resolution scheme for complaints involving credit unions which are members of the **Credit Union Dispute Resolution Centre (CUDRC)**. Disputes with participating credit unions (which abide by a code of practice) are handled without charge to credit union members. The Centre has jurisdiction to handle a complaint concerning up to $100 000. The Centre's decision is binding on the credit union but not on the customer. Phone 1300 780 808; www.cudrc.com.au

Australian Association of Permanent Building Societies Building societies do not have their own dispute resolution scheme, but have officers trained to handle complaints. Contact the head office of the society or go to the Financial Co-operative Dispute Resolution Scheme website for information on what to do. Phone 1300 139 220; www.fcdrs.org.au

Financial Industry Complaints Service Limited This scheme handles disputes involving financial advice. There is no charge for the service. An award in the consumer's favour can be made up to a maximum of $6000 per month for income protection insurance,

$250 000 for life insurance and $100 000 for funds management, stockbroking, investment and financial advice. Phone 1300 780 808; www.fics.asn.au

Insurance Ombudsman Service This scheme primarily handles complaints involving motor vehicle property damage and your insurance company, but also provides free advice about general insurance: property, contents, landlord's policies and more (though not life insurance). The services are free of charge and the limit on disputes is $280 000. Phone 1300 780 808; www.iecltd.com.au

The Insurance Brokers' Disputes Limited This service handles disputes with insurance brokers. It is a free service and can handle complaints for general and life insurance. Phone (02) 9964 9400; www.niba.com.au

Mortgage & Finance Association of Australia (MFAA) This is the industry body for non-bank mortgage providers, brokers and mortgage managers. There is a code of practice—check the website. Phone 1300 554 817; www.miaa.com.au

The MFAA complaints scheme handles customer complaints about its members, provided the customer has already attempted to resolve the dispute directly with the member but is not satisfied with the outcome. Members of the MFAA agree to abide by a code of practice, part of which includes an obligation to empower the Credit Ombudsman Service to investigate, negotiate and ultimately make a decision on a customer's complaint. The Ombudsman's decision is binding on the Association member. An award can be made in favour of the customer up to a maximum of $250 000. The process is free of charge to the customer. Phone 1800 138 422, or in Sydney 9273 8400; www.creditombudsman.com.au

PROPERTY REPORTS AND MARKETING

Many real estate agents have their own individual websites. Contact them for the address. Here is a selection of more general property sites.

Domain A Fairfax publications site, www.domain.com.au, Domain is a good place to check real estate advertisements from the Fairfax publications around Australia. You can get a suburb snapshot, ask to be alerted electronically when a particular type of property is advertised and can save individual property ads to your own shortlist file. A mortgage comparison tool is also available.

Australian Property Monitors This site sells property reports—you can select by postcode, suburb or even by street name. Auction results and a free email newsletter keep you up-to-date; www.homepriceguide.com.au or www.apm.com.au

HomePath This is an information site which is a subsidiary of the Commonwealth Bank. Free registration gives you access to information on aspects of buying, selling and investing in property, including calculators, some price data and a personalised property alert function; www.homepath.com.au

Property This is a general website of interest with information on searching for properties, getting an agent, finance, etc.; www.property.com.au

PropertyWeb Although the focus here is largely on commercial and industrial property, there is still good information for those looking for homes or residential investments. Auction clearance rates and volumes (in price brackets) are a highlight feature. An interesting range of articles can be found here too; www.propertyweb.com.au

Realestate A property-searching site which includes predictions for growth suburbs; www.realestate.com.au

Residex Here, for a fee, you can get hold of price information and reports for Queensland and New South Wales; www.residex.com.au. Performance predictions are a feature. Residex links to www.findmeahome.com.au, where you can search for a property and mortgage.

YOUR FINANCES

Reserve Bank of Australia Phone (02) 9551 8111 or 1800 300 288; www.rba.gov.au

Interest rates

Here are some sites where you can find current interest rates for loans from a wide range of financial institutions:

Cannex: www.cannex.com.au
InterestRate: www.interestrate.com.au
Ninemsn: www.money.ninemsn.com.au
Yahoo: www.finance.yahoo.com.au
EChoice: www.echoice.com.au
Rate City: www.ratecity.com.au

Financial product comparison

If you want some guidance and assistance with comparing various financial products (banking, loans, deposits, managed funds), try these websites:

Cannex: www.cannex.com.au
Infochoice: www.infochoice.com.au
AFR Smart Investor: www.afrsmartinvestor.com.au
Your Mortgage: www.yourmortgage.com.au

Financial planning

Here are some useful places for information on integrating your financial and investment projects:

Ninemsn: www.money.ninemsn.com.au

Moneymanager: www.moneymanager.smh.com.au (part of the f2 network)

ING/Financialpassages: www.ing.com.au

AMP: www.amp.com.au (a fine personal finance site)

Investorweb: www.investorweb.com.au (good for property trusts)

Financial Planning Association: www.fpa.asn.au (information on licensed financial planners and assistance via an online referral service)

Online conveyancing

Legalmart: www.legalmart.com.au. This is an online conveyancing company which will quote for jobs in New South Wales and Queensland.

Magazines

Here are four of my favourite financial information sites prepared by magazine publishers. They have useful calculators and carry helpful articles in a magazine style:
AFR Smart Investor www.afrsmartinvestor.com.au
Australian Property Investor magazine: www.apimagazine.com.au
Your Mortgage: www.yourmortgage.com.au
CHOICE www.choice.com.au

Online mortgage providers and brokers

There are so, so many of these now. Don't know which loan is right for you? Online mortgage finders will help you. Here is a selection to get you started.
www.echoice.com.au
www.wizard.com.au
www.homeloansnow.com.au
www.eloan.com.au
www.mortgagechoice.com.au
www.mortgagehouse.com.au
www.onedirect.com.au
www.peachhomeloans.com.au
www.yeshomeloans.com.au

Financial institutions

Looking for the website for a particular bank or other lender? Try typing in the institution's name, as in these examples:

www.anz.com.au
www.aussiehomeloans.com.au
www.commbank.com.au (Commonwealth Bank)
www.imb.com.au (IMB Banking & Financial Services)
www.national.com.au (National Australia Bank)
www.westpac.com.au

Credit

Your credit record At Veda Advantage, for a fee you can check your credit record and see what it says about you. Go to www.mycreditfile.com.au

Consumer Credit Code Find out about a lender's obligations under the Credit Code, including the mandatory use of a comparison rate in advertising; www.creditcode.gov.au

TAXATION

Stamp duty/duties

For inquiries and information, call your State or territory revenue office or go to its website.

Australian Capital Territory: Phone (02) 6207 0028; www.revenue.act.gov.au

New South Wales: Phone 1300 130 624; www.osr.nsw.gov.au

Northern Territory: Phone (08) 8999 7949 or 1300 305 353; www.nt.gov.au/ntt/revenue

Queensland: Phone 1300 300 734; www.osr.qld.gov.au

South Australia: Phone (08) 8226 3750; www.revenuesa.sa.gov.au

Tasmania: Phone (03) 6233 3566 www.treasury.tas.gov.au

Victoria: Phone 13 21 61; www.sro.vic.gov.au

Western Australia: Phone (08) 9262 1100 or 1300 368 364; www.dtf.wa.gov.au

Land tax

For inquiries and information, call your State or territory revenue/land tax office.
Australian Capital Territory: Phone (02) 6207 0047; www.revenue.act.gov.au
New South Wales: Phone 1300 139 816 or (02) 9689 6200 outside New South Wales; www.osr.nsw.gov.au
Northern Territory: not applicable; www.nt.gov.au/ntt/revenue
Queensland: Phone 1300 300 734; www.osr.qld.gov.au
South Australia: Phone (08) 8204 9870; www.revenuesa.sa.gov.au/taxes
Tasmania: Phone (03) 6233 3068 or 1800 001 388; www.treasury.tas.gov.au
Victoria: Phone 13 21 61; www.sro.vic.gov.au
Western Australia: Phone (08) 9262 1400 or 1300 368 364; www.dtf.wa.gov.au

Income tax and GST

Australian Taxation Office: www.ato.gov.au
Business Tax Infoline: 13 28 66
Income tax withholding variation: 1300 360 221
Personal Tax Information Line: 13 28 61
Translating and Interpreting Service: 13 14 50

BUILDER LICENSING AUTHORITIES AND ASSOCIATIONS

Australian Capital Territory: ACT Planning and Land Authority (ACTPLA), builders' licensing section. Phone (02) 6207 1923; www.actpla.act.gov.au
New South Wales: Department of Fair Trading. Phone 13 32 20 or (02) 9895 0111; www.fairtrading.nsw.gov.au
Northern Territory: Department of Planning and Infrastructure—Building Advisory Services and the director

Building Control. Phone (08) 8999 5511; www.ipe.nt.gov.au or www.nt.gov.au/lands/building, phone (08) 8999 8960

Queensland: The Queensland Building Services Authority (BSA). Phone 1300 272 272; www.bsa.qld.gov.au

South Australia: Office of Consumer and Business Affairs, Builders Licensing. Phone (08) 8204 9644; www.ocba.sa.gov.au

Tasmania: Department of Justice, Director of Building Control. It is not a general licensing system but a scheme for accreditation of the 'principal builder' on the site. Phone 1300 366 322; www.wst.tas.gov.au/industries/building

Victoria: Building Commission Victoria. Phone (03) 9285 6400 or 1300 557 559; www.buildingcommission.com.au

Western Australia: Builders Registration Board. Phone (08) 9476 1200; www.brb.org.au

Housing Industry Association Ltd This is a national association (with State branches) for the building trades. Phone (02) 6245 1300; www.hia.com.au

Master Builders Australia This is the major Australian association for the building and construction industry. There are State and national organisations. Phone (02) 6202 8888; www.masterbuilders.com.au

INDEX